IRISH LAW TEXTS

EMPLOYMENT LAW

by

Ferdinand von Prondzynski, B.A., LL.B., Ph.D.

Lecturer in Industrial Relations,
Trinity College, University of Dublin

and

Charles McCarthy, M.A., Ph.D.

Professor of Industrial Relations,
Trinity College, University of Dublin

Foreword by

John Horgan

Chairman, Labour Court

LONDON
SWEET & MAXWELL
1984

Published in 1984 by
Sweet and Maxwell Limited of
11 New Fetter Lane, London
Computerset by Promenade Graphics Limited, Cheltenham
Printed in Scotland

British Library Cataloguing in Publication Data

von Prondzynski, Ferdinand
   Employment law.—(Irish law texts)
   1. Labor laws and legislation—Ireland
   I. Title   II. McCarthy, Charles
   III. Series
   344.17041125   KDK802

   ISBN 0–421–31240–8

©
Sweet & Maxwell
1984

Introduction

Both Irish jurisdictions have long suffered from the problems associated with the lack of a developed local legal literature. This lack of development has been particularly acute in the Republic of Ireland, where it is only in the last few years that any works at all have appeared in the main fields of law and where many gaps still remain. The combination of the small market for law books in the Republic and a considerable lag between the achievement of political independence and the emergence of a corpus of indigenous law deterred the production of legal literature. For many years law students and the legal profession made do with the older editions of English textbooks or else did without. In Northern Ireland, the problems were never so acute since the local law generally kept pace with changes in Britain. Nevertheless, there are also significant differences between the available works on English law and procedure and the law taught and practised in that jurisdiction.

Over the last two decades a variety of factors has brought about change. In the first place there is a much greater output of local law both in legislation and through court decisions. The number of students in the universities and other third level colleges who are studying law has increased enormously. There has also been a proportionate increase in the numbers engaged in the full-time teaching of law with correspondingly a greater number of academic lawyers available to undertake research and writing. The size of the legal profession has doubled in both jurisdictions in the last decade.

One happy result of the new circumstances has been the coincidence of acute concern about the dearth of works devoted to Irish law and sufficient local demands to encourage authors to write and publishers to publish. It was in these circumstances that *Irish Law Texts* was conceived. The series aims to produce reasonably priced works on the main fields of Irish law to meet the needs of the broadest legal population.

Books in the series are concerned primarily with the law of the Republic of Ireland, which is the larger Irish jurisdiction and the one which has seen the greatest changes in legal principles and statute law from Britain. However, wherever possible, reference will be made to the law of Northern Ireland, particulary the decisions of the courts. *Irish Law Texts* therefore hopes to make a contribution to the needs of students and the professions in both parts of the island.

Kevin Boyle
Series Editor

Foreword

Following the publication of the Report of the Commission on Industrial Relations in 1981 there has been a protracted, if muted, debate on the role of law in industrial relations. The protagonists have adopted the expected postures. Trade union reaction, supported by a good many commentators with little direct experience of the cut and thrust of industrial conflict, have argued that the law has simply no role to play and that all legal intervention is sooner or later damaging. The other side of the debate might similarly be simplified and paraphrased as: "All other areas of social and economic conduct are subject to the law and so should the totality of interactions known as Industrial Relations."

Despite the fact that the spate of protective legislation of the 1970s introduced by the then Minister for Labour, Mr. Michael O'Leary T.D. flows uneasily between these opposing factions, the debate for the most part has been a barren one.

This book has within it the seeds of an alternative framework of thinking. The authors have carefully analysed the law as it stands and, more importantly, as it is being interpreted and applied. As in so many areas of controversy, a detached examination of reality rewards the prudent investigator with new insights and creative solutions.

A recurring theme of this work is that employment law as it has developed is faulty in many respects. It is often not the servant of industry; the law confuses and at times frustrates the honest and sensible intention of unions and employers and indeed the legislators themselves. Where this happens the fault can almost always be traced to the importation of inappropriate legal concepts. For example, it would be foolish to expect that each and every concept of contract law, as applied to commercial contracts for instance, should have a counterpart of equal relevance in the construing of employment contracts. Neither should all the equitable doctrines which work well in land law serve an equal purpose in the difficult area of the agency powers of trade unions. Too much labour law is based on partial immunity from common law maxims which were never pertinent in the first place.

This theme points towards a new way of thinking. Instead of bringing "the law" into industrial relations, why not bring industrial relations concepts which are found generally acceptable to employers and trade unions into law? This is not to suggest that notions inherent in workplace custom and practice should be reformed or deformed for the sole purpose of fitting into the conven-

vii

tional framework of civil and criminal law. Perhaps a new branch of law, which need not apologise for being different, needs to be created. It could develop at its own pace to serve the interests of employers and employees and not be forced into the moulds formed by generations of lawyers unfamiliar with the reality of modern industry in a developing economy. In other words, labour and employment law needs to develop on its own terms just as historically all other branches of law have done.

Without wishing to develop the point here, I am of the opinion that the correct jurisprudential approach to the development of labour law is represented by the Social Contract school of thought. The parties to industrial relations agreements themselves form a consensus as to the duties and obligations which they owe to each other arising out of their agreements. They can and do (with increasing frequency) agree amongst themselves mutually acceptable sanctions for non-compliance. From these can emerge a set of enforceable norms, codes or laws. It does not matter what they are called provided they continue to command respect as to their fairness from the majority. The role of the State and of the constitutional judiciary in all this should be to facilitate this process and not to impose or prescribe laws of their own making except the basic laws necessary for the preservation of public order.

John Horgan
Chairman
Labour Court

Preface

It has been suggested by some of those engaged in industrial relations that it is an area in which the law has no place. This is intended to convey that in the area of collective bargaining and industrial disputes there should not be recourse to a court of law, on the grounds that such a procedure is not likely to yield a just or an appropriate result. A number of reasons are cited for this, particularly by trade unionists. It is suggested that lawyers are prejudiced against trade unions by reason of their social background and their educational formation. It is suggested that the law has difficulty in practice in taking account of the rights of collectivities, that is to say of trade unions, in view of the strong common law tradition of emphasising individual rights. It is suggested finally that lawyers tend to see industrial disputes from the point of view of judgment rather than the point of view of the actors in the industrial relations process; it is the lawyer's approach, as one of the present authors has described it elsewhere, to "see things primarily from the point of view of the court, of the adjudicator, of the person engaged in the application of the law rather than of the person who is painfully identifying it in the course of his own activity" (Charles McCarthy, *Elements in a Theory of Industrial Relations*, 1984, p. 6). In these circumstances there has grown a widely held view that the law should be kept out of industrial relations, a view which has frequently been described as voluntarism and which has influenced large numbers of industrial relations practitioners and academics.

However, since the 1960s the law has, in a particular area, made significant advances into the industrial relations field. These advances have come largely in response to international instruments, many of them passed under the auspices of the International Labour Organisation, which have held that a civilised society must guarantee certain minimum standards in the employment relationship. The resulting statutes, together with the few Acts which had already existed previously, now form the substantive corpus of what we may call employment law, or individual labour law as it is sometimes known. The Statutory framework exists alongside and is heavily influenced by the common law construct of the contract of employment, which in turn is governed by the more traditional lawyer's approach. Both the common law and the protective statutes protect individual rights, but from very different perspectives, and the relationship between them is at best uneasy. It is finally to be noted that the labour market consists of two sectors. Those employees who make up the latter tend to be part-time or temporary

ix

workers, frequently unorganised by trade unions; it appears that within the labour market a gradual redistribution is taking place between these sectors from the primary to the secondary, leaving an increasing number of workers unprotected by the provisions of employment law, which itself is a feature largely of the primary sector. This may create social problems with which the Oireachtas will need to concern itself.

This book covers employment law, or individual labour law, although we have endeavoured to place the subject by explaining the general context in which it arises. For an analysis of collective labour law, readers might consult the forthcoming book by Gerry Whyte and Tony Kerr, *Trade Union Law in the Republic of Ireland*. The relationship between collective labour and industrial relations is explored in more detail by the present authors in two further books: by Charles McCarthy in *Elements in a Theory of Industrial Relations* (*op. cit.*), and by Ferdinand von Prondzynski in the forthcoming book *Freedom of Association and Industrial Relations*.

It has been our objective in this book not merely to provide a descriptive account of the present law—although we do that as well—but also to attempt a critical analysis of it and an assessment of its success in providing the kind of protection for which it was designed. We have done this by paying special attention to the context in which the actors in the industrial relations process would meet the legal provisions. In the course of our research it became clear to us—or rather we were confirmed in our view—that the framework of employment law in this country is still unsatisfactory. There are gaps in the legislation, some caused by draftsmanship and some by interpretation, and there is on the whole an inadequate understanding of the functions and substance of the law. To some extent this may be put down to the absence of relevant Irish literature, a situation which we here hope to begin to redress.

Our thanks are due to various persons who very kindly gave us advice or information or who read drafts of some of the chapters. These include Dr. Brian Napier of Queens' College, Cambrige, Mr. Tony Kerr of University College, Dublin, Miss Caroline Simons of the Employment Equality Agency, and Mr. Willam O'Shaughnessy of the Employment Appeals Tribunal. Needless to say, any mistakes which remain are the responsibility of the authors. We are also grateful to Sweet & Maxwell who were helpful and patient during the preparation of the book. Finally, we would like to thank Miss Wendy Richards for her assistance in proof-reading the book.

Trinity College, Dublin   Ferdinand von Prondzynski
August 1984   Charles McCarthy

Contents

Table of Cases and Decisions

For the purposes of the table of cases, the following abbreviations apply:

A.C.	Appeal Cases (U.K.)
All E.R.	All England Reports (U.K.)
C.C.	Circuit Court (unreported)
H.C.	High Court (unreported)
I.C.R.	Industrial Cases Reports (U.K.)
I.L.R.M.	Irish Law Reports Monthly
I.L.T.R.	Irish Law Times Reports
I.R.	Irish Reports
I.R.L.R.	Industrial Relations Law Reports (U.K.)
I.T.R.	Industrial Tribunal Reports (U.K.)
Q.B.	Queen's Bench (U.K.)
S.C.	Supreme Court (unreported)

Decisions of the Employment Appeals Tribunal (E.A.T.), the Equality Officers and the Labour Court are generally not reported in any of the law reports. Mimeographed copies are however issued by the E.A.T. and the Labour Court, and these have reference numbers of the following kind:

DEE 23/84	Labour Court determination under the Employment Equality Act 1977
DEP 23/84	Labour Court determination under the Anti-Discrimination (Pay) Act 1974
EE 23/84	Equality Officer recommendation
EP 23/84	Equality Officer recommendation
M 23/1984	E.A.T. determination under the Minimum Notice and Terms of Employment Act 1973
P 23/1984	E.A.T. determination under the Maternity Protection of Employment Act 1981
UD 23/1984	E.A.T. determination under the Unfair Dismissals Act 1977
23/1984	E.A.T. determination under the Redundancy Payments Acts

The decisions of the E.A.T. may have more than one reference number. For example, if a case involves both unfair dismissal and minimum notice issues, then its references will be something like the following: Smith v. Jones Ltd. M 23/1984; UD 30/1984. In such circumstances the case list below will give only the reference number relevant to the text in the book.

In all reported cases, page references in the text of the book are to the report given in the list below; the case may of course also be reported elsewhere.

Table of Cases and Decisions

Table of Statutes

*[Page references in **bold** indicate the page upon which the statute is written out verbatim.]*

Irish Statutes

(a) *Statutes of the Parliament of the United Kingdom of Great Britain and Ireland*

(b) *Acts of the Oireachtas*

[The following Bills, referred to in the text, had not yet passed into law at the time of writing:

British Statutes

Statutes from other Jurisdictions

Table of Statutory Instruments

Constitution of Ireland (1937)

EEC Instruments

Treaty of Rome

EEC Regulations

Code of Practice (for the Elimination of Sex and Marital Status Discrimination and Promotion of Equality of Opportunity in Employment (issued by the Employment Equality Agency in 1984))

1 Irish Labour Law and Industrial Relations

TRADE UNION LAW

In the Republic of Ireland a trade union, whether of workers or of employers, is essentially a body licensed to engage in collective bargaining. Strictly speaking, a trade union is validly a trade union under the law whether it is licensed or not for collective bargaining purposes, but so central is collective bargaining to its *raison d'etre* that the licence can be seen as the characteristic which distinguishes the trade union from other organisations. There are naturally exceptions, the major one being that, in common sense, there can be no impediment to workers negotiating directly with their own employer, but the existence of a licence, at least of some kind, remains a requirement in all other cases. It is necessary to consider briefly how this came about.

The law as it evolved in England applied in great measure to Ireland up to 1921 since Ireland, up to that time, was part of the United Kingdom. Since then there has been some parting of the ways, in particular because Ireland gave itself a written Constitution. Nevertheless, the law of England continued to influence development here. This is particularly so in the matter of case law, which, while not binding on the courts here, is nevertheless highly persuasive in that traditionally the Irish courts follow English practice quite closely and frequently cite English decisions in their judgments. Since 1971 however, there have been substantial statutory developments in England which have not been followed here and there have been some unique developments in Ireland particularly

1

from 1977 onwards. Despite this however the similarity in the legal systems is considerable.

The idea of a licence for trade union activity arose in the context of a trade union's intrinsic unlawfulness under the common law and the need, in common sense, to provide it with some degree of legitimation. In the traditions of English law, trade unions were seen to be unlawful because their purposes were in restraint of trade. Although there has been much development within the law in the last 50 years this is still largely the case. Lord Wedderburn remarked in 1971:

> "The courts have more lately reverted to the earlier attitude; and today most unions, especially if they have rules for calling strikes and disciplining members or if they operate a closed shop, are thought to be unlawful at common law by reason of restraint of trade." (K.W. Wedderburn, *The Worker and the Law* 1971, p. 315).

This might appear at first sight to be a rather artificial, if not a remote reason, for making so many associations unlawful. It has been suggested that the common law is strongly opposed to the notion of collective might and holds both trade unions and employers' associations to be unlawful as being in restraint of trade for that reason (Bryn Perrins, *The Trade Union and Labour Relations Act 1974* 1975, p. 2). Perhaps there are two separate ideas here. In the first place the common law attributes fundamental rights to natural persons; every collectivity however is a *persona ficta* to which rights might be attributed artificially but which cannot possess them in any antecedent way; this is the case with a limited liability company for example. In the second place there is a long tradition that the rules of the market, while permitting competition, and indeed very vigorous competition between individual traders, regard competition by a collectivity of traders as being improper and in the nature of a conspiracy.

But the reason for the sanctity of the notion of freedom of trade goes deeper than that. It was associated with the idea of progress and economic expansion, the importance of which was regarded as overwhelmingly self-evident in the later nineteenth century. Such ideas of economic individualism were seen as protected by the correlative duty not to interfere with a man's right to trade whether that trade was in regard to goods or in regard to labour. Trade unions manifestly offended against this. Sir William Erle, a nineteenth century jurist whose views have been quoted with approval in the High

Court here by Budd J. in *Educational Company of Ireland* v. *Fitzpatrick (No. 2)* (1961) set out, as explicitly as any, the manner in which the common law viewed activities by trade unions which were in restraint of trade. In his tract of 1868 he put the position as follows:

> "Every person has a right under the law as between himself and his fellow subjects to full freedom in disposing of his own labour or his own capital according to his own will. It follows that every person is subject to the correlative duty arising therefrom and is prohibited from any obstruction to the fullest exercise of this right which can be made compatible with the exercise of similar rights by others" (Sir William Erle: *The Law Relating to Trade Unions*, 1869).

It followed that "a stop in the supply of labour is obviously a damage in every trade; the causing of the stop is a restraint of trade, and all restraint of trade is as above stated, presumed to be unlawful until the contrary is shown."

Sir William Erle was chairman of the Royal Commission on Trade Unions which reported in 1869, and the majority report, following his principles, recommended that only those unions should have the protection of the law which in their rules declared explicitly against picketing, much strike action, closed shop arrangements, limiting apprentices and the like. There was however a minority report, one which attempted to domesticate the trade union movement, at least to some degree, within the juridical system as it then existed; it was this minority report, not the majority report, which the government followed when they introduced the Trade Union Act 1871, which still partly governs the position of trade unions in Ireland.

THE TRADE UNION ACT 1871

The 1871 Act and those of 1875 and 1876, which developed somewhat on it, sought to make trade unions lawful. The 1871 Act began by stating that trade unions were not criminal conspiracies. Section 3 of the Act is of great importance. Up to then, when a trade union had, among its principal purposes, objects which were in restraint of trade, that trade union was seen as being unlawful, not so much as to render it liable for damages or for penalty, but rather in that because of its unlawfulness the courts would do nothing to assist the parties in carrying out even their lawful objects. This meant that the law would do nothing to protect the property, contracts and trusts of such trade unions. Section 3, therefore, of the Trade Union Act 1871 provided that "the purposes of any trade union shall not by reason merely that they are in restraint of trade, be unlawful so as to render void or voidable any agreement or trust."

This created a further problem, because now it might appear that the courts could be called upon to enforce an agreement between members concerning their conditions of work, the payment of subscriptions and so forth. The Act therefore went on in section 4 to declare that while such agreements were lawful they would nevertheless be unenforceable in the courts, at least directly. The agreements which were seen by the Act as being lawful but unenforceable could be summarised as follows: agreements between members concerning conditions on which they should be employed; agreements for the payment of penalties and subscriptions to trade unions; agreements between trade unions; agreements relating to the application of the funds of a trade union; and agreements to secure the performance of such agreements.

To say that an agreement is lawful but cannot be enforced by the courts is of course something which the law is very reluctant to do. It is not surprising therefore that this particular provision in the 1871 Act is very tightly construed. Unless the agreement is of a kind which is specifically mentioned in the Act then it is enforceable. For example a member can enforce his right to vote in elections, his right in the winding up of a trade union, his right to restrain persons who attempt to exclude him from membership and so forth. Furthermore, the only methods of enforcement that are excluded are those specifically mentioned in the Act. Other forms of enforcement would still remain open in regard to the agreements that are excluded. Therefore these would be a basis for an action on an account stated, for the application of an arbitrator's award, for the purpose of a declaratory judgment, or for the recovery of funds that had been misapplied. The only matters which are excluded are proceedings for damages or for direct enforcement.

The third objective of the 1871 Act was to encourage trade unions to bring themselves under the wing of the law, as it were, by a system of registration. The registrar for this purpose was to be the Registrar of Friendly Societies. The rules of the union had to correspond with the provisions of the Act, but once a certificate of registration was issued it was conclusive evidence that the regulations in respect of registration had been complied with and that the combination was indeed a trade union. It was also provided that any unregistered union could apply to the Registrar of Friendly Societies for a certificate that it was a trade union.

A number of things follow from registration. Before registration a union had little or no legal personality. Upon registration it became an entity with some legal personality that was independent of its members. It was not in fact clear, on the face of the 1871 Act, that a trade union had legal personality conferred on it and indeed the matter was in some dispute until the decision in the case of *Taff Vale Railway Co.* v. *Amalgamated Society of Railway Servants* (1901), in which it was held that the Act had conferred "quasi-corporate" status on trade unions. In these circumstances a trade union can sue and be sued in its registered name, and indeed it has sufficient character to be the subject of defamation. However it cannot hold property in its registered name. Both real and personal property vests in its trustees for the use and benefit of its members.

The earlier sections of the Act apply to all trade unions which fall within the definition contemplated by the Act whether registered or not. The definition therefore of a trade union is of the first importance; it appeared first in the Act of 1871 and was amended by the Act of 1876 and again by the Act of 1913. In its amended form it runs as follows:

> "The expression trade union for the purposes of the Trade Union Acts 1871 (to 1913) means any combination whether temporary or permanent, the principal objects of which are under its constitution statutory objects . . . whether such combination would or would not, if the Trade Union Act 1871 had not been passed, have been deemed to have been an unlawful combination by reason of some one or more of its purposes being in restraint of trade . . . The expression 'statutory objects' means . . . the regulation of the relations between workmen and masters, or between workmen and workmen, or between masters and masters, or the imposing of restrictive conditions on the conduct of any trade or business, and also the provision of benefits to members."

There are a number of points of a general kind which can be made. A trade union, for the purposes of the Act, is a combination "whether temporary or permanent," thus covering any passing group of workers, once one of the objects of the combination falls within the Act. A trade union is therefore a trade union because its objectives make it so. In order further to emphasise the impermanence of the body which the law would recognise as a trade union it is interesting to note that the word constitution, as used in the definition, does not necessarily require that there should be any formal document or rules (Trade Union Act 1913, ss.2(2) and 3). The Registrar, it appears, is entitled to look at the actual practice of the combination and the manner in which it carries out its objectives.

To summarise therefore, the 1871 Act set out to register trade unions and to confer on them certain advantages by reason of their being registered. Furthermore it required them to do certain things in relation to rules and so forth before registration. On the other hand it recognised quite clearly that trade unions existed irrespective of the registration procedure and the Act recognised trade unions which, by reason of defect in rules might not be eligible for registration. When therefore one comes to consider matters like unofficial industrial action, one must recognise that for the purposes of the law a group of workers can be regarded as a trade union although they are acting in a manner contrary to the rules of the association or union of which they are members.

TRADE DISPUTES LAW

The Act of 1871, then, attempted to legitimate trade unions within the law by this system of registration. This endeavour, however, met with failure. It met with failure principally because the activities of a trade union when engaged in industrial action were virtually impossible to accommodate within the law as it stood. It was not surprising then that a number of very explicit difficulties began to arise. First it was established that the 1871 Act had not gone far enough in regard to the doctrine of conspiracy. In the famous case of *Quinn v. Leathem* (1901) it was established that if two or more persons combine together without legal justification to injure another, they are liable for damages for conspiracy.

However there was worse to come. Before 1871 it had been virtually impossible for persons injured by the activities of a trade union to obtain a judgment which was enforceable by any process of law against the funds of the union itself. Individuals were proceeded against, but the individuals concerned were often men of straw. However, because the Act of 1871 gave a certain legal personality to registered trade unions and also because of the enactment of the Judicature Act 1873, which improved court procedure, the courts held in the *Taff Vale* case (1901, see above) that a registered trade union could be sued in its registered name, and the union concerned found itself liable for £23,000 in damages and for a substantial sum in respect of costs as well. Indeed trade unions had been to some extent domesticated within the law by the Act of 1871 but that domestication had resulted not in their redemption from unlawfulness as much as in an increase in their vulnerability as institutions to the activities of the law. Domestication therefore was largely abandoned as a solution and instead Parliament proceeded to consider the conferring of immunities on trade unions in certain circumstances, that is to say recognising the inherent unlawfulness of what they were doing, but exempting them specifically from any penalty that might follow. This was a very basic change in the whole approach of the law. It manifests itself in the very important Trade Disputes Act 1906. This Act still applies in Ireland, although its provisions have been largely re-enacted in another form in the United Kingdom; more recently the Employment Acts of 1980 and 1982 have significantly taken away from the statutory protection in that jurisdiction.

In view of its vast influence on trade union law, both philosophically and in practice, the Trade Disputes Act 1906 is remarkably brief, consisting of five sections only, and capable of being written on a single sheet of paper. It set out to remedy directly and explicitly the difficulties which had arisen by reason of the courts' interpretations of the Act of 1871.

The problem facing the legislators was the manner in which one could confer immunity on trade union activity and not have it extended to any group of citizens acting in combination. We have seen how difficult it is to identify a trade union, and probably because of this the legislators turned instead to a definition, not of the body engaged in the activity as much as the circumstances in which the activity takes place. In a word they decided to confer immunity by and large only in regard to those acts which were done "in contemplation or furtherance of a trade dispute." This is why the definition of a trade dispute becomes of such extraordinary significance. Upon it turns the question of immunity.

Let us consider what the Act set out to do. First, it provided that a conspiracy is not actionable unless the act which is contemplated by the conspiracy would, if done by one person alone, be actionable (s.1). It provided that peaceful picketing is lawful where its purpose is peacefully to communicate or obtain information or persuade persons to work or not to work (s.2). Finally it provided that inducing a breach of contract of employment and interference with the trade, business or employment of another person are not of themselves actionable (s.3). It will be noticed that the first and third of these activities are here not made lawful. What the legislators in fact set out to do was to render these activities immune from legal proceedings; that is to say, they limited the jurisdiction of the courts in their regard. In the case of picketing, however, they actually legitimated the activity if it was peaceful. As we have pointed out, all these immunities require as a necessary condition that those engaged in them should in fact be acting "in contemplation or furtherance of a trade dispute" and this we shall take up in a moment. It is necessary however to recognise that there is a further provision, which does not depend on the actions being in contemplation or furtherance of a trade dispute and which in fact deals directly with trade unions that are registered under the 1871 Act. Those who constructed the 1906 Act provided in general that a trade union could not be sued in respect of any tortious act committed on its behalf (s.4). The intention here of course was to protect the funds of trade unions in the aftermath of the *Taff Vale* case.

This brings us therefore to a consideration of the phrase "in contemplation or furtherance of a trade dispute" (referred to by K.W. Wedderburn as the "golden formula"). Almost every single word of this little phrase has been tested, distinguished and scrutinised by the courts. In a word it has been the subject of what has been described as strict interpretation. The reason of course is plain enough. The law sees itself as dealing with essentially unlawful activity on which by statute certain immunities have been conferred. It follows from this that the immunities must apply only where they are clearly required by the Act. To interpret the Act in any other way would, in the eyes of the courts, run counter to the general thrust of the law. It is not surprising therefore that the history of the Trade Disputes Act 1906 has been a history of continuous limitation and refinement. While phrases like "in contemplation of" or "in furtherance of" gave rise to much discussion, perhaps the phrase that created most difficulty was the phrase "trade dispute." This in turn had been further defined by section 5(3) of the same Act to mean "any dispute between employers and workmen, or between workmen and workmen, which is connected with the employment or non-employment or the terms of employment, or with the conditions of labour of any person, and the expression 'workmen' means all persons employed in trade or industry, whether or not in the employment of the employer with whom a trade dispute arises . . . ." In this country perhaps the phrase which has given rise to most debate was that which restricted the application of the Act to "persons employed in trade or industry," a phrase interpreted by the courts in a manner which excluded public servants and all those not involved in commercial or industrial activities. After much contention, the matter was resolved by the Trade Disputes (Amendment) Act 1982 and the traditional immunities were extended to all employees other than the police and defence forces.

TRADE UNION ACT 1913

Before proceeding to consider the legislation as it was enacted by the Oireachtas in this country, it might be well to mention one further piece of legislation which was enacted before we secured our own independent legislature, this being the Trade Union Act 1913. It arose because in 1910 the House of Lords held in the case of *Osborne* v. *Amalgamated Society of Railway Servants* (1911) that trade unions were not entitled to raise or expend funds for political purposes. This meant that a trade union acted *ultra vires* if it attempted to engage in political activity. The Trade Union Act 1913 provided an entitlement for a trade union under certain conditions, to create and maintain a political fund.

THE IRISH TRADE UNION MOVEMENT

We must now take account of the manner in which Irish industrial relations diverged from those in the United Kingdom, since this divergence gave rise to certain features which were unique to Ireland.

When the new and independent state was created in Ireland in 1922 the six North-eastern counties, indeed themselves forming a separate statelet, remained part of the United Kingdom. In 1894, a trade union congress or centre to which virtually all the trade unions were affiliated had been established for Ireland, reflecting the creation of a similar centre, the Trades Union Congress, in Britain some decades earlier. While some Irish workers were organised in local Irish unions, the majority of Irish workers were organised in the large amalgamated unions, spread throughout the United Kingdom and with headquarters in Britain. The Irish branches of these great unions and the local Irish unions made up the Irish Trades Union Congress. When the new State was created in 1922, this congress, which catered for all unions North and South, continued; and indeed the present Irish Congress of Trade Unions is still organised in this manner.

The same great nationalist impulse that brought the independent

State of Ireland into being also caused some of the large British unions in Ireland to fragment, as some of their members broke away to form exclusively Irish-based unions. Nevertheless a great number of members remained loyal to their original unions; and these persist to the present day, some quite powerful, and if anything growing in influence.

In the Republic of Ireland therefore we have craft unions that are Irish-based and craft unions that are British-based, organising workers of the same skill; we have general unions that are Irish-based and general unions that are British-based, sometimes co-existing in the same employment. Of course a bare description such as this can give a much more intractable picture than actually exists. As one would expect there is a wide network of arrangements of various kinds; and in a small country such as Ireland personal relations are important.

These events also had their consequences as far as legal status was concerned. The Irish Transport and General Workers' Union had been formed by James Larkin in 1909. In 1921 there was formed in the United Kingdom the Transport and General Workers' Union, bringing together a number of different unions and these existed in Ireland no less than in Britain. In Dublin therefore there were two head offices established (actually in the same street) one, that of the Irish Transport and General Workers' Union, and the other that of the Transport and General Workers Union, with all the potential for confusion and ambiguity. In order to overcome the difficulty the Irish Transport and General Workers' Union instituted proceedings in 1922 in the Dail Eireann Courts (which were then of doubtful constitutionality) and in June of that year got an order restraining the amalgamated union from using the name Transport and General Workers' Union. As a result of this the latter union by rule decided that in Ireland it would be known as the Amalgamated Transport and General Workers' Union, and the amended rule was recorded with the Registrar of Friendly Societies in Saorstat Eireann in August 1925.

This however was by no means the end of the case. During the years that followed, Irish nationalism developed a rough and exclusive character and particularly in the leadership of the Irish Transport and General Workers' Union we find a growing determination to exclude British-based unions from the Irish Free State, as it was then described. An opportunity to undermine the legitimacy of the amalgamated trade unions in Ireland lay in the Act of 1871. This as we know provided for the voluntary registration of trade unions and the Trade Union Amendment Act 1876 provided that a registered trade union operating in more than one of the three countries, England, Scotland and Ireland, then constituting the United Kingdom, should be registered in the country in which its registered offices were to be situated, but that if it wished to operate in another of the countries, it should then send its rules to the Registrar there who would record them. This was regarded as sufficient for its being seen as a registered union in that country. It did not therefore have to seek registration there.

This naturally was the procedure followed by the amalgamated unions in Ireland, and in particular by the Amalgamated Transport and General Workers' Union. By virtue of section 3 of the Adaptations and Enactments Act 1922 the name Ireland came to mean Saorstat Eireann but this radically altered the whole purport of the section, which as Judge Meredith stated in his judgment in 1935 in *Irish Transport and General Workers' Union* v. *Transport and General Workers' Union* (1936) was based on a legislative union of the three countries. The fact was that the British legislation never contemplated a situation where a trade union, established and controlled outside the United Kingdom, operated within the United Kingdom; and when the same legal construct was imported automatically into the law of the Free State a situation of mutual exclusivity arose. Meredith J. therefore decided that "the recording in the Registry of Trade Unions in Saorstat Eireann of the rules of the Transport and General Workers' Union or of the Amalgamated Transport and General Workers' Union or of any amendment of the said rules is inoperative and of no legal effect" (p. 484).

The amalgamated unions nonetheless decided to make no issue of this matter but continued to handle their business in the ordinary way, conscious of the fact that their legitimacy as trade unions sprang from the intention of their members primarily and that registration merely provided certain advantages under the law but was not anything more radical than that. The upshot of it is that in Ireland today, amalgamated, or British-based, unions are on the whole not registered with the Irish Registrar and, more than that, this special situation is recognised by the Trade Union Act of 1941 and they are not at a disadvantage to any great extent on that account.

TRADE UNION ACT 1941

The Trade Union Act of 1941 is the second major instrument of structural reform in trade union affairs. It was conceived and enacted during a period when industrial unrest was seen as a major peril for the country. This also was the period during the last war when the Irish nation appeared to be at considerable risk. It followed therefore that the citizens were prepared to accept from the government a degree of regulation in their own lives which might not normally be the case. At the time there was a widespread belief that industrial unrest was greatly aggravated, if not caused, by two structural defects in the trade union movement, first the very large number of trade unions, fragmented and unco-ordinated, and secondly the presence in the country of a substantial number of British-based unions whose activities were seen by many, quite wrongly as it turned out, to be sinister and hostile to the best interests of the nation.

The Trade Union Act of 1941 set out in particular to exclude certain trade unions from operating. This had to be so if the trade union movement was to be reorganised and in particular it was necessary if it was intended to exclude British trade unions altogether.

Since trade unions could not be disestablished by law, the legislators instead set out to distinguish between the existence of a trade union and the exercise by that trade union of certain fundamental functions, principally the function of collective bargaining or negotiation. It was thought that although one could not disestablish a trade union one could however regulate the function of negotiation, licensing certain trade unions for the purpose and excluding others from such activity. This was the central idea behind the 1941 Act. It was decided therefore to provide that trade unions should, if they wished to engage in collective bargaining, have a negotiating licence and those bodies that proceeded to negotiate without such a licence committed an offence.

Naturally enough there had to be certain exceptions to this general provision. We have seen that one must always permit an employer to negotiate directly with his own workers. Other exemptions were made in the case of civil service bodies and also teachers' unions and associations. This appears to have arisen from the idea that civil servants could not enter into a conflict with their employers because in some sense such a conflict constituted a degree of disloyalty to the State. This was one of the reasons too why civil servants were excluded from access to the Labour Court which was established under the Industrial Relations Act 1946.

The appropriate minister was thus empowered to recognise such associations or unions and once he did so they could legitimately exercise the function of negotiation. Of course their position was far less secure than that of a trade union with a negotiating licence because a trade union, once it fulfilled certain conditions, was automatically granted a negotiating licence, while in the case of civil service associations and other excepted bodies the minister concerned could always exercise a degree of discretion. The conditions which qualified a collectivity to receive a negotiating licence concerned the size and stability of the organisation and were represented essentially by the capacity of the organisation to deposit a sum of money in the High Court. Once the objects of the association were those of a trade union and once the sum of money was in fact lodged then it followed that a negotiating licence would be issued. The Trade Union Act 1971 subsequently required that notification of the intention to seek a negotiating licence must be given by the trade union in question to the Minister for Labour and to the Irish Congress of Trade Unions not less than 18 months before the application is made. Furthermore it required that a union should have 500 members at least at the date of application and also at the date 18 months earlier. Finally the appropriate deposit must be made with the High Court, now of a sum not less than £5,000 (the actual amount depending on the size of the union).

The trade union movement in Ireland today is therefore still a very fragmented body, the trade union centre, the Irish Congress of Trade Unions, having in membership unions both North and South and therefore still continuing, however uncertainly, as an all-Ireland institution. In the Republic of Ireland the total number of employees organised in trade unions is approaching the 500,000 mark and the number of unions is about 90. Yet this can be misleading since a small number of large unions represent the overwhelming majority of all employees; 19 unions in fact represent 82 per cent. of the total membership. As we have already recognised, the unions differ in their nature; there are craft unions and general unions; there are industrial unions; there are unions with headquarters in Britain and unions with headquarters in the Republic of Ireland. In such circumstances there was always pressure for reform largely by way of amalgamation and simplification but these on the whole have failed principally because of the intractable difficulties associated with reconstructing unions which are often traditional and well established.

An endeavour by the government to engage in widespread reform, which was also essayed in the 1941 Act under Part III, was declared to be repugnant to the Irish Constitution. In recent years the government has fostered amalgamations, if not to any great effect, and this is represented by the Trade Union Act 1975.

EMPLO .

When we turn to employers we find that in the private sector the Federated Union of Employers is the most significant and influential of the organisations. It originated as an organised resistance to the activities of James Larkin during the period from 1909 to 1911, and in 1941, by reason of the provisions of the Tra· · Union Act of that year, it became the Federated Union of Emp.. ers and secured a negotiating licence as a trade union.

Once the Labour Court was established in .946 (which we deal with below) the services of the FUE rapidly increased and so did the membership so that today it is a highly developed centralised body, organised in four regions of the country and with nearly 3,000 industrial and commercial establishments in membership. The employment content of member companies of the FUE is in the order of 250,000. There are also a number of other prominent employers' federations, such as the Irish Printing Federation and the Electrical Contractors' Association, both in close association with the Federated Union of Employers, and (with a more independent stance), the Construction Industry Federation. These federations represent the management side of industry and business in all matters concerning industrial relations, labour and social affairs. The Federated Union of Employers in particular does not purport to represent industry in its general policy-making role as for example the Confederation of British Industry does. This function is discharged by the Confederation of Irish Industry.

Apart from the federations of employers in the private sector there are also two other categories of employers, the semi-State or parastatal bodies and the State itself. The semi-State or State-sponsored bodies are very numerous and very diverse in character. Some are straightforward trading enterprises or nationalised industries, differing from the general run of private enterprise only in their shareholding and control. These, as we shall see in Chapter 2, have become particularly significant in the Irish experiments in worker participation at board level. In contrast, there are committees and councils whose members, appointed by the State, serve without remuneration and employ virtually no labour. The State-sponsored bodies in fact were established as the need was seen, and therefore do not appear to be governed by any very coherent philosophy of creation and development. We are concerned here only with those which are significant employers, and some are very large indeed. The five semi-State bodies represented on the Employer-Labour Conference employ in all very nearly 45,000 persons, with one, the transport authority Coras Iompair Eireann, employing over 16,000, and the Electricity Supply Loard employing over 11,000.

The State itself employs, through its civil service, approximately 30,000 persons. Up to January 1, 1984, the largest department of State was the Department of Posts and Telegraphs, employing 29,000 persons. It was decided by the Government to create two State-sponsored bodies to discharge the functions of the Department, greatly reducing the numbers in this category.

The local government system, although highly centralised in its control, is undoubtedly very diverse, including local authorities and also various specialised local bodies. The common distinguishing characteristic of all these bodies is a territorially limited jurisdiction. The number employed as a whole by all these bodies is approximately 35,000.

COLLECTIVE BARGAINING IN IRELAND

While regulation has some role in collective bargaining, it is in Ireland a very minor one. Regulation is certainly evident in the area of trade union activity; it is evident in the notion of a floor of rights in employment; but in the area of collective bargaining the thrust of statute is to construct institutions which assist the parties to reach an accommodation. Of course, statute is by no means the only method by which the government may facilitate an accommodation. Not only can it promote non-statutory institutions but it can promote as well framework agreements of a national character which greatly stabilise the bargaining process. These we shall discuss in due course.

The outstanding fact about a collective agreement is that there is a collectivity at work at least on the part of the workers. A collectivity for our purposes here is not a unitary group, such as a board of directors, but a widely dispersed group the members of which by definition cannot have a direct involvement in the bargain but at best an indirect one. Furthermore, as we have seen, the actions of a collectivity in the market place are viewed with suspicion by the law, whether the collectivity is one of traders or of workers. We therefore must expect that in the field of collective bargaining the rights, obligations and purposes of the parties, and the manner in which these are viewed by the public authority and by the courts, will sometimes be complex and difficult to resolve in a common understanding.

We begin by distinguishing between, on the one hand, the process of bargaining, and on the other, the rights and obligations which arise from a bargain once it has been made. The process of bargaining simply means that the parties are recognised to have conflicting objectives which the process is intended to resolve. This conflict of objectives is described in industrial relations theory as a conflict of interest, in contrast to the conflict of rights which can arise where the parties have bound themselves by agreement or are under some obligation by reason of statute or by reason of the common law.

A conflict of interest is distinguished by the fact that the objective of each party to the conflict is legitimate. Sometimes, as with certain forms of industrial action, the means of advancing that objective may be illegitimate, but the objective itself is not. In a word, it is in no way illegitimate for a worker to seek an increase in pay, and in no way illegitimate for an employer to resist it. If a number of workers join together to advance their common interest in the matter of pay, they may indeed find themselves in doubtful territory under the common law, but the objective of increased pay of itself is unexceptional.

If, then, a group of workers and their employer, determined on some civilised resolution of such a conflict of interest, present themselves before some tribunal or other, it is clear that they are not asking the tribunal to declare one party's objective to be legitimate and the other party's to be illegitimate in some mutually exclusive way. On the contrary, they are asking essentially for a prudent and respected view which both sides might consider. Let us contrast this with the notion of judgment where a tribunal declares one side to be right, and in doing so declares the other to be wrong. This will arise where one party claims against another that he has breached an agreement or a bargain, already made and binding in some sense. This is what is described as the area of conflicting rights. In the area of conflicting interests, however, the notion of judgment is wholly inappropriate. On the other hand it must not be thought that a conflict of interest is without passion and conviction. Industrial disputes frequently manifest the very contrary. But no matter in what imperative terms the objectives of the parties are described, the reality is that there can be applied to these conflicting interests no rule, no law, which would identify one as right and exclude the other.

A very practical point follows from this. A tribunal acting in relation to a conflict of interest has no grounds for enforcing its view on the parties, at least under Irish practice, although from time to time this has been suggested. It was suggested for example in the Report of the Commission of Inquiry on Industrial Relations (1981) in the case of trade union recognition disputes and inter-union disputes. So-called compulsory arbitration usually means that the parties, in advance of the tribunal's opinion and irrespective of its import, undertake to accept it. The compelling nature of the recommendation obviously springs not from the character of recommendation in itself but from a prior agreement of the parties in its regard. One can by law create an enforceable arbitration process as with the New Zealand Arbitration Board, but such a board would appear in fact to exercise a delegated legislative function of some kind rather than a judgment.

The process of collective bargaining is distinguished by another important characteristic. It takes place in the context of a strong and continuing relationship between the parties, a relationship which is greatly structured in rights and obligations, sometimes arising from earlier agreements, sometimes from convention and frequently in later times from statute. If it is in its character a market place activity, it takes place very much within a relationship of mutual dependence, so extensive that the actual bargaining itself may become obscured. (For quite a contrasting view one might see Allan Flanders, *Management and Unions* 1975, p. 216). All this is much in contrast with a simple bargain such as buying apples in a market stall where if a bargain is not struck the parties go their way quite unflurried, while in the case of collective bargaining in employment there is a great imperative to find an accommodation. This is what may give rise to the desire of the parties for an institution of facilitation and the concern of the public authority to provide it.

ENFORCEABILITY OF COLLECTIVE AGREEMENTS

We turn now to the question of the collective bargain once it has been made. We can lead into the heart of the topic by asking ourselves why, in practice, in Ireland as in the United Kingdom, collective agreements are not enforceable at law. We use the term "in practice" because the question as a legal proposition is somewhat shrouded in doubt. Although the issue has not been conclusively decided, the *dicta* by two Supreme Court judges in the case of *Goulding Chemicals Ltd.* v. *Bolger* (1977) appear to suggest that the Irish courts favour the idea of legal enforceability of all agreements not covered by section 4 of the Trade Union Act 1871. In general, however, there is no great desire for such enforceability among industrial relations practitioners.

But why should this be so? Once again we must return to the fact that at least one of the parties to the bargain is a collectivity and must conduct its affairs through a representative, a trade union official. When the official concludes an agreement with an employer therefore, he does so not merely with the intention of binding himself but of binding often a large and disparate group. He will frequently ballot the members but the validation here is merely by way of majority and often a very slender one. What then is the relationship between the members and the agreement? It could be suggested that while it is of course indirect, their obligation to their union is not, and in that regard they have undertaken to be bound by majority decision even where they are personally in profound disagreement. But the trade union is a voluntary association, sometimes in competition with others, often fissiparous in character, and a trade union official is a servant of his members and not their master; therefore the problem of discipline and penalties is particularly difficult. An attempt can be made by statute (as was done in the United Kingdom in 1971) to make the trade union and the official constructively liable under the law for the wrongdoing of their members, but this, in our general tradition of the common law, is of doubtful propriety in the light of the strong traditional doctrine regarding the limits of vicarious responsibility. But quite apart from this difficulty, collective agreements, particularly in relation to pay and conditions, are peculiarly subject to deterioration because of changing market place conditions; and finally one must not forget the reluctance of trade unions to have their agreements made justiciable in the courts of law, a disposition even more marked in Ireland than in Britain.

Although all these difficulties exist, a collective agreement once made is indeed binding and does indeed impose rights and obligations, although the sanction appears to be essentially a moral one. Nevertheless it must not be discounted. There is by and large a considerable commitment by both parties to the observance of collective agreements. The strong and continuing relationship between them, though often full of tension, requires it. One can see then yet another function for some tribunal in the area, a function which is in the full sense that of judgment, in relation to breaches of agreement or conflicts of interpretation. In practice they are unenforceable, but they are nevertheless judicial acts, quite unlike the recommendations which are made in the area of conflicting interests.

We recognise too that in the area of statutory rights in employment, the "floor of rights" as it has been called, the public authority frequently avails of tribunals of a special kind (see Chapter 9), special, that is, to industrial relations, although it could just as well avail of the ordinary courts of law. Here however the decisions are clearly judgments and are enforceable. Their enforceability provides no great difficulty since in all such cases the tribunal is dealing essentially with individual and not collective rights and the problems of the collectivity do not arise.

Finally behind all these institutional devices stand the courts of law to which any citizen may have recourse to right a wrong or secure a remedy, but here, in the tradition of the law, the individual, the person, is the bearer of the right, particularly (as is frequently the case in industrial relations) where tortious matters are involved. For reasons which we have already discussed, the collectivity on the whole makes a poor showing.

INSTITUTIONS OF THE MIDDLE GROUND

What functions then should we seek from institutions in the collective bargaining field, that is to say those which take up the middle ground and which the public authority may have an interest in providing? First we must recognise that in the vast majority of cases the parties successfully strike their own bargains and successfully maintain them. In the case of intractability, however, we can distinguish the following functions. As an aid to the process of bargaining, there is the function of conciliation, that is to say the function of bridging and of exploration of positions. This has two quite distinct aspects which some institutions such as the Northern Ireland Labour Relations Agency and the corresponding institutions in Britain keep quite strictly apart. These are the function of conciliation where the conciliator's skill lies not in offering a view himself but in facilitating the bargaining process; the other is where a view is explicitly offered, a function which may frequently be described as arbitration. None of these functions is judicial in character. However, as an aid to the maintenance of a bargain, there is the function of interpreting the collective agreement and identifying where a party has breached it. This is quite clearly a judicial function, although in Ireland and in the United Kingdom (but not in some major European countries) the judgment, as a rule, is not legally enforceable. And finally there is the function of vindicating personal rights in employment whether these be statutory in character or perhaps constitutional. This is also a clear judicial function and as a rule such judgments are indeed enforceable.

Against this background let us consider the institutions which the public authority in Ireland has created for these various purposes. The Industrial Relations Act 1946 established the Labour Court, the principal institution in Ireland for facilitating the settlement of industrial disputes. The Act provided that the Court could establish Joint Labour Committees and register certain collective agreements (see Chap. 4). The Act also provided that the Court could register, and therefore foster, voluntary Joint Industrial Councils. But these were of minor significance compared to the Court's two major functions, conciliation and the investigating of industrial disputes. Conciliation was effected by means of Conciliation Officers, now known as Industrial Relations Officers, all appointed by the Court but in practice drawn exclusively from the civil service. The investigating of industrial disputes was carried on by the Court itself sitting publicly, hearing submissions and making recommendations. The function of the conciliation officer was largely one of assisting the parties, and the function of the Court that of recommending the terms on which a dispute might be settled, a form of non-binding arbitration. Most of these functions were not judicial in character. The title "Court" therefore is quite misleading, made even more difficult by the powers given to the Court to summon witnesses under penalty and to take evidence under oath, powers which in fact it has never used. Indeed the government itself, reflecting the concern of the trade unions, has never appointed a chairman to the Court who was professionally competent in the law, and until such time as the Court was given certain powers under the sex discrimination legislation (which we deal with in Chap. 6) there had been only one occasion where a party before the Court was represented by counsel and solicitor.

The Court originally consisted of a chairman a deputy chairman and four wing men, all appointed by the government but of course in consultation with the trade unions and the employers, and in the case of the wing men, on their nomination. The Court has greatly developed since then and now there are three deputy chairmen and eight wing men, the Court sitting in four divisions (see also Chapter 9).

Originally, section 3 of the Industrial Relations Act 1946 excluded from access to the Court civil servants and local government employees, giving rise to the establishment of the separate system of conciliation and arbitration schemes which we deal with below. However, there has been a steady broadening of access. Under the

Industrial Relations (Amendment) Act 1955 access was extended to many local authority employees, and the Industrial Relations Act 1969 gave the Minister for the Public Service powers at his discretion to extend access to any group of public service employees with the exception of established civil servants.

Section 68(1) of the Industrial Relations Act 1946 set out criteria which should guide the Court in regard to its recommendations. They were contradictory and therefore confusing:

> "The Court, having investigated a trade dispute, shall make a recommendation setting forth its opinion on the merits of the dispute and the terms on which, in the public interest and with a view to promoting industrial peace, it should be settled, due regard being had to the fairness of the said terms to parties concerned, and the prospects of the said terms being acceptable to them."

Under the 1969 Act they were much simplified, now reading in section 19:

> "The Court, having investigated a trade dispute, may make a recommendation setting forth its opinion on the merits of the dispute and the terms on which it should be settled."

This new criterion was intended to reflect a current belief in the Court itself that it should approach its task in a wholly pragmatic and flexible way. In fact the Court was viewing with growing concern not only the occasional government attempts to use it in order to influence pay policies, but much more than that the practice of trade unions and employers to enter into overarching national pay agreements, which were intended to govern virtually all pay and conditions for a stated period. The agreements which were by and large successful created inevitably some industrial tension since the parties were vigorous in attempting to ensure the observance of their terms and naturally they expected the Labour Court to take the same view. But the Labour Court at the time was impatient of such constraints and anxious to be free to settle disputes exactly as it saw fit, that is to say, to maintain the role of promoting an accommodation in the circumstances of the case, not making a judgment. In the later 1970s however, the Court, though emphasising that it had no obligation to do so, followed in its recommendations the terms of the national pay agreements, interpreting them and urging their implementation, although not without misgivings. In this it fulfilled a judicial function, although of course its recommendations continued to be unenforceable.

The drift towards a more juridical character for the Court continued in legislation. The Industrial Relations Act 1969 had also provided for the appointment of Rights Commissioners, persons of experience in industrial relations, whose task was to attempt to resolve individual cases which did not bear on pay and conditions. An appeal however lay from their recommendations to the Labour Court. But much more was to follow. While a special tribunal, the Employment Appeals Tribunal, was established for the purposes of the Redundancy Payments Acts and the Unfair Dismissals Act 1977, the Court itself became the appeals board from decisions of the Equality Officers under the Anti-Discrimination (Pay) Act 1974 and the Employment Equality Act 1977 (see chaps. 6 and 9). Yet despite this substantial growth in straight judicial business the Court continued to insist on its essentially non-judicial character and has from time to time expressed a growing unease, an unease which is shared by many employers and trade union officials and which has given rise to certain proposals for reform.

SCHEMES FOR STATE EMPLOYEES

We have already seen that under section 3 of the Industrial Relations Act 1946 civil servants, among others, were excluded from access to the Labour Court. In 1949 however, a conciliation and arbitration scheme was agreed for civil servants, introduced on a trial basis in 1950 and eventually made permanent on April 1, 1955. Other important groups followed, teachers in the 1950s and in 1962 the police, to be followed in 1963 by local authority staff. The schemes have two major features, these being agreed procedures for the discussion of claims between staff and management (*i.e.* the conciliation level), and in the event of disagreement at that level arrangements for arbitration under an independent chairman appointed by the government in agreement with both sides. Unlike the Labour Court, the chairman in these schemes is frequently a prominent member of the bar or a judge. The process is orderly and the recommendations of the chairman are usually accepted, but despite this the functions performed by the arbitration board are by and large not judicial in character. They are essentially designed to promote accommodation between the parties, despite the air of finality which they possess.

Although in these matters the government is acting as an employer, it cannot escape its wider responsibilities as government, and since a civil service settlement can have considerable knock-on effects (perhaps more in the past than now) it can have an impact not only on the public purse but on pay policy generally. The civil service scheme provided therefore that where the government considered that a pay increase could have such a consequence they could introduce a motion in Dail Eireann to reject it or modify it. Although this provision was an agreed one, its application met with vigorous resentment from the staff on the one occasion on which the government availed of it. The chairmen of these arbitration boards have a further problem in that they find it difficult to make an evaluation of government arguments in relation to the national economic consequences of their recommendations, and one recent chairman therefore discounted such submissions, claiming that the government had its own remedies if the public interest were imperilled. Nevertheless, with the outstanding exception of certain low-paid grades, the schemes have worked well.

Large employers, and in particular the commercial state companies, frequently develop their own conciliation systems which normally provide, as a final step, reference to the Labour Court, or in the case of one very large institution, the Electricity Supply Board, to a joint industrial council.

Finally in the area of government initiatives there is the Review Body on Higher Remuneration in the Public Sector which was established in 1969 with the object of recommending on the pay of higher civil servants, chief executives of State bodies and such others as the government might decide. In practice its recommendations extend to the judiciary and ministers for government as well. In an early report in 1972 it attempted to establish certain objective criteria in dealing with such different groups, emphasising the overriding significance of external comparisons between jobs of a like responsibility, and these criteria they have repeated in subsequent reports. At best however they are guides, and do not provide rules upon which a judgment can be made. While the Review Body in the nature of things offers a view which is regarded as final, nevertheless its status is that of a third view, *i.e.* an opinion, not a judgment.

NATIONAL BARGAINING

Finally there are the national pay agreements, fostered by the government, but in fact created by the national employer and trade union groups acting in a bipartite manner. It is possible to see in national agreements little more than an understanding nationally on the maximum pay which trade unions undertake to claim; but they hold out greater promise than that, although for much of the 1950s and early 1960s they were little more. In Ireland it was unusual to find at industry or company level wide-ranging collective agreements particularly in regard to procedures, and disputes tended to be disputes as to interests, and in the absence of rule quite intractable. The notion of a national agreement therefore that would set out procedures for negotiation and the resolution of disputes offered the hope of a more orderly system where, in substantial areas, rights and obligations were created which could be the subject of adjudication. This was the objective in the first national pay agreement to be concluded. It was secured in 1948 by the chairman of the Labour Court of the time, R.J.P. Mortished, and it not only determined pay but it provided procedures for dealing with disputes during the currency of the agreement in which the Labour Court had a significant role. However the stresses of the time overwhelmed the system, and no further attempt was made until 1964. This too, while very much more ambitious, ran into difficulties (see Charles McCarthy, *The Decade of Upheaval* 1973, Chap. 3).

The series of national pay agreements which spanned most of the decade of the 1970s were very much more elaborate and had a number of special characteristics, not least a joint body which both negotiated them and supervised them, the Employer-Labour Conference. This body at quite an early stage established a steering committee and also an interpretation committee and an adjudication committee. The last named had the function of adjudicating on performance, that is to say of judging whether a party to the agreement had departed from its terms. It can be seen therefore that both in interpretation and in adjudication the Employer-Labour Conference had a clear judicial role. However, the steering committee was the major subcommittee of the Conference and dealt with all these questions in a manner more marked by conciliation than adjudication, although some remarkable adjudications were in fact made by the adjudication committee. The Labour Court had a role under the national pay agreements which was not dissimilar. In its more formal setting, however, it found itself confronted with the task of applying the national pay agreements to disputes coming before it, which, as we have seen, it did with reluctance, believing that it distorted its traditional flexibility in resolving disputes. That there should be some ambiguity in the roles of these bodies is not unexpected, and in practice, the Employer-Labour Conference did not, in later years pursue its adjudicating role.

The government's role in all this was particularly interesting. At the outset the employers' side to the Employer-Labour Conference consisted of the private sector federations and some of the large State companies; but the government itself was a major employer in its own right, and by 1972 was a member of the Conference, but only in its role as employer. The trade unions had adopted an unswerving policy that the Conference should be a bipartite one, and so it was (certainly in theory and largely in practice) since the government as an employer was represented by civil servants, while the government in its role as government when it wished to consult the parties did so through the agency of its ministers. In 1979 and again in 1980 there was a further development in this system of bargaining. The agreements of these years were called "National Understandings"; they consisted of understandings in relation to wider political matters (employment, taxation, social welfare provisions, and so forth) worked out between the government and each side of the Conference, against the background of which the parties negotiated bilaterally a national pay agreement in accordance with the older model. There have been no national agreements or understandings since 1980, although there have been two movements in pay, both of a reasonably orderly kind, the orderliness being due as much to the difficulties of the recession as to any other reason. It is true that the government's role in this is somewhat ambiguous, and were it not for the trade unions' traditional commitment to bipartite bargaining it would undoubtedly have been larger. There has been evidence of late of the government attempting to exercise a more direct influence in bargaining, but this is resisted in particular by the trade unions.

But despite the government's apparently lesser role in the negotiating of the terms of national pay agreements they have regarded them as of considerable significance, have carefully encouraged them and supported them where it appeared appropriate. The outstanding example was that of the dispute in the commercial banking system where neither the trade union of bank officials nor the bank employers were affiliated to any body involved in the Employer-Labour Conference and therefore in the national pay agreement of the time. The banks therefore, despite pressure from the government, decided to yield to the demands of the union to pay increases in excess of the *maxima* set out in the national pay agreement. This would have greatly damaged the acceptability of the national agreement of the time, and the government in the circumstances enacted the Banks (Remuneration and Conditions of Employment) (Temporary Provisions) Act 1973 which prohibited the banks under penalty from paying more than that set out in the national pay agreement. Legislation in such an area was not something which the trade unions would normally have accepted, but in this case they made no comment. Of course the incident was a most unusual one since it would be difficult to find another substantial employer and trade union unaffiliated to either party to the Employer-Labour Conference; nevertheless it does indicate that the government viewed this quite bilateral arrangement as having some sort of national legislative character, since they expected it to govern all pay movements and conditions of work, whether the persons who negotiated them were parties to the national pay agreements or not.

There is one final point to be made. While there does not exist at present any national agreement or national understanding, the Employer-Labour Conference continues in existence, and therefore we must assume that some national arrangement in the future would not be unexpected.

INDUSTRIAL CONFLICT

It is frequently asserted in the media and stated by commentators that Ireland has a particularly "bad" record for industrial conflict. International comparisons, some of which are referred to in the *Report of the Commission of Inquiry on Industrial Relations* (1981), do not entirely back up the assertion. They show that some industrialised countries, such as the United States of America, Italy, and Australia have over the past years consistently had a greater number of man-days lost due to strikes than has the Republic of Ireland. Furthermore, figures recently released by the Department of Labour show a continuing decline in the number of man-days lost due to strikes during the last 10 years (with the sole exception of 1979, in which a large number of lost days were accounted for by the lengthy dispute in the Department of Posts and Telegraphs). Public and media awareness of an apparent growth of industrial conflict is therefore wrong, and probably based more on the dramatic nature of some of the more publicised strikes than on any real figures or facts.

It is also in the area of industrial conflict that the principles of voluntarism, to be discussed in Chapter 2, become most controversial. Strike law in the Republic of Ireland is governed primarily by two statutes passed by the Westminster Parliament prior to independence. These Acts are, respectively, the Conspiracy and Protection of Property Act 1875, and the Trade Disputes Act 1906, as amended by the Trade Disputes (Amendment) Act 1982 (see above). In broad terms, as we have seen, these two Acts remove the criminal law and the law of torts from acts committed "in contemplation or furtherance of a trade dispute." In particular, sections 1–3 of the 1906 Act give protection against actions in tort for conspiracy, watching and besetting (picketing) and inducement to break employment contracts.

The protection afforded by the 1906 Act has been criticised in two senses and from two directions. On the one hand the Federated Union of Employers, supported by some other employer and semi-State opinion, has consistently argued that the protection given to strikers by the Act is excessive and should be restricted so as to compel strikers to follow certain specified disputes procedures. These views were broadly accepted and followed by the Commission on Industrial Relations in its report (see in particular P. III and P. V.)

On the other hand, trade unions have consistently argued that the interpretation of the 1906 Act by the courts has removed a large measure of the protection which the Act was designed to provide. This, it is claimed, has come about through, firstly, the restrictive interpretation by the judiciary of the Act's provisions, and secondly, through the excessive and irrational granting of interlocutory injunctions to employers in trade disputes. Both of these problems were highlighted by the case of *Talbot (Ireland) Ltd.* v. *Merrigan* (1981).

The Department of Labour, in its recent *Discussion Document on Industrial Relations Reform* (1983), has acknowledged that changes in strike law and in particular the imposition of restrictions as advocated by the FUE, can only be successfully implemented if broadly accepted by both employers and trade unions. Since such broad support is unlikely to materialise in the near future, one must assume that the broad framework of strike law will remain the same as it presently is. However, there are some areas in particular which have been singled out for likely amendments, including the area of unofficial strikes, and the question of the principles upon which interlocutory injunctions should be granted in trade disputes.

2 The Nature of Irish Employment Law

VOLUNTARISM AND THE ROLE OF THE STATE

The Irish industrial relations system, like that of Great Britain, is generally described as a voluntaristic one. What this means is that, as a matter of tradition, the law has not played a major role in regulating industrial relations practice. The *Report of the Commission of Inquiry on Industrial Relations* (P1. 114, July 28, 1981) described the Irish system as one in which "the parties to the industrial relations process are free to agree, or not to agree, on the substantive principles which are to govern their mutual rights and obligations and to regulate their behaviour, without the intervention of the State." The Commission found that this characteristic of the Irish industrial relations system has the "general support of both trade unions and employers." (p. 10)

The reason for the strong adherence to voluntarism, at any rate on the trade union side, can partly be explained by reference to the shared industrial relations history of both Ireland and Great Britain. The unfavourable attitude of judges towards trade unions and trade union action during the nineteenth and early twentieth centuries led to a desire that the courts should be kept out of the industrial relations process. This general attitude has also meant that when legal intervention, particularly in the area of industrial conflict, does take place, it is frequently unsuccessful. Some examples of this would include the failure of the Electricity (Special Provisions) Act 1966 to prevent picketing in the strike by ESB employees in 1968, as well as the failure of the courts to prevent or bring to an end the occupation of the Ranks factories in Dublin and Limerick in 1983. As was noted recently by the Department of Labour in its *Discussion Document on*

Industrial Relations Reform (November 1983), legal intervention in industrial relations will only work if it has the general consent of those whose conduct is to be regulated.

Nevertheless, it would be quite wrong to conclude from all this that there is no substantive labour law in the Republic of Ireland. Apart from the common law, there is now a large corpus of statute law dealing with industrial relations matters. This statutory intervention, which may be said to have the support of the majority of industrial relations practitioners, arises out of the recognition that the State must ensure minimum civilised standards for all employees. It must however be noted that these statutes deal primarily with the individual employment relationship. It would still be true to say, in a general way, that legal intervention has not proved successful in the procedural or collective arena. At the same time, it must be doubted whether the idea of voluntarism, as it has been traditionally stated, still has much relevance in industrial relations theory and practice. It cannot really be argued any longer that the law has no place in industrial relations, since economic and social developments make legal intervention of some kind fairly inevitable. The argument should instead probably centre on the question of the exact nature of the legal intervention, rather than on whether it should take place at all. In this sense, the continued resistance of trade unions to legal restrictions on their freedom to take industrial action is still understandable. But at the same time, legal intervention to ensure adequate social and economic conditions for the national workforce is certainly required. It is this kind of motivation which underlies the majority of the statutes which we are to discuss below. As will become clear from the discussion, there is a lot which still needs to be done by the Oireachtas.

EMPLOYMENT LAW AND THE CONTRACTUAL RELATIONSHIP

Largely as a result of the tradition of voluntarism, as explained above, there is in Ireland relatively little of what on the continent of Europe would be described as "collective labour law." This means that the regulation of the employment relationship takes place almost exclusively at the individual contractual level. In broad terms, therefore, employment law is based on the assumption that an employer and an employee, or "master" and "servant" in the old parlance, enter into a contractual relationship, on equal terms, setting out the terms and conditions of employment.

Irish employment law is therefore an extension of the law of contract, in that almost all of its substance relates to contract law. This
is true even to the extent that statutory provisions with what one
might call a collective intent, as, for example, section 6(2)(a) of the
Unfair Dismissals Act 1977, introduce the protection they provide
through individual contractual means. The effect of that will be discussed in later chapters. The fact that the terms and conditions of
employment of the overwhelming majority of employees in the State
are determined exclusively through collective bargaining carried out
by trade unions and employers or employers' associations does not
become apparent in employment law at all. There are only occasional, usually veiled, references to the social importance of collective
agreements, such as in section 9(4) of the Minimum Notice and
Terms of Employment Act 1973, section 5 of the Anti-Discrimination (Pay) Act 1974 and section 10 of the Employment Equality
Act 1977. (See Chapters 3 and 6).

STATUS AND CONTRACT

The contractual element inherent in employment law is in part a
result of what Sir Henry Maine called the movement "from status to
contract" which is the hallmark of "progressive societies" (*Ancient
Law*, chap. V). In Maine's analysis the movement from status to
contract was progressive in that it was a movement away from feu-
dalism and towards self-determination by individual citizens. As
was explained by the late Sir Otto Kahn-Freund in an article in
1967, in strict legal terms the move from status to contract has not
been reversed since Sir Henry Maine's day in the area of employment law ("A Note on Status and Contract in British Labour Law"
[1967] 30 M.L.R. 635). This was so because the individual worker,
although his terms and conditions of employment might be largely
determined through collective agreements, still took the ultimate
and crucial decision to apply for a job himself. The decision to enter
into an employment relationship was therefore still one taken at the
individual contractual level.

While that analysis is undoubtedly true from a strict legal point of
view, it must nevertheless be asked whether it reflects a common
understanding of what the modern employment relationship is
about. The development of collective bargaining, which in turn as
we have seen is underpinned by the tradition of voluntarism, has
ensured that individual employees have little if any input into the
process which determines their employment conditions and their

pay. This was particularly notable in Ireland during the 1970s, when the wages of the overwhelming majority of the national work-force were determined centrally through national agreements entered into by the employers' associations on the one hand (includ-ing the State) and the trade unions on the other. While, therefore the formation of the employment relationship might depend, at any rate for the most part, on an individual deciding to apply for work, all other forms of regulation of that relationship are carried out at another level. To some extent it would therefore be creating a wrong impression if one were to say that the employment relationship was indicative of contract rather than status. Indeed it is the general emphasis on contract law, as we shall see in later chapters, which has served both to confuse and to frustrate much employment law and it must therefore be treated with great care.

JOB PROPERTY

The nature of the employment relationship has also in recent times been much discussed in the context of another question. Certain statutes which have been enacted, in particular since 1967, have greatly fettered the discretion of employers to hire and fire. Above all the Unfair Dismissals Act 1977 has narrowed down the grounds upon which an employer may legally dismiss an employee. (See Chapter 7). This development has to some extent called into ques-tion the idea that the employment relationship is merely a contrac-tual one. Mary Redmond stated in her Thomas Davis lecture of 1979:

> "The Unfair Dismissals Act 1977 is the greatest signpost to date on the road to recognition of *proprietas* or property rights in employment." ("The Law and Workers' Rights," in *Trade Unions and Change in Irish Society*, (ed.) Donal Nevin, 1980, p. 89).

Similar sentiments were expressed by the then President of the Industrial Tribunals in Britain, Sir Diarmuid Conroy, who said in 1968:

> "Just as a property owner has a right to his property and when he is deprived he is entitled to compensation, so a long term employee is considered to have a right analogous to a right of property in his job . . . " (*Wynes* v. *Southrepps Hall Broiler Farm*).

Whether these developments genuinely indicate the emergence of some concept of job property is a matter for debate. It is possibly more sensible to state that the development of statutory rights in the field of employment reflects an acceptance of the need to formulate and apply a social policy approach to this very important area of people's lives, which may ultimately require an extension of the idea of what constitutes "property" in the modern welfare State.

Whichever way one views these developments, there is implicit in them a recognition that employees have a greater stake in their jobs than the mere sum of their contractual entitlements, and that this stake must in some way be legally protected. Whether the existing protection as contained in the statutes passed since 1967 adequately reflects this development is another matter. It can certainly be argued that a much greater amount of legislation is required in this field than has hitherto been presented, and that the effectiveness of the existing statutory framework even within its limited application is unsatisfactory.

WORKER PARTICIPATION

In contrast with developments in most other Western European countries (with the exception however of Britain), there is no very advanced scheme of industrial democracy or worker participation in Ireland. The Irish Congress of Trade Unions has maintained a fairly constant interest in the development of industrial democracy, beginning with a resolution passed at the 1967 annual conference instructing the Executive Council to examine the matter, which in turn resulted in a special conference in 1968. The 1968 annual conference of Congress then passed a resolution calling on the government "to commence the application of industrial democracy, in consultation with the trade union movement, within the State sector" (Irish Congress of Trade Unions, *Annual Report*, 1967, p. 221). At the same time other suggestions were also made, as in the *Interim Report of the Committee on Industrial Relations in the Electricity Supply Board*, and the *Final Report of the Committee on Industrial Relations in the Electricity Supply Board* (1969) (chaired by Professor Michael Fogarty). These reports outlined participative measures which, it was suggested, the ESB could introduce.

Ireland's entry into the European Economic Community in 1973 also meant that the European Commission's draft proposals for a Fifth Directive on the harmonisation of company law, first made in 1972, became relevant. This draft directive envisaged the introduction of board level representation of workers, but its proposals, perhaps largely because they were geared to continental company structures unfamiliar here, have been the source of much controversy since they were first published. New versions are still being drafted, and it is not clear when implementation of the directive will follow.

One development which in fact has taken place relates to the State sector. Following the publication of a White Paper in 1975 the Oireachtas enacted the Worker Participation (State Enterprises) Act 1977. The Act related originally to seven State-owned companies—this is now being extended to further companies—all of which are more or less commercial in character, and it provides that one third of the board members of these companies should be worker representatives (s.23). These representatives are elected, having been nominated by trade unions or other representative groups recognised for collective bargaining purposes, to a single-tier board, where they act as ordinary company directors. All the seven original companies have now elected worker directors, and some of the directors concerned have greatly added to the general discussion through comments which they have made on their own role and performance. The National Understanding of 1980 proposed the extension of the system to other State enterprises, and this is now being effected.

Finally, the Department of Labour issued a discussion paper in 1980 on the further development of industrial democracy. This document does not in any concrete way make specific suggestions, its principal intention being to promote public discussion and set the scene. However, the paper does indicate some possible developments, including the opportunity for companies to create a two-tier board structure should they so wish (*Worker Participation: A Discussion Paper*, March 1980, p. 8). The paper also analyses measures short of board level or formalised participation, such as increased levels of consultation. The idea of works councils is also taken up and given some support in the discussion paper.

Again, however, it must be said that not much action has followed the publication of the paper. Contributing to this state of affairs is the reluctance of the employers' associations to get involved in any worker participation schemes, as well as the fact that the trade unions, while being very much in favour in principle, do not always actively push the idea of worker participation. Although there is much interest in this area, it cannot be said that any great sense of urgency has been in evidence.

3 The Contract of Employment

INTRODUCTION

Until recently it would have been fairly accurate to describe much of employment law as merely a branch of contract law. The employment relationship, as we have already noted, is based on contract, and contractual principles were therefore virtually the only principles of substance relevant to individual labour law; only in very limited contexts were these qualified by statute. With the arrival of the protective legislation which we outline in later chapters there has been some change, but nevertheless the contract of employment is still at the heart of employment law today.

It can be said that the contract of employment as a direct and exclusive source of rights, obligations and remedies has lost much of its importance, at any rate for all but very highly paid employees or those to whom special circumstances apply. However, the contract is still very important when it comes to the interpretation and application of statutory rights. As we shall see, it would for example be very difficult to understand many of the decisions on unfair dismissal (see Chapter 7) without some knowledge of contract law. Whether this is a desirable state of affairs is another day's work, but for the moment it must be accepted as the way in which employment law operates.

IDENTIFYING A CONTRACT OF EMPLOYMENT

For the most part, employment law applies only to persons who have entered into (or, in some cases, intend to enter into) a contract of employment. Arrangements which do not involve a contract are thus outside its scope: see *e.g.* the decision of the English Court of Appeal in *President of the Methodist Conference* v. *Parfitt* (1983). However, the same is true also of other contractual arrangements which do not give the parties the status of employer and employee; these are of course subject to ordinary contractual rules, but not specifically to those of employment law, whether they arise under the common law or the statutes regulating the employment relationship which give protection only to "employees." It is therefore of great importance to distinguish between contracts of employment, traditionally referred to by lawyers as "contracts of service," and other contracts, known as "contracts for services." To put it another way, the employee (or "servant" in the old common law terminology) must be distinguished from the independent contractor. As a rule it is only the employee or servant who can avail of the protection which modern employment law affords.

The traditional method of identifying a contract of employment was by considering the degree of control which the employer (or "master") exercised over the employee (or "servant"). For example, in a string of cases the former Irish Court of Appeal held that what mattered was not whether the relationship was temporary or permanent, whether the labour was casual, how the worker was paid, and so forth, but rather whether the worker was, when given instructions, "bound to work": see *e.g. O'Donnell* v. *Clare County Council* (1913). More recently, in the case of *Roche* v. *Patrick Kelly & Co. Ltd.* (1968) Walsh J. in the Supreme Court put the position in a similar way (p. 108):

> "While many ingredients may be present in the relationship of master and servant, it is undoubtedly true that the principal one, and almost invariably the determining one, is the fact of the master's right to direct the servant not merely as to what is to be done but as to how it is to be done."

Seen in this way the contract of employment was primarily a contract of subordination, and indeed this was reflected in the terms used to describe the parties, *i.e.* "master" and "servant."

The English decision of *Ready Mixed Concrete (South East) Ltd.* v. *Minister of Pensions and National Insurance* (1967) extended the criteria somewhat. Here MacKenna J. held in the Queen's Bench Division that the existence of a contract of service depended on three conditions being fulfilled, these being: (a) the agreement by the servant to "provide his own work and skill in the performance of some ser-

vice for his master" in consideration of a wage or other remuneration; (b) the agreement that "in the performance of that service he
will be subject to the other's control in a sufficient degree to make
that other master," whereby "control includes the power of deciding
the thing to be done, the means to be employed in doing it, the time
when and the place where it shall be done"; and (c) the fact that
"the other provisions of the contract are consistent with its being a
contract of service" (p. 515). In this way, according to MacKenna
J., the control of the work by the other party is "a necessary, though
not always a sufficient, condition of a contract of service" (p. 517);
factors such as the provision of tools and materials may affect the
nature of the contract if they are a significant feature of it. This has
been called the "mixed test."

Whether these criteria are still exclusively applicable is a matter
of doubt. The complexity of a modern employment relationship
might make it difficult to reduce everything to a question of control.
What is more, it may be undesirable, in view of the growing acceptance of the changing status of an employee in his relations with the
employer. In *Wilson* v. *Racher* (1974) Edmund Davies L.J., in the
English Court of Appeal, pointed out that employment in this century is no longer a "Czar-serf" relationship and that "we have by
now come to realise that a contract of service imposes upon the parties a duty of mutual respect" (p. 430). It therefore seems reasonable
that other indicators should be considered in addition, examples
being the payment of P.A.Y.E. and social insurance contributions,
the provision of equipment and materials for the job, the so-called
"integration test" suggested by Kahn-Freund (*i.e.* was the worker
integrated into the employer's organisation?—1951, *Modern Law
Review*, Vol. 14, p. 504), and so forth.

This indeed was the approach of the industrial tribunal in the
recent English case of *O'Kelly* v. *Trusthouse Forte Plc* (1983). The tribunal declared that it had to "consider all aspects of the relationship, no single feature being in itself decisive, and each of which may
vary in weight and direction," and this was approved by the Court
of Appeal (p. 374). As the English Employment Appeal Tribunal
(E.A.T.) further held in *Wickens* v. *Champion Employment* (1983),
there are cases in which control would be "quite an inappropriate
test" (p. 369), while in other cases it could be crucial. An illustration
of this was provided in the recent English case of *Nethermere (St.
Neots) Ltd.* v. *Taverna* (1984), in which the Court of Appeal held that
the appellants, who were homeworkers with very flexible terms and
conditions, were working under contracts of employment; clearly the

degree of control exercised over workers in such employment is relatively small, so that control could not have been the deciding factor.

In *Lamb Bros. Dublin Ltd.* v. *Davidson* (1979) Costello J. in the High Court declared that what is often decisive is the intention of employer and worker, or as he put it colloquially, "what they both considered they were about." Following this and some other recent British authorities the Employment Appeals Tribunal (E.A.T.), in cases under the Unfair Dismissals Act 1977 (see Chapter 7), has held that what must be done is to "consider the reality of the relationships": see *e.g. Kirwan* v. *Dart Industries Ltd.* (1980). In doing so a court or tribunal must of course bear in mind that the parties may, for reasons of their own (often illegal), attempt to attach a label to the relationship which does not reflect the real state of affairs; for example, a worker may be described as a sub-contractor in order to avoid the P.A.Y.E. and P.R.S.I. liability. This sort of arrangement may not however have legal effect. MacKenna J. put it as follows in the *Ready Mixed* case (p. 513):

> "It may be stated here that whether the relation between the parties to the contract is that of master and servant or otherwise is a conclusion of law dependent upon the rights conferred and the duties imposed by the contract. If these are such that the relation is that of master and servant, it is irrelevant that the parties have declared it to be something else."

More recently Lord Denning M.R. stated it similarly in *Massey* v. *Crown Life Insurance Co.* (1978) (p. 579):

> " . . . If the true relationship of the parties is that of master and servant under a contract of service, the parties cannot alter the truth of that relationship by putting a different label on it."

This was followed by Costello J. in *Lamb Bros.* when he stated that the intention of the parties is not found in their express statements if such arrangement is "in any way a fiction," particularly if the purpose of the fiction is to defraud the revenue.

Taking all this together it appears therefore that the existence of a contract of employment is determined on the basis of a more flexible test than merely that of control by the employer; the primary criterion is the real intention of the parties. In *Massey* Lord Denning held that the agreement between the employer and the worker is "the best material from which to gather the true relationship between them" (p. 580). In all cases, however, the ordinary contractual requirements of offer, acceptance, consideration and intention to create legal relations apply also to employment contracts; for an analysis of these contract law textbooks should be consulted.

OFFICE-HOLDERS → *Judges, Chairpersons Presidents, etc.*

An employee must further be distinguished from an "office-holder." The significance of the distinction lies in the fact that office-holders are in some respects subject to different legal principles than employees; for example, it has long been held that office-holders are entitled to the benefit of the principles of natural justice before being removed from office (see below), while on the other hand certain office-holders are not eligible to claim under the Unfair Dismissals Act 1977 (see Chapter 7).

It is not entirely easy to define an office-holder. He may work under a contract of employment, but the legal basis of his position is something else, or at any rate something additional. A definition of a kind was put forward by Kenny J. in *Glover* v. *B.L.N. Ltd.* (1972):

> "The characteristic features of an office are that it is created by Act of the National Parliament, charter, statutory regulation, articles of association of a company or of a body corporate formed under the authority of a statute, deed of trust, grant or by prescription; and that the holder of it may be removed if the instrument creating the office authorises this" (p. 414).

In general, it might be said that, as Redmond has put it, the concept of an office-holder in modern employment law refers to a person "whose employment involves a special status" (*Dismissal Law in the Republic of Ireland*, 1982, p. 49). Often this special status flows from statute, although the office will not necessarily have been created by the statute; the special status may further flow from a charter, articles of association, a trade union rule book, and so forth: see *e.g. Stevenson* v. *United Road Transport Association* (1976).

English law further makes a distinction between an ordinary office and an office "held at pleasure," that is to say, held (in the British case) at the will and pleasure of the Crown. In *Garvey* v. *Ireland* (1979) it was held by the Supreme Court that no such distinction, or anything equivalent, operates under Irish law.

THE TERMS OF THE CONTRACT

Identifying the terms of a contract of employment is not as straightforward in our system of employment law and industrial relations as it is in some other countries. On the Continent of Europe, for example, employees are almost invariably presented with a comprehensive document setting out all terms and conditions of employment, and this is signed by both parties before the employee takes up work. In Ireland, as in Britain, written contracts are by no means always drawn up, and even when they are they may not set out all the terms.

(1) Statement of particulars

Terms implied by statute (many others).

In order to achieve some measure of certainty for the employee, the Oireachtas has created a statutory device by which he can receive a written statement of his terms and conditions of employment. Section 9 of the Minimum Notice and Terms of Employment Act 1973 provides that an employee may, "for the purposes of ascertaining or confirming any term of his employment," require the employer to furnish him, within one month of a request to do so, with a written statement containing certain particulars, including:

    (a) the date of commencement of the employment;
    (b) "the rate or method of calculation of his remuneration";
    (c) the times at which the employee is paid and the intervals between payments;
    (d) particulars relating to hours of work and overtime;
    (e) particulars relating to holidays, sickness and pension arrangements; and
    (f) the period of notice "which the employee is obliged to give and entitled to receive," or (in the case of fixed-term contracts) the date of expiry of the contract.

Section 9(5) further provides that the employer must in any case furnish these particulars to all new employees within one month of the employee commencing work. Non-compliance with these obligations is a criminal offence; prosecutions are brought by the Minister for Labour.

It is important to note that the statement of particulars given under the 1973 Act does not constitute the contract of employment. First, only certain details must be given under the Act, so that additional terms of the contract may not be included in the statement. But even apart from that, the particulars merely constitute what the employer *thinks* are terms of the contract, or perhaps what he would like the employee to think are terms of the contract; in other words, the employer's statement may not be an accurate one.

[handwritten annotation: To the benefit of the employee where the employer cheats.]

If this is so, the parties may possibly be estopped from denying the accuracy of the particulars at a later date. In the English case of *Smith v. Blandford Gee Cementation Co. Ltd.* (1970) the respondents had issued to the applicant a statement under the equivalent British provision—now in section 1 of the Employment Protection (Consolidation) Act 1978—despite the fact that they were not actually his employers. The Divisional Court held however that they were estopped from denying, for the purposes of the redundancy payments legislation (see Chapter 8), that they were the employers.

By the same token it might be thought that an employee who accepts an inaccurate statement would be estopped from subsequently denying its accuracy. However, in the case of *Robertson v. British Gas Corporation* (1982) this conclusion was not drawn by the English Court of Appeal. Ackner L.J. pointed out the undesirable nature of estoppel if applied in such cases (p. 357):

> "If the statutory statement did not accurately set out the terms of the contract, then the employer would be in breach of his statutory obligation, and I find it difficult to accept that a failure to comply with a statutory obligation could redound to the benefit of an employer and create an estoppel against the employee from saying the employer got it wrong."

However, it is probably still advisable, in cases of doubt, to challenge the statement immediately.

Finally, section 9(4) of the 1973 Act allows the employer, instead of specifying the required particulars, to "refer the employee to a document containing those particulars which the employee has reasonable opportunities of reading during the course of his employment, or which is reasonably accessible to him in some other way." This is generally taken to be a reference to collective agreements setting out the terms of employment. Where such an agreement is sufficiently comprehensive, the employer can refer the employee to it and so discharge his obligations under the Act.

(2) Incorporation of collective agreements

The provisions of section 9(4) of the 1973 Act are in many ways an acknowledgment of the importance of collective agreements as a source of terms and conditions of employment. In cases where an employer recognises a trade union or a group of unions for collective bargaining purposes he will almost invariably enter into regular agreements covering pay and other conditions. Copies of these collective agreements will, as a matter of practice, frequently be given to individual members of the workforce, and equally it is not uncommon for workers to be asked to sign a statement by which they accept that the agreements contain their terms and conditions of employment; an example of such a procedure is set out in the case of *Becton, Dickinson & Co. Ltd.* v. *Lee* (1972) (see p. 5 of the report). Where this is done we speak of the "incorporation" of the collective agreement, by which is meant that the substantive terms of the agreement become terms of the individual contracts of employment of the workers.

It must be stressed that the legally binding nature of the substantive terms of a collective agreement as between the employer and an individual employee—that is to say, the incorporation of the agreement—is unrelated to the enforceability or otherwise of the agreement as between the collective parties, the employer and the trade union or unions. As we have seen in Chapter 1, there is some doubt as to whether collective agreements are legally enforceable, but there is nothing to stop an employer and an individual employee from agreeing in a binding contract to apply the terms of a collective agreement which is itself not legally enforceable at a collective level. Furthermore, once a collective agreement is incorporated into a contract of employment its substantive terms remain terms of the contract until such time as the contract is validly varied or terminated; the fact, for example, that the collective agreement itself has expired will not necessarily affect the individual contract: see *Robertson* v. *British Gas Corporation* (1982, above). The issues of enforceability of the collective agreement and incorporation into the contract of employment must thus be kept strictly apart. For this reason the comments by Murphy J. in the recent case of *Allied Irish Banks Ltd.* v. *Lupton* (1983), in which he indicated that the absence of an intention to create legal relations in respect of an agreement between the plaintiffs and a trade union called into question the incorporation of that agreement into the defendant's contract of employment, must be considered to be wrong.

The form of incorporation outlined above, by which employer and employee expressly adopt the terms of a collective agreement as part of a contract of employment, is generally known as "express" incorporation. The matter becomes more difficult if the intention to incorporate is to be found in something other than an unambiguous, express statement of the parties. The sometimes mooted argument that a trade union, in concluding a collective agreement, acts as a contractual agent for its members and thus binds them individually,

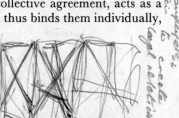

cannot be sustained. The rules of agency are precise and are not met in a collective bargaining situation. Thus in *Goulding Chemicals Ltd.* v. *Bolger* (1977) Kenny J. held in the Supreme Court that "membership of a corporate body or of an association does not have the consequence that every agreement made by that corporate body or association binds every member of it" (p. 237). Furthermore the English E.A.T. has held that the mere silence of an employee cannot be taken as his acceptance of the terms of a collective agreement: *Jones* v. *Associated Tunnelling Co. Ltd.* (1981). Before there can be incorporation, therefore, some more tangible evidence of acceptance by the employee who is to be affected is required.

That still leaves the question whether the substantive terms of a collective agreement can be implied into a contract of employment. It seems to be accepted, on the basis of some older English cases, that implied incorporation is possible, for example where there is a custom in a particular industry that terms and conditions of employment are regulated in accordance with collective agreements negotiated from time to time. In general, the ordinary common law tests for implying terms would apply in such cases.

Finally, it will be noted that we have referred throughout to the incorporation of "substantive" terms. Sir Otto Kahn-Freund argued in his book, *Labour and the Law* (see 3rd ed., 1983, Chapter 6), that collective agreements have "contractual" and "normative" functions, resulting in procedural and substantive terms respectively. It is generally thought that only substantive clauses, *i.e.* those relating to the individual worker's terms and conditions of employment, are suitable for incorporation into that worker's individual contract. Procedural terms such as, say, terms about facilities for union officials or about union-management meetings, are clearly not appropriate in a contract of employment of an ordinary employee. Technically this should apply also to a "no-strike" clause, which is essentially collective and procedural, but that seems to be in doubt as a result of the House of Lords decision in *Rookes* v. *Barnard* (1964).

(3) Obligations of the parties

It has been held by the judiciary in both Britain and Ireland for some time that there are certain characteristics in an employment relationship which require that the parties observe certain obligations towards each other. In fact the courts have tended to be rather more explicit about the duties owed by employees than about those of employers, but nevertheless it is accepted that there are mutual obligations, among them being the "duty of mutual respect" mentioned by Edmund Davies L.J. in *Wilson* v. *Racher* (above). These obligations are implied into the contract of employment. As Lord Tucker in the British House of Lords put it in *Lister* v. *Romford Ice and Cold Storage Co. Ltd.* (1957), they "derive in the main from the common law by which they have become attached in the course of time to certain classes of contractual relationships" (p. 594), in this case the relationship between employer and employee. Viscount Simonds in the same case declared that the existence in a contract of employment of such implied terms was "a question of status" (p. 576).

Attempts to provide a list of such implied duties are in some respects of rather doubtful value, since many of them are based on cases which, when read in their entirety, hardly reflect a modern, twentieth century understanding of the employment relationship. The employee's duty of obedience, for example, still probably exists in some form, and yet a literal approach to it cannot really be squared with the more participative view of the employment relationship now generally favoured; the duty of obedience should therefore perhaps now be described, as Hepple and O'Higgins suggest, as the "duty of co-operation" (*Employment Law*, 4th ed., 1981, p. 137). The obligations listed in cases decided as recently as *Lister* v. *Romford Ice* (1957, above) tend at least to some extent to portray the relationship as an authoritarian or paternalistic one, and cannot therefore be reliable guides today.

In Ireland it is necessary to point out that the Constitution is an important source of obligations. In *Meskell* v. *Coras Iompair Eireann* (1972) Walsh J. emphasised that constitutional rights and obligations are superior to the common law. So, for example, the employee has a right not to be discriminated against on the grounds of sex: *Murtagh Properties Ltd.* v. *Cleary* (1972); or on the grounds of religious profession, belief or status: *Mulloy* v. *Minister for Education* (1975). Whether these rights can be waived in the contract of employment by way of an express term is unclear. In *Murphy* v. *Stewart* (1972) the question was considered by Walsh J. in the Supreme Court but not decided; however, if they can be waived it is clear that the waiver must be clear and unambiguous and must be understood by the party waiving his rights.

It must also be pointed out that certain statutes, to be reviewed in subsequent chapters, imply terms into the contract of employment, or alternatively modify existing terms of the contract or render them void. For example, the Anti-Discrimination (Pay) Act 1974 inserts into each contract of employment an entitlement in certain circumstances to equal pay as between men and women (see Chapter 6), and the Unfair Dismissals Act 1977 renders void any attempt to waive the right to redress in the case of an unfair dismissal in all but certain fixed term contracts (see Chapter 7). In general it would be accurate to say that the contract of employment cannot be used as a means of evading the obligations imposed on the parties to an employment relationship by protective legislation.

It is clear that there are also still in existence a number of obligations implied by operation of the common law. In the *Ready Mixed* case (above) MacKenna J. held that, at the least, there must be a duty of the employer to pay remuneration and a duty of the employee to provide "work and skill" (page. 515). These are the essential ingredients of an employment relationship and there can be no contract of employment without them. Beyond that there are also duties of co-operation, care and fidelity which, in different ways, affect both parties. For the employee this means that he must do the work with reasonable care and skill, that he must be "honest and diligent" (*per* Lord Tucker in *Lister* v. *Romford Ice*, above, at p. 594), that he must generally obey instructions, provided they are both reasonable and lawful, that he must not wilfully disrupt the employer's business or other activities (*per* Lord Denning M.R. in *Secretary of State for Employment* v. *ASLEF* (*No. 2*), 1972, at p. 967), that he must not disclose confidential information or trade secrets, and so forth. For the employer it means that he must provide a safe place of work, safe equipment and processes, that he must provide adequate training and instructions, that he must not require the employee to do anything illegal or unreasonable, and so forth. It might be noted that although the employer must pay wages or other remuneration, he is not required to provide any actual work for the employee to do, except perhaps where the employee requires work to develop or maintain special skills relevant to the job; this general principle was confirmed recently by the English Court of Appeal in *Nethermere* (*St. Neots*) *Ltd.* v. *Taverna* (1984). However, if the employee is on piece work the situation is different, since he will need to be provided with work in order to qualify for remuneration: *Devonald* v. *Rosser* (1906).

The most difficult of the employee's obligations is perhaps that of fidelity. This is so partly because it is an obligation which can extend beyond the end of the employment relationship. It has been held in a number of cases that the duty of a former employee not to disclose certain confidential information or to use it to the detriment of the degree of anger or dissatisfaction felt by the employer which matters, so that the fact that the employee has, for example, used bad language in an argument with the employer is not necessarily a good ground for summary dismissal, particularly if the employee was provoked: *Wilson* v. *Racher* (1974). In any case, the Supreme Court held in *Carvill* v. *Irish Industrial Bank Ltd.* (1966) that the employer may only justify a summary dismissal by using grounds known to him at the time; subsequently discovered acts of misconduct are inadmissible, since it would be "quite illogical to say that an employer may be heard to say that he dismissed his servant on a ground unknown to him at the actual time of dismissal" (*per* O'Keefe J. at pp. 345–6). In the case of *Glover* v. *B.L.N. Ltd.* (1972) Walsh J. added to this that "the misconduct, if known but not in fact used as a ground for dismissal at the time, cannot be relied upon afterwards in an effort to justify the dismissal" (p. 426).

(3) Wrongful dismissal

A summary dismissal not justified by the employee's conduct is a wrongful dismissal. It is "wrongful," or unlawful, because it amounts to a breach of the contract of employment, and the same is true therefore of any other dismissal in breach of the contract. In most cases that rather reduces the possibilities, since a dismissal with due notice will not be wrongful, almost regardless of the circumstances. However, that needs to be qualified in three ways. First, if the contract of employment states categorically and unequivocally that a dismissal may be effected only for certain specified reasons (which very few contracts will state), then it appears that a dismissal for any other reason is wrongful; this point arises out of the House of Lords decision in *McClelland* v. *N.I. General Health Services Board* (1957), and it appears to have been affirmed by Budd J. in *Walsh* v. *Dublin Health Authority* (1962). Secondly, if under the contract of employment a certain dismissal procedure is stipulated, for example involving warnings and a hearing, then a dismissal in breach of this procedure will be wrongful; this was held by the Court of Appeal in *Gunton* v. *Richmond-upon-Thames London Borough Council* (1980) and was accepted, at any rate by strong implication, by Murphy J. in the case of *Allied Irish Banks Ltd.* v. *Lupton* (1983). In this context it is particularly relevant to consider whether, in a given case, a collective agreement containing a disciplinary procedure has been incorporated into the contract of employment.

Thirdly, it is clear from *Meskell* v. *Coras Iompair Eireann* (1972) that

former employer is implied into a contract of employment. Most recently in the English case of *Faccenda Chicken Ltd.* v. *Fowler* (1983) Goulding J. held that specific trade secrets may never be used or disclosed, while other kinds of information only remain confidential during the continuance of the employment relationship. An employer may further, through express terms in the contract, restrict the freedom of an employee to compete with him after the employment has ceased "within reasonable limits of time and space" (*per* Goulding J. in *Faccenda Chicken*, above, p. 65). That such restrictions, if reasonable, are legally valid has been accepted for some time: see *e.g. Nordenfelt* v. *Maxim Nordenfelt Guns and Ammunition Co. Ltd.* (1894, House of Lords).

In a general way, it might be said that the obligations imposed on the parties and implied into the contract of employment are based on three considerations: (a) that both parties (but in particular the employee) are under an obligation not to do anything which will impede, endanger or prejudice the work process or the employer's business interests; (b) that both parties (but in particular the employer) should adhere to minimum standards expected of them on social grounds; and (c) that there is, as the Employment Appeals Tribunal has put it in a number of unfair dismissal cases, in the employment relationship an essential "bond of mutual trust" which neither party is entitled to break: see *e.g. Skelly* v. *S.A. Roantree and Sons Ltd.* (1983). It is these principles which will determine the substance of the parties' obligations under the contract. (See Chapter 7).

TERMINATION OF EMPLOYMENT

Until 1977 the contractual principles relating to termination of employment were of considerable importance in the absence of statutory regulation. In fact the common law provided only minimal protection which in turn was attractive only to a very small number of employees, usually those in highly paid positions. The significance of the contract of employment to these employees remains, but in the overall scheme of employment law attention has switched to statutes such as the Redundancy Payments Acts, the Minimum Notice and Terms of Employment Act 1973 and, in particular, the Unfair Dismissals Act 1977; all these are analysed in depth in later chapters. These Acts have become the primary focus not only because they have introduced new substantive legal protection, but also because this protection is administered through new tribunals which make unnecessary the use of the formal and very expensive civil court procedures. In fact, as we shall see in later chapters, neither the statutes nor the tribunals are entirely satisfactory, but they have nevertheless changed the picture of employment law in the area of termination of employment. At the same time the use of contractual principles by the courts and tribunals in interpreting and applying the statutes has meant that the contract remains highly significant, albeit in a new statutory setting. We examine the substance and implications of this in Chapter 7, and in the present context we intend merely to outline briefly the remaining marginal role of the contract of employment as a source of rules and remedies in its own right.

(1) Notice

It is a general principle of employment law that all contracts of employment, other than those for a specified fixed term, can be unilaterally terminated. Thus Lord Denning M.R. held in *Richardson* v. *Koefod* (1969) that "in the absence of express stipulation, the rule is that every contract of service is determinable by reasonable notice" (p. 1816). This is so because it is thought that "the contract of employment is subject to an implied term allowing it to be terminated by the unilateral act of giving notice" (Redmond, *op. cit.*, p. 52). Therefore a term with this effect is implied into a contract which is silent on the matter. The unusual feature of this principle is that it appears to apply even where the express terms of the contract would suggest otherwise. Where, for example, a contract of employment states that it is "permanent," this does not apparently mean that it cannot be terminated by notice. In the case of *Walsh* v. *Dublin Health Authority* (1962) the plaintiff, who was employed by the defendants as a carpenter, was told that "his appointment was on a permanent basis" (p. 85). He was subsequently dismissed, and he challenged the legality of the dismissal. Budd J., following some *dicta* of the law lords in *McClelland* v. *Northern Ireland General Health Services Board* (1957), held that what mattered was what the parties had intended; in ordinary cases "permanent" employment meant "employment for an indefinite duration and not more and therefore subject to reasonable notice to terminate it" (p. 90); this however could be different if the contract or its surrounding circumstances indicated that there was an intention to create an employment relationship which could not be terminated (save, presumably, by consent) or could only be terminated in certain circumstances.

If a contract of employment may be terminated by notice, the question remains of course as to what period of notice must be observed. If the period is specified in the express terms there is obviously no problem; if it is not, then under the common law there is an implied term that there should be "reasonable notice": see Scott L.J. in *De Stempel* v. *Dunkels* (1937) (at p. 261). What is reasonable will depend on factors such as custom and practice, as well as the position and status of the employee; in the case of manual employment the period of notice which was traditionally implied was one week. This common law position has now been modified significantly by the Minimum Notice and Terms of Employment Act 1973. (See Chapter 7.)

(2) Summary dismissal

If almost every contract can under the common law be terminated by notice, then the employer's discretion to fire is almost unfettered and is subject only to his having to observe the contractual period of notice (leaving aside the provisions of legislation). In fact even the notice requirement does not apply where an employee is guilty of serious misconduct. Where this is the case the employer may dismiss summarily, *i.e.* without giving notice. In the case of *Carvill* v. *Irish Industrial Bank Ltd.* (1966) Kenny J. in the High Court stated that:

"The grounds relied on, to justify a dismissal without notice of an employee, must be actions or omissions by the employee which are inconsistent with the performance of the express or implied terms of his contract of service" (p. 335).

In the English case of *Sinclair* v. *Neighbour* (1966) Sachs L.J. held that:

"It is well-established law that a servant can be instantly dismissed when his conduct is such that it not only amounts to a wrongful act inconsistent with his duty towards his master but is also inconsistent with the continuance of confidence between them" (p. 289).

The obligations which arise under a contract of employment which we have discussed above, provide some basis for an assessment of what conduct will justify a summary dismissal. However the test is an objective one: the entitlement to dismiss summarily depends on the circumstances of the case and, it appears, on status of the employee (see Redmond, *op. cit.*, p. 58). It is not

a dismissal is wrongful where the ground for dismissal is unconstitutional under the 1937 Constitution. Walsh J. held in the Supreme Court that the exercise of "what may loosely be called a common law right of dismissal" will be illegal if it is intended "as a method of compelling a person to abandon a constitutional right" since the Constitution must take precedence over the common law (p. 135). Thus a dismissal connected with, say, religious belief, or a person's desire to exercise his property rights or other constitutional rights may be termed wrongful.

A number of English and Irish cases dealing with special employments have opened up the possibility that a dismissal in breach of the requirements of natural justice may be a wrongful dismissal (see Redmond, *op. cit.*, pp. 68–81). This began with the decision of the House of Lords in *Ridge* v. *Baldwin* (1963), and has included the Supreme Court decisions of *Glover* v. *B.L.N. Ltd.* (1972), *State (Gleeson)* v. *Minister for Defence* (1976) and *Garvey* v. *Ireland* (1979). However, although these cases contain some hints that natural justice might apply to the termination of employment generally, none of them can be considered an authority for this proposition. Furthermore, there are two recent *dicta* by High Court judges, in the cases of *National Engineering and Electrical Trade Union* v. *McConnell* (1983) and *Allied Irish Banks Ltd.* v. *Lupton* (1983), that repeat the old view that natural justice applies only to the removal of office-holders, and not to the dismissal of other employees. It may be that this narrow view should now be extended, particularly in view of the development of the concept of "constitutional justice": see *e.g. East Donegal Co-operative Livestock Mart Ltd.* v. *Attorney General* (1970).

Where a court finds that there has been a wrongful dismissal, the redress awarded will as a rule be damages for the loss suffered, subject to the obligation of the employee to mitigate his loss: see the House of Lords decision in *Westwood* v. *Secretary of State for Employment* (1984). There is a strong legal tradition that a court will not decree the specific performance of a contract of employment, and in a number of cases it has been held that the courts will neither compel a worker to work nor an employer to employ; as Lord Denning put it in *Hill* v. *C.A. Parsons & Co. Ltd.* (1971), "it is inconsistent with the confidential nature of the [employment] relationship that it should continue contrary to the will of one of the parties thereto" (p. 314). Curiously the Court of Appeal actually decided in that same case to make an exception, based on the unusual facts of the case, thus suggesting that the general rule is not immutable. Furthermore there is a suggestion in the judgment of Walsh J. in *Meskell* v. *CIE* (1972) that reinstatement may be available in the case of a dismissal which is unconstitutional (p. 135).

(4) Other forms of termination

For reasons analysed in more detail in Chapter 7, one of the more curious, and as we would argue less desirable, effects of statutory protection in the area of dismissal has been a surge of cases in which employers argue that what might have looked like a dismissal was in legal (if not in commonsense) terms something else. Of course contract law knows a number of forms of contractual discharge, and dismissal as commonly understood—*i.e.* termination by the employer—is merely an example of one of these. The main forms of discharge, to use the categories adopted by Clark (*Contract*, 1982, Chapter 16), are: (a) through performance; (b) through agreement; (c) following from a breach; and (d) by operation of law. All of them are capable of being applied to contracts of employment.

The law in this area demonstrates the inappropriateness of a strict contract law approach to employment matters. Attempts to apply doctrines which are entirely straightforward in the context of a commercial contract introduce sometimes insurmountable problems in the context of an employment contract; they also tend to obscure the social implications of certain kinds of conduct or events by reducing them to legalistic principles.

The forms of discharge which have created the greatest problems are repudiation and frustration; we discuss the meaning and implications of these terms in Chapter 7. The difficulties which one encounters are illustrated in particular in cases involving repudiation, which is, according to Clark (*op. cit.*, p. 202), "a decision by one party that he will not perform his contractual obligations." The same author states that this "does not of itself terminate a contract," for otherwise "a person could, by his own act, put an end to his contractual obligations" (p. 201). Instead the innocent party can elect either to accept the contract as discharged or to treat it as remaining in force. An unaccepted repudiation, as it was put by Asquith L.J. in *Howard* v. *Pickford Tool Co. Ltd.* (1951), "is a thing writ in water and of no value to anybody" (p. 421).

Because of the reluctance of the courts to compel the parties to an employment relationship to carry out their main contractual obligations against the will of either party, this general contractual rule has caused much judicial heart-searching whenever it has been canvassed in an employment setting. In the case of *Vine* v. *National Dock*

Labour Board (1957) it was suggested in the Court of Appeal and the House of Lords that repudiation *always* discharged a contract of employment, but after a string of cases (listed in some detail by Buckley L.J. in *Gunton*, below) debating the issue it was held by the English Court of Appeal in *Gunton* v. *Richmond-upon-Thames LBC* (1980) that an unlawful repudiation of a contract of employment had to be accepted by the innocent party to result in the termination of the contract, as is the case with other contracts. What exactly this means in practice is not altogether clear. It does *not* mean, apparently, that the employee can, where the employer has repudiated the contract, insist on continuing in employment (see Brightman L.J. in *Gunton*, p. 778); he merely retains some residual contractual rights and, subject to the duty to mitigate, a right to claim for damages. But whether for example it entitles him to extend his notional period of continuous employment to make him eligible to claim under the various protective statutes is uncertain.

The uncertainties of the kind outlined above, and those which we shall consider in Chapter 7, illustrate the difficulties experienced by the courts in trying to marry contractual doctrines with social policy in the employment field. It is, perhaps, an attempted marriage of incompatibles, which leads us to note again that the legal basis for employment law, the contract of employment, is in urgent need of a fairly fundamental overhaul.

4 Protective Legislation and Conditions of Employment

INTRODUCTION

There is now a fair amount of legislation and delegated legislation regulating pay and conditions of employment. However, while it is extensive in terms of sheer volume it is still relatively insignificant in terms of substance. The growth of protective legislation has centred mainly around dismissal and, to a lesser extent, sex discrimination, while the impact on terms and conditions of employment has been much less noticeable.

Partly this must be put down to the continuing strength of voluntarism. There is still a strong feeling, particularly in trade union circles, that terms and conditions of employment should not be regulated by the State, but should be settled instead by collective bargaining between employers and unions. The problem is that this approach does not sufficiently take into account the needs of those employees who are unorganised or represented by weak trade unions and so does not fully meet the requirement of civilised standards for all employees.

It has therefore come to be recognised that the law must fulfil what Sir Otto Kahn-Freund called its "regulatory" role, that is to provide a "code of substantive rules to govern terms and conditions of employment" which would supplement the terms provided by collective agreements ("Industrial Relations and the Law: Retrospect and Prospect," 1969, *British Journal of Industrial Relations* 301). This chapter will outline the existing law, as well as point out some of the defects and inconsistencies of the legal framework. It will not

52

cover health and safety at work, which will be dealt with separately in the following chapter.

YOUTH EMPLOYMENT

Various statutory restrictions are imposed on the employment of young persons. Historically these became necessary because of the appalling exploitation of child labour in the wake of the Industrial Revolution. During the nineteenth century the Westminster Parliament introduced legislation imposing a minimum age for employment and regulating hours and conditions of work, and after Irish independence the Oireachtas extended this protection in Part II of the Conditions of Employment Act 1936. It is now to be found in the Protection of Young Persons (Employment) Act 1977.

For the purposes of its provisions the 1977 Act distinguishes in section 1 between a "child," who is a person under the current school leaving age (*i.e.* at present 15), and a "young person," who has reached the school leaving age but is less than 18 years old. This distinction has to be kept in mind since different rules apply to each category.

(1) Restrictions on employment

The Act imposes an absolute minimum age for employment; under section 4, an employer may not under any circumstances (subject perhaps to section 17, discussed below) "employ" a child under the age of 14 "to do work." There is a possible weakness in the Act here, since "employ" is defined in section 1 as offering "employment under a contract of service or a contract of apprenticeship," so that it would appear that employers could attempt to circumvent the Act by entering into a contract for services with the child or his guardian. This certainly does happen, at any rate on a minor scale; at one stage, for example, it was discovered that under-age children were working on paper rounds in Cork, but it was impossible to prove that they were "employed" by anyone for the purposes of the Act. Whether this amounts to a serious social problem would be hard to say, but if such arrangements are considered to have been made in order to contravene the Act, then the employer, and any parent or guardian who aids or abets him, can be prosecuted for a criminal offence (see below).

Under section 6 of the Act the Minister for Labour may by order raise the minimum age, after consultation with employers and trade unions, for particular kinds of work. Up to the time of writing no orders of this kind have been made. For other children, that is for persons aged between 14 and 15, section 4(2) does permit certain limited employment; they may be employed "to do light non-industrial work" which is "not harmful to the health or normal development of the child" and will not affect his or her school attendance or instruction. All "industrial" work is prohibited, and under section 2 this covers all those activities mentioned in section 3 of the Conditions of Employment Act 1936, such as manufacturing, repairing, packing, construction, quarrying, printing and so forth. Also prohibited under the 1977 Act are work in mining and transport, as well as any other activity declared by the Minister for Labour to be industrial work for the purposes of the Act; agricultural or domestic work are not prohibited. In all cases the employer must under section 5(1)(*b*) obtain the consent of the parent or guardian before he can employ a child.

There are no restrictions, in a general way, on the employment of "young persons," although the conditions of employment of such employees are regulated to some extent. However, before an employer can employ either a young person or a child he must under section 5(1) require the production of a birth certificate. Employers must also maintain a "register or other satisfactory record" containing particulars (including name, age, working hours and pay) in respect of each child or young person employed.

(2) Conditions of employment

Where children or young persons are employed, the employer must observe certain provisions in the Act relating to terms and conditions of employment. The most important of these relate to maximum working hours. Again, there is a distinction in this respect between children and young persons. Children are in general permitted to work for not more than 14 hours per week during school term and 35 hours during holidays, but this is subject to various qualifications which can be found in section 4(3) and (4) of the Act, and indeed the maximum hours can also be varied by ministerial order.

Sections 7 to 10 of the Act specify the "normal" and "maximum" working hours for young persons, whereby a distinction is made between those who are over and those under 16 years of age. All hours worked in excess of the "normal" working hours must be paid at overtime rates. For example, the "normal" working week for an employee under 16 years of age is $37\frac{1}{2}$ hours, and the "maximum" is 40 hours; such an employee can therefore work for 40 hours, but if he does $2\frac{1}{2}$ of these must be counted as overtime. For employees over 16 the figures are 40 hours and 45 hours respectively, but further details will need to be checked in sections 7 and 9, as well as any varying orders, or any varying agreements which the Act permits; under the Hours of Work Bill 1984 (see below) it is proposed that such agreements may not permit employment "in excess of fifty hours in any week" (s.7). Time spent on vocational training is deemed to be within normal working hours under section 11.

Under section 12 rest periods of half an hour are required every four hours for a child and every five hours for a young person, but these need not be paid and the requirement does not apply at all to industrial shift work. A rest period must also be interposed between the end of the normal working hours and any overtime worked which exceeds an hour and a half, and under section 13 there must be a rest period of 24 consecutive hours every week (except in certain cases).

Finally, sections 14 and 15 prohibit or restrict night work for children and young persons, and section 16 prohibits double employment.

(3) Enforcement

As has already been noted in specific contexts, breaches by employers, and in some circumstances by parents or guardians, of the Act's provisions are criminal offences. In the case of offences by bodies corporate, their officers (such as directors, managers, and so forth) can also be convicted personally. The penalties are specified in section 24, and range from a maximum fine of £100 for a first offence to £200 for subsequent offences. A continuing offence may further be punished by £10 to £20 per day. These penalties are clearly too low, and it is not difficult to envisage an employer saving more than the maximum £20 per day fine by violating the Act's provisions.

Policing is carried out by inspectors of the Department of Labour, and these are empowered under the Act to enter premises (though not normally private dwelling houses) to examine the employer's records and interview the employer or employees. Prosecutions may be brought under section 23 by the Minister for Labour, by a trade union or by the parent of guardian of an affected employee. In 1982 only three prosecutions were brought by the Minister, on the basis of 1,266 inspections (*Labour Inspection Report* 1982, pp. 74–7).

(4) Exemptions

As with much Irish protective legislation, the Act does not necessarily give an accurate overall picture of the existing law. The Minister for Labour has, as already noted in some contexts, wide-ranging powers to issue statutory instruments varying the Act's provisions. Under section 17 he has further been given the power to make regulations which "modify any provision of this Act," although he must first consult representatives of employers and employees and publish his intention, giving at least three weeks for objections to be received. At the time of writing no regulations under section 17 have been made.

Beyond that, the Minister can also grant licences exempting "any class of employers from complying with any provision of this Act or of regulations under this Act" if, in his opinion, compliance "would be impracticable" or if the employers are participating in an education or training scheme. To date the Minister has used this power only once, in order to exempt employers of close relatives.

Powers to exempt of this kind must of course be seen in conjunction with the principles of administrative law which limit ministerial discretion to make statutory instruments. For example, any regulations or licences which appeared to defeat the purposes of the Act, in so far as these can be clearly discerned, would probably be held to be *ultra vires*: see, *e.g. East Donegal Co-op Ltd.* v. *Attorney-General* (1970). However, this would be difficult to prove, and ultimately legal proceedings would involve the judiciary second-guessing the Minister as to what is socially desirable and required in relation to the protection of young employees. The exempting powers are hedged about with duties to consult, but it would be far better to restrict such powers much more than the Act has done. Exploitation of young workers is, or ought to be, a sensitive topic, and one would want the Oireachtas to err on the side of caution.

(5) Youth employment and training schemes

Certain government schemes and programmes are in operation to promote youth employment and training. The Industrial Training Authority, or An Chomhairle Oiliuna (AnCO), was set up under the Industrial Training Act 1967 to run training programmes. These involve courses in AnCO training centres as well as apprenticeship schemes, and of course young people in particular are able to benefit. Furthermore, the Youth Employment Agency was set up under the Youth Employment Agency Act 1981 as a limited company with the function of encouraging, developing and extending "schemes for training and employment of young persons." It is financed by a special "youth employment levy." It was estimated in June 1982 that the Agency had created almost 3,000 potential jobs or training places for young persons (*Manpower Information Quarterly*, 1982 Vol. 4, No. 1, p. 9).

HOURS OF WORK

The permitted working hours (as well as some other conditions of work) of employees other than children and young persons are at the time of writing regulated in outline by the Conditions of Employment Act 1936, as amended by the Conditions of Employment Act 1944. These Acts apply to "industrial work," as defined in section 3(1) of the 1936 Act; not covered therefore is agricultural, commercial and domestic work, as well as fishing and transport, but hours of work for these employees may in some cases be regulated elsewhere. Shop assistants, for example, have their hours regulated under the Shops (Conditions of Employment) Acts 1938 and 1942, miners under the Mines and Quarries Act 1965, bakery workers under the Night Work (Bakeries) Act 1936 and transport workers under the Road Traffic Acts 1961 and 1968 and under EEC Regulations 543/69 and 1463/70.

The provisions of the 1936 Act are very complex, and it must further be stressed that they merely set certain norms which can be, and are, varied or suspended for particular employers and industries by ministerial orders and licences. Exemptions are on the whole freely granted, so that the actual picture which emerges in industry is altogether different from what the Act appears to portray. While the current legal position is set out in the 1936 and 1944 Acts, the Government has introduced a new Bill to regulate some of these matters, the Hours of Work Bill 1984. This will cover a wider range of workers; under section 2 of the Bill it is provided that it will apply to "all workers except where otherwise provided," and the section goes on to exclude members of the Defence Forces, the Garda Siochana and the prison service, any person employed by a close relative who resides and works in the employer's home, persons employed in the transport industry, fishermen, medical employees, and residential caretakers. Under section 2(3) and section 3 the

Minister for Labour may make regulations extending the coverage of the Act or excluding further categories of workers. Interestingly, the Bill does not (apart from one instance) propose to repeal any provisions of the 1936 and 1944 Acts, but merely to add additional rules to the existing framework, which will however have the effect of making at least some provisions of the Acts obsolete; some parts of the original legislation will on the other hand continue to set out the relevant law.

(1) Working hours

Under section 38(1)(*b*) of the 1936 Act work must not be continued after 8p.m. on any working day (other than a "short" day, where it is 1p.m.), nor must the working day be longer than nine hours. The working week must not exceed 48 hours. Section 4 of the Hours of Work Bill proposes to limit the working week to 40 hours, with special provisions applying where the hours vary from week to week or where the work is of a seasonal kind. Under section 8 of the Bill double employment, *i.e.* work for more than one employer, is restricted in that the employee may not in aggregate work for more than the permitted period.

(2) Overtime

Under section 41 of the 1936 Act, overtime (that is work going beyond the normal working hours just referred to) must not exceed two hours per day, or 12 hours per week, or 240 hours per year, or 36 hours in a period of four consecutive weeks. This can be extended under section 42 by ministerial permit. Overtime pay is governed by section 43. Under section 5 of the Hours of Work Bill overtime is to be restricted to 40 hours in four consecutive weeks or 100 hours in twelve consecutive weeks. Section 5(3) deals with overtime in relation to work where hours of work vary, and section 6 permits the Minister to make regulations extending the permitted overtime.

(3) Shifts

Under section 32 of the 1936 Act shift work is unlawful unless it is done on "continuous process," *i.e.* if it "requires to be carried on without intermission." However, if the work in question does not fit that description a "shift work licence" can nevertheless be obtained from the Minister for Labour, and the restrictions do not apply at all to the printing and publishing of newspapers. Shifts may under sec-

tion 33 not exceed nine hours, nor may a worker work on two consecutive shifts, and there must be an interval of at least eight hours
between shifts. Again, there are over 60 ministerial regulations permitting shifts in particular industries of longer duration (usually 10
to 12 hours). The Hours of Work Bill does not propose any changes
in this context.

(4) Working hours for women

Perhaps the most controversial part of the 1936 Act is that which
prohibits night work for women. Section 38(1)(a) provides that a
woman may not "commence work earlier than the hour of 8a.m. on
any day," and section 46 declares it unlawful for an employer "to
permit any woman to do for him any industrial work at any time
between the hour of 10 p.m. on any day and the hour of 8 a.m. on the
following day"; it also provides that there must be an interval of at
least 11 hours between working days.

These provisions were made necessary by ILO Convention No. 89
(Night Work for Women), ratified by Ireland, which in turn was
prompted by the desire to outlaw the exploitation of women at work.
At the same time it is felt by many today that such measures deprive
women of employment opportunities and experience and are thus
not justifiable in this form. In fact a fairly large number of exemptions have been granted by the Minister for Labour, but such
exemptions usually depend on the initiative of the employers concerned. Following the criticisms by the Employment Equality
Agency of these provisions in its 1978 *Annual Report* (p. 36) the
Government decided early in 1983 to denounce the ILO Convention, and it was expected that new statutory provisions on this matter would be contained in the Hours of Work Bill 1984. In the event
the Bill does not make any changes in relation to this matter, and
additional legislation must be awaited.

(5) Enforcement

Non-compliance with any of the above provisions, in the absence
of a ministerial exemption or licence, is a criminal offence. Under
section 9 of the 1936 Act (as amended), prosecutions may be
brought by the Minister, or by a worker or his trade union. Inspectors of the Department of Labour exercise a policing function. In
fact prosecutions are now rare, and there were none at all in 1981,
the most recent year for which figures are available (*Labour Inspection
Report* 1981, p. 32); no information at all is provided for subsequent

years. Under the Hours of Work Bill prosecutions are to be brought, under section 13, solely "at the suit of the Minister"; it will further be possible to bring such prosecutions against both employers and workers who have contravened the provisions of the proposed legislation.

HOLIDAYS

The entitlement of employees to holidays and leave is governed by the Holidays (Employees) Act 1973. Under this Act all but some exempted workers are entitled to a specified number of annual public holidays and a specified period of annual leave. Under section 2 the Act does not cover outworkers, agricultural workers, seafarers, fishermen, persons employed by or under the State, and relatives living with and maintained by the employer. Agricultural workers, it might be noted, are separately governed by the Holidays (Agricultural Workers) Regulations 1977 (S.I. No. 64 of 1977).

(1) Public holidays

The public holidays are governed by section 4 of the Act, as amended from time to time by ministerial regulations (most recently in 1977). At the time of writing there are eight annual public holidays, on which employees are entitled to a paid day off or to an extra day's pay.

(2) Annual leave

Annual leave is governed primarily by section 3 of the Act. This provides that in every year after "one qualifying month of service," each employee is entitled to three working weeks leave for the full year. Employees with less than 12 months service during the full year are entitled to a proportionately shorter period of leave, but in order to qualify at all an employee must work at least 120 hours per month (or 110 hours if the employee is under 18 years of age). All workers entitled to annual leave must, under section 6(3) of the Act, be given full pay for the period of leave, paid in advance at the "normal weekly rate."

Under section 6 of the Act the exact timing of the annual leave is determined by the employer, but this is subject to some qualifications. First, the employer must consult the employee or his trade union in the matter. Secondly, where an employee has at least eight months service during the year, he must under section 3(5) get an "unbroken period equivalent to two working weeks" of annual leave.

(3) Enforcement

Failure to comply with any of the Act's provisions is a criminal offence, for the fines payable on conviction the Act should be consulted. Furthermore, under section 10 an employer must keep precise records, for at least three years, of holidays and leave taken by his employees, and these may be inspected by inspectors of the Department of Labour.

JOINT LABOUR COMMITTEES

Terms and conditions of employment, and in particular minimum rates of pay, may also be determined for some workers by Joint Labour Committees. Ireland does not have a statutory minimum wage, but the Industrial Relations Act 1946, as amended by the Acts of 1969 and 1976, does provide for a system of guaranteed minimum pay and conditions for certain sections of industry. This system was first set up by the Westminster Parliament under the Trade Boards Act 1909; the purpose was to improve terms of employment in the "sweated industries" where pay was chronically low and union representation either inadequate or non-existent. It was further extended by the Trade Boards Act 1918.

In Ireland five trade boards were originally set up, in the tailoring, paper box, shirt-making, confectionary and food preserving, and linen and cotton industries. A further 14 boards were created in 1921, and the whole system was overhauled and to some extent changed by Part IV of the 1946 Act, through which the trade boards were transformed into Joint Labour Committees.

(1) Establishment of JLCs

A Joint Labour Committee (JLC) is set up by the Labour Court in accordance with a procedure set out in detail in the Act. Under section 36 an application is made either by the Minister for Labour, or by a trade union, or by any other organisation claiming to represent workers or employers. Before the Labour Court can set up the JLC, it must be "satisfied" that one of the following conditions applies: (a) that there is "substantial agreement" between the workers and employers who will be affected; or (b) that the existing machinery for determining pay and conditions of employment, is inadequate or is likely to cease or to cease to be adequate; or (c) that "having regard to the existing rates of remuneration or conditions of employment" it is "expedient" that a JLC should be established (s.37).

If at least one of these conditions is satisfied the Labour Court can proceed to make an "establishment order." Under section 38 it does this by consulting affected parties and publishing its intention to make the order, stating that it will receive objections. If serious objections are made, the Court will hold a public inquiry; otherwise it will make the establishment order. A JLC consists of an equal number of trade union and employer representatives, and of independent persons nominated by the Minister for Labour. The actual number of members can vary from case to case.

(2) Employment Regulation Orders

The function of a JLC, once established, is to determine minimum wages and other conditions of employment for all workers covered by it. This is done in the form of an "employment regulation order" (ERO), which is drafted by the JLC and put into force by the Labour Court. An ERO is drafted in the course of negotiations by the members of the JLC. Recent experience and case law have established that the draft terms need not be agreed by all parties and can therefore be passed by a simple majority. In other words, the independent and trade union members could for example push through certain terms against the opposition of the employer members. In such cases, however, the JLC must seriously consider the objections put forward by the dissenting members, or the resulting ERO will be invalidated: see *Burke* v. *Minister for Labour* (1979).

Once a draft ERO is completed, it is submitted to the Labour Court, which can under section 43 either refer it back to the JLC or publish a notice in the newspapers that a draft ERO has been submitted and where it can be inspected. Interested persons can then raise objections within 21 days, and where this happens the objections are referred back to the JLC which may or may not as a result amend the draft order. When this procedure is completed the Labour Court can either make the full order or refuse to make it; it cannot however itself amend the draft ERO.

Where an ERO is in force, it has the effect of automatically amending the contracts of employment of all workers covered by the JLC to give them the entitlement to the minimum pay and conditions; more favourable terms contained in the contracts remain in force. An employee thus has a contractual entitlement to the minimum terms, but beyond that, section 45 provides that an employer who fails to observe the minimum terms is guilty of a criminal offence and is subject to a fine. A court may also order a convicted employer to pay compensation to the affected workers, and if it can be proved that the employer committed a similar offence within the three preceding years, the court may order the employer to pay the difference between what he paid and what he ought to have paid to the workers during that period. Under section 50 an employer may in certain circumstances seek to have another person brought before the court to show that that person was in fact responsible for the breach of the ERO.

Again, policing functions are carried out by inspectors of the Department of Labour, who are given powers to enter premises and inspect records.

(3) Effectiveness of JLCs

At the end of 1982 there were 20 JLCs in existence. Of these, 16 were described as "active" by the Labour Court in its 1982 *Annual Report* (p. 14); the remaining four had "not met for some time," and this, the Court felt, "would suggest that the need for Joint Labour Committees in these areas has diminished." In 1984 these four JLCs have been abolished; at the same time, the Labour Court has established an additional JLC in the contract cleaning industry, and an inquiry into the establishment of a JLC for workers in architecture and engineering consultancy is due to be held. During 1982 16 new EROs were made, with the minimum pay ranging from about £23 per week (Waterford City Messengers, age 18), to £115 (law clerks). Industries covered include hotels and catering, shirtmaking, tailoring, hairdressing, and so forth, and under the Industrial Relations Act 1976 a special JLC was set up for agricultural workers, with representation on the JLC for the main farming organisations.

During recent wage rounds, in which both the Government and the main employers' organisations sought to keep wage increases at a low level, much attention focussed on the JLCs, and they were subjected to some criticism. In February 1982 the Federated Union of Employers claimed that pay increases determined by JLCs were inflationary and were damaging the competitiveness of some of the industries concerned. Earlier, in 1978, the employers covered by the Hotels JLC had brought a legal challenge against an ERO submitted to the Labour Court in spite of the opposition of the employer members. The action succeeded, and the Supreme Court held in *Burke* v. *Minister for Labour* (1979) that the JLC had, in not giving consideration to some material submitted by the employers, acted *ultra vires*. The Labour Court in its 1982 *Annual Report* also noted the criticism of employers covered by the Clothing JLC that minimum wage rates were being put into force against their opposition and in spite of the depressed state of the industry (p. 14).

There is therefore some element of controversy in the operation of JLCs at present, and indeed also some uncertainty as to the legal position in the wake of the Supreme Court decision in *Burke's* case. In general it would not seem unreasonable to argue that JLCs should be abolished in those industries where there is adequate trade union organisation and therefore sufficient scope for free collective bargaining; it is not in the long-term organisational interests of the unions to get a statutory safety net of this kind.

However where there is no effective union representation of workers the argument is altogether different, for in such cases JLCs give some degree of support to workers who cannot get it elsewhere. In these circumstances the question of the "competitiveness" of the minimum pay rates has to be handled with great care. If JLCs are really being asked to implement "competitive" increases in the minimum wage rate, then what is being envisaged is competitiveness *vis-à-vis* the relevant industries in countries like Korea, Hong Kong and Japan. In view of the wage rates obtained in those countries, which were specifically listed in the 1982 FUE statement, that would in effect mean a return to the "sweated" industries, and it must really be asked whether there is not a better and more socially desirable solution, including if necessary import controls. It might be noted that the average ERO minimum wage in 1982 of around £75 to £80 was less than half the national average blue-collar wage at that time.

In the meantime, the enforcement of EROs may need to be stepped up. The 1982 Labour Court Annual Report notes that the inspectors of the Department of Labour had to collect arrears in many cases when inspections were made. Employers do not therefore appear to apply ERO minimum rates consistently.

REGISTERED EMPLOYMENT AGREEMENTS AND FAIR WAGES CLAUSES

Under Part III of the Industrial Relations Act 1946 it is also possible, if certain conditions are met, to register collective agreements with the Labour Court. Where this is done the agreements become legally binding on all employers and workers covered by them, even those not involved in or represented at the negotiations. Relatively little use is made of this procedure, the original purpose of which was to deprive employers who did not recognise trade unions of the opportunity to engage in unfair competition, by economising on pay, with competitors who engage in collective bargaining.

The system of registered employment agreements, as it stands, is too complex and involves some risks for the participants, since once registered, an agreement remains legally binding until *all* parties to it agree to its de-registration. In this way some very old agreements are still on the register, generally kept there by employers who feel more secure with a legally binding collective agreement incorporating, as all these agreements must, a no-strike clause. For these reasons the scheme has really failed, and a more effective procedure, possibly along the lines of the Fair Wages Resolution, might be preferable.

The Fair Wages Resolution was, in its present (Irish) form, passed by the Westminster Parliament in 1908; it has since been first amended and now rescinded in Britain, but that has not affected the Irish position. The Resolution was approved after independence by the Government Contracts Committee in 1922. In line with this the Government now requires all its contractors to "pay rates of wages and observe hours of labour not less favourable than those commonly recognised by employers and trade societies (or, in the absence of such recognised wages and hours, those which in practice prevail among good employers) in the trade in the district where the work is carried out," or in the nearest district where such "recognised" or "prevailing" rates can be found.

PAYMENT OF WAGES

While for the majority of employees there is no statutory entitlement to a particular rate of pay there are however rules concerning the methods and forms of payment. This is to be found under the Truck Acts of 1831, 1887 and 1896 and under the Payment of Wages Act 1979. The Truck Acts were passed to prohibit various practices such as payments in kind and unexplained or unjustified deductions from wages, all of which were common at the start of the nineteenth century. However, they apply only to workers engaged in manual labour. Hairdressers and domestic servants, for example, have been held to be excluded from the statutory protection; see *R.* (*Holywood*)

v. *Justices of Co. Louth* (1900) and *Cameron* v. *Royal London Ophthalmic Hospital* (1941). The 1979 Act was introduced to allow, in certain circumstances, payment of wages otherwise than in cash.

The basic purpose of the truck legislation can be found in section 3 of the Truck Act 1831, which provides:

> " . . . The entire amount of wages earned by or payable to [the employee], in respect of any labour by him done, shall be actually paid to such [employee] in the current coin of this realm, and not otherwise."

This will need to be examined more closely and qualified to some extent, but broadly it means that: (a) the wages must be paid to the worker himself; (b) the entire amount must be paid to the worker without deductions; and (c) the wages must be paid in cash, except where the 1979 Act applies.

(1) Payment to the worker

One of the main purposes of the Truck Acts was, as it was put in the House of Lords in the case of *Penman* v. *Fife Coal Co. Ltd.* (1936) quoting Bowen L.J. in an earlier case, to ensure that the employer would not be "both payer and payee" in respect of any part of the wages. This was necessary because it was at one stage common practice to require workers to be members of "social clubs" and suchlike controlled by the employer, and to deduct "membership subscriptions" from their pay. Under section 3 of the 1831 Act this became illegal. Similarly, the employer cannot deduct other amounts of money not connected with the employment relationship. In *Penman's* case, for example, it was held that the employers could not, without the employee's consent, deduct from his pay rent owed to them by his father.

There is however an important exception to this. Where the employee consents in the contract of employment to have certain amounts of money deducted from his wages and paid to a third party who is entirely independent of the employer, this is not illegal under the Truck Acts. This was established in the case of *Hewlett* v. *Allen* (1894) and was confirmed more recently in *Williams* v. *Butlers Ltd.* (1975). The latter case concerned the "check-off" system, whereby trade union subscriptions are deducted from wages and paid over directly to the union, and the English Divisional Court held that this did not violate the 1831 Act, even where the employee in question had later withdrawn his consent to the deductions. Michael Davies J. emphasised in his judgment that there was an important distinction between "contracts and deductions made to benefit the employer and those relating to payments to a third party" (p. 896). However, one must suppose that subscriptions to a house union or staff association dominated or controlled by the employer cannot legally be deducted at source in the case of manual workers.

(2) Fines and deductions for bad workmanship

The 1831 Act requires that the "entire amount of wages" be paid to the employee, but this is subject to an exception permitted under the Truck Act 1896. Sections 1 and 2 allow employers to deduct fines, or payments "for or in respect of bad or negligent work or injury to the materials or other property of the employer," but only if a number of conditions are satisfied: (a) the contract of employment must clearly and explicitly allow such deductions and must moreover be displayed in a notice at the place of work or other place easily accessible to the employee; (b) the amount of the deduction must be "fair and reasonable, having regard to all the circumstances of the case"; (c) deductions for bad workmanship or damaged goods must not exceed the amount of the actual loss to the employer; and (d) each deduction must be notified and explained in writing to the employee. Similar conditions must be observed under section 3 in respect of deductions for materials supplied to the employee.

To an extent the effectiveness of the above provisions has been called into question by some judicial decisions. In *Deane* v. *Wilson* (1906) Andrew J. held that the deduction of two shillings, for non-attendance by the employee for part of a day, from the normal pay was not illegal since the amount was equal to a "full attendance bonus" which the employee through her absence simply had not earned. As he put it, "the non-payment took nothing from her to which . . . she had become entitled" (p. 409).

This approach was extended by the English Court of Appeal in *Sagar* v. *Ridehalgh* (1931), in which the employer deducted one shilling for an allegedly faulty piece of work. The Court held that this was not a deduction (which would have attracted the procedural obligations of the 1896 Act) but rather simply a non-payment of what had not been earned on account of the bad workmanship. Similarly, in *Bird* v. *British Celanese Ltd.* (1945) the Court of Appeal concluded that suspension without pay was not regulated by the

Truck Acts, since there could be no "deduction" where no sum was contracted to be paid. Taking these decisions into account it is not easy to see how any fine or deduction for bad workmanship will still be covered by the 1896 Act, and there is therefore a serious loophole in the statutory scheme.

(3) Other deductions

Section 5 of the Payment of Wages Act 1979 provides that every time an employer makes a deduction from an employee's salary or wages, he must give the employee a written statement explaining the "nature and amount of the deduction." This statement must be given "at the time of the payment," unless the payment is by credit transfer, in which case it must be given "as soon as may be." It should be noted that while the 1979 Act in its other provisions applies, like the Truck Acts, only to manual workers, section 5 applies to all employees, in whatever capacity or sector they may be employed.

(4) Forms of payment

Under the 1831 Act wages must be paid in "current coin of the realm," that is in cash. However the Payment of Wages Act 1979 has allowed the use of other forms of payment, including cheques, bills of exchange, postal orders and credit transfers (section 3), provided that certain conditions are satisfied. These conditions are:

(a) there must be agreement between the employer and the employee (or his representative) on this form of payment; this must be in writing, but a written collective agreement covering the employee will suffice;

(b) the agreement must contain a term which provides that this form of payment can be terminated, either on a fixed date or on the giving of notice;

(c) the form of payment must not be stipulated in the contract of employment, as a condition of employment.

The above conditions do not need to be satisfied in the case of an employee who is at the time of payment working away from his usual place of work or who is absent due to illness. In such circumstances the non-cash forms of payment can be used without a written agreement, but if the employee notifies the employer in writing that he objects to this, the wages must be paid in cash.

(5) Evaluation of the legislation

The Truck Acts have for the most part now been in force for a very considerable period, and it is occasionally suggested that they should be radically amended or even repealed. The social and economic conditions, it is thought, which made the 1831 Act necessary no longer obtain, and even if they did, it is hard to see why manual workers only should be given protection. On top of that judicial interpretation has seriously eroded some of the intended effect.

In Britain in 1961 a Government-appointed Committee advocated that the Truck Acts be repealed in their entirety and replaced by more modern legislation which should apply to all employees (*Karmel Committee on the Truck Acts*, 1961 H.M.S.O.). Furthermore, the British Department of Employment has recently issued a discussion paper in which the legislation is further examined (*Proposals for updating the law relating to the payment of wages*, 1983). The Truck Acts, the paper points out, stand in the way of a quicker move towards cashless pay, and on the whole the legislation is "complex, outdated and full of anomalies and uncertainties in terms of its aims and scope" (p. 4). The British Government has subsequently announced its intention of repealing the Acts and inserting new forms of protection into the Employment Protection (Consolidation) Act 1978.

It seems clear that some protection for workers is still necessary. Employers should not be permitted to make unexplained or unjustified deductions from wages, and to leave these matters to be regulated exclusively by contract or through collective agreements will not sufficiently protect unorganised workers. At the same time the legislation must clearly be updated and extended, and the question whether it hinders more desirable methods of non-cash payment must be examined. All of this will probably require new legislation, rather than amendments of the existing statutes.

TRANSFER OF EMPLOYMENT

An increasing amount of legal protection for employees is now being made necessary by Ireland's membership of the European Economic Community. An example of this is provided by the EEC Council Directive 77/187, "on the approximation of the laws of the Member States relating to the safeguarding of employees' rights in the event of transfers of undertakings, businesses or parts of businesses" (generally known as the "Acquired Rights Directive"). The purpose of the Directive is to safeguard the interests of employees in cases where the undertaking or business which employs them is transferred to, or merged with, another employer.

To give effect to this the Minister for Labour issued the European Communities (Safeguarding of Employees' Rights on Transfer of Undertakings) Regulations 1980. The effect of these regulations is (a) to protect employees and their rights where the identity of their employer changes and (b) to impose an obligation to inform and consult on both the old and the new employers where there is a transfer. A breach of these obligations is a criminal offence punishable by fines of up to £500.

(1) The safeguarding of workers' rights

Under regulations 3 and 4 all existing rights and obligations under a contract of employment or a collective agreement are transferred with the business, so that the transferee is bound by the contracts and agreements in the same way as previously the transferor. The only exception is that benefits under private pension schemes (*i.e.* outside the Social Welfare Acts) need not be continued for persons other than former or retired employees of the transferor.

Regulation 5 provides that "the transfer of an undertaking, business or part of a business shall not in itself, constitute grounds for dismissal by the transferor or the transferee." However, dismissals coinciding with the transfer for "economic, technical or organisational reasons entailing changes in the workforce" are permitted.

(2) Information and consultation

Under regulation 7 both the transferor and the transferee (*i.e.* the old and new employers) must inform "the representatives of their respective employees affected by the transfer" of the reasons for the transfer, the "legal, economic and social" implications of the transfer, and the "measures envisaged in relation to the employees." If in fact any "measures" are envisaged, the relevant employer must "consult his representatives of the employees in good time."

(3) Evaluation of the regulations

Rather strangely, the method chosen to implement the Acquired Rights Directive was a statutory instrument rather than a statute. More strangely still, the regulations have largely adopted the wording of the EEC Directive, which could lead to problems of interpretation because of the major differences between Irish and European legal terminology. For example, the regulations (following the Directive) refer to the "rights and obligations" arising under collective agreements. However, under Irish law some collective agreements (at the very least those covered by section 4 of the Trade Union Act 1871) are not legally enforceable, so that the relevant provisions of the regulations must either be taken to have no effect at all or else to have created an exception, in the case of transfers of employment, to the existing law on collective agreements.

In fact the regulations on their own are also incomplete, since for definitions one has to consult the Directive itself. Indeed some concepts are nowhere defined, an example being the "measures" referred to in regulation 7. Also, the regulations do not establish any connection with existing law such as the Unfair Dismissals Act 1977 and the Redundancy Payments Acts, which again could cause problems in hearings under those Acts before the Employment Appeals Tribunal. Enforcement is again to be effected exclusively in criminal proceedings brought by the Department of Labour. Overall, therefore, the regulations must be considered to be fairly unsatisfactory.

INTRODUCTION

It is perhaps not sufficiently recognised that, apart altogether from statute, employers have common law duties to their employees in health and safety matters, and this duty of care "involves the provision of a safe place of work, competent staff, proper equipment and a safe system of work." (*Report of the Commission of Inquiry on Safety Health and Welfare at Work*: Dublin Stationery Office P1 1868, 1983, p. 39.) Failure to do so provides a basis for compensation. But for the nineteenth century employer it was not a sanction of any great significance. It did not arise until an injury actually occurred and in time the sanction itself became very limited by reason of the doctrine of *volenti non fit injuria* and also by reason of the doctrine of common employment as it developed in the mid nineteenth century. (See Declan Madden *Regulating Safety*: unpublished thesis Trinity College Dublin 1983).

When the State began to intervene it did so primarily in order to prevent injury arising in the first instance, and for that purpose it set out to regulate the workplace. This was the central focus of the legislation that followed. In the early nineteenth century we see in the United Kingdom first an endeavour by statute to protect children and young persons, and then we see this principle of regulation gradually extended, albeit with reluctance, to all factory workers, leading eventually to consolidation under the Factories and Workshops Act 1901.

THE CURRENT LEGISLATION

The early British legislation also formed the basis of the law in Ireland until 1955 when the Factories Act of that year was enacted, consolidating and codifying the practice up to then but adding little that was new. This was followed in 1980 by the Safety in Industry Act (the legislation is cited as the Safety in Industry Acts 1955 and 1980.) The Acts deal exclusively with the safety, health and welfare of workers, and are further limited in their operation to manufacturing industry, the construction industry, and those workplaces which fall within the scope of a "factory" as defined by the Act, covering docks, wharves, quays, warehouses, electrical stations and certain institutions and training establishments. The number of workers concerned is about 20,000. The Act is administered by the Department of Labour and is supervised by the Industrial Inspectorate (See *Report of the Commission of Inquiry on Safety Health and Welfare at Work, op. cit.*)

While the Act of 1955 followed the traditional pattern, providing for the safe use, construction and maintenance of machinery, proper work practices, training, supervision, fire precautions and so forth, the 1980 Act, following developments in the United Kingdom (as in the Health and Safety at Work Act 1974) provided for a general duty of care, for obligatory consultation with employees, and for more immediate sanctions. More specifically, the Act provided for a system of compulsory joint consultation in factories, through "safety representatives" and "safety committees." Safety committees are elected in workplaces where there are 20 or more employees, while in those with less than 20 employees a safety representative or a safety committee is appointed. The committee or representative acts on behalf of the workforce in all matters relating to health and safety; they are informed of visits of an inspector, whom they are entitled to accompany, and they are entitled to make recommendations to the employer which the latter must at any rate "consider."

Furthermore, under section 39 of the 1980 Act an employer who in any premises employs more than 10 employees must prepare a written "safety statement," which must specify the manner in which the health and safety of employees is to be secured. The statement must be given to the safety representative or the safety committee, or if there are none to each individual employee.

There are other statutes dealing with the health and safety of workers. The Mines and Quarries Act 1965, which came into force in 1970, covers all mines and quarries but not exploration; about 6,000 workers are involved. The Office Premises Act 1958 applies to all offices in which more than five persons are employed on clerical work. The Shops (Conditions of Employment) Acts 1938 and 1942 apply to the wholesale and retail trades and hotels in the Dublin area and provide some limited protection.

Finally there are those statutes which are general in their intent, but which nonetheless provide workers with protection. One might mention the Dangerous Substances Acts 1972 and 1979, the Road Traffic Acts 1961 to 1978 (in particular in relation to hours of driving and the construction and use of vehicles), the Railways Act 1925, the Explosives Act 1975 (regulating the import, conveyance and storage of explosives), the Poisons Act (Paraquat) Regulations 1975, and the Nuclear Energy Act 1971.

ENFORCEMENT

The principal supervisory body is the Industrial Inspectorate of the Department of Labour and to this we have already referred. The inspectors regularly visit factories and other workplaces; they may prosecute persons in breach of the statutory obligations, but this tends to happen only if the breach has been blatant or serious. The Minister for Labour may also issue a "prohibition notice" under section 11 of the 1980 Act, which has the effect of suspending work in a factory until specified activities have ceased or a particular situation has been remedied which involved a risk of serious bodily injury to workers. There are also other enforcing authorities, the local authorities and health boards, in relation to shops and offices and also in relation to fire hazards, the police in some cases, and certain other Departments of State in relation to the more general regulations. Nor must we overlook the fact that apart altogether from their powers and duties under statute, government departments and State agencies promote health and safety in a substantial way.

THE STATUTORY OBLIGATIONS

The actual substantive obligations on employers and employees are contained in part in the statutes mentioned above and, for the greater part in terms of volume, in statutory instruments made under the Acts. Taken together there is a very extensive list of obligations, so extensive that a comprehensive enumeration would in the present context not be feasible. It could however be said that the obligations fall into three categories, these being health, safety and welfare.

(1) Health

The legislation, and the regulations made under it, set out detailed obligations in relation to all matters arising out of the conditions in which people perform the duties of their employment. More specifically, the matters covered include cleanliness, overcrowding, temperature, noise, ventilation, lighting and sanitation. The actual substance of these obligations varies from Act to Act.

(2) Safety

Section 12(1) of the Safety in Industry Act 1980 provides that "every place at which any person has at any time to work shall be made and kept in a safe condition." The most important obligation is contained in section 23(1) of the Factories Act 1955, which provides that "every dangerous part of any machinery, other than prime movers and transmission machinery, shall be securely fenced." Machinery is considered to be "dangerous" if, in accordance with the test put forward by the British House of Lords in *Close* v. *Steel Company of Wales* (1962), the danger of injury from the machine to persons acting in a way that one might reasonably expect them to act, in circumstances that one might reasonably expect to occur, is reasonably foreseeable. More specific obligations also deal with the handling and repair of machinery, the construction and use of lifting machines (such as hoists, lifts, ropes etc.), protection of eyes, gassing, and so forth. The Mines and Quarries Act 1965 contains specific provisions regarding safety at places of work to which it relates.

(3) Welfare

Welfare provisions contained in the legislation cover such matters as washing facilities, suitable accommodation for boiling water and taking meals, the availability of first-aid boxes, and so forth. Again, the exact content of the obligations varies from Act to Act (this no longer relates to "Welfare").

The precise details of the statutory obligations under the above three headings can be obtained from the Department of Labour.

Under section 8(1)(*a*) of the Safety in Industry Act 1980 employees are also under an obligation, this being the duty to take care for their own safety and health and that of any other persons who might be affected by their acts or omissions at work. The case of *Kennedy* v. *East Cork Foods Ltd.* (1973) does however suggest that the

courts will not hold an employee legally responsible unless a high
degree of carelessness can be established.

ASSESSMENT OF THE CURRENT FRAMEWORK

As a result of the recently issued *Report of the Commission of Inquiry on
Safety Health and Welfare at Work* (1983, the Barrington Report) it is
clear that some fairly extensive legislative changes to the current
framework will need to be effected in due course; however, it looks
increasingly unlikely that the Government will introduce legislation
in the near future. The Commission made a number of criticisms of
the present system, which appear to fall into three categories, the
excessive legalism of the system, its limited scope, and its defects in
implementation.

In regard to the legalism of the system, there is first the criticism
of its incoherence; there are a number of statutes, a mass of regulation and no discernible policy framework. Much of the legal texts
lack clarity and there is much uncertainty regarding definitions;
technical detail has been incorporated in the legislation which technological development has often rendered out-of-date; and the law
as it stands is excessively reliant on prohibitions rather than on a
general duty of care. The Commission summarised the position as
follows:

"Our report is characterised by a certain distrust of legalism.
We doubt if safety and health can be advanced by an excessive
reliance on detailed and increasingly complex regulations
imposed on workplaces from outside. Rather, we see the problem in terms of reform within the workplace based on clearer
ideas about the responsibilities of employers, workers, the self-
employed and others. The law has a role to play in relation, for
example, to dangerous substances and to setting the framework
within which managers and workers operate, but it is no substitute for a sense of commitment based on responsibilities which
are clearly defined and understood." (*Report op. cit.* p. 3).

The second major criticism concerns the scope of the legislation.
It refers almost exclusively to factories, mines and quarries and to
the construction sector. True, some office and shop workers are
covered, but not only are the regulations indifferently enforced,
there is also widespread ignorance of their existence. Excluded from
the legislation are workers in agriculture, forestry, fishing, transport,

laboratories and hospitals. Finally there is no cover for
employed.

The third major criticism concerns the wide field of imp
tation. The courts appear to have a very limited role, in a s
which ostensibly is based on regulation supported by penalty.
Direct court intervention is relatively rare, apart from civil actions
by injured workers. There are 21,000 factories on the Inspectors'
Register, and about 4,000 accidents are reported annually; yet the
number of occupiers prosecuted each year is between 60 and 70.
The Minister has the power to seek a court order prohibiting
dangerous conditions, but very rarely does so. Penalties are low,
but that apart, the courts are lenient in their administration. The
average fine imposed by the courts in respect of offences under the
Factories Act 1955 was less than £30 in 1981, although in most
cases fines of £300 could have been imposed (Madden, *op. cit.*,
p. 138).

The difficulties in part could be attributed to the enforcing authorities. The role of the inspectors appears to be highly ambiguous;
on the one hand it is seen as regulative, minatory and ultimately as
that of a prosecutor, on the other hand it is seen as supportive,
informative and advisory. In a substantial way one role tends to
exclude the other. In the case of the local authorities, there is very
little information on inspection, and it appears to have a very low
level of priority. Furthermore no formal liaison exists between the
local authorities and the Minister for Labour.

COMPENSATION FOR ACCIDENTS AND INJURIES

Finally there is the question of compensation for occupational accidents and injuries. There are two sources for such compensation, the
Occupational Injuries Benefit Scheme of the Department of Social
Welfare (based on the Social Welfare Occupational Injuries Act
1966), and payments arising from civil liability in tort, that is to say,
the common law remedy. It is estimated by the Commission (*op. cit.*
p. 155) that in 1982 over £17 million was paid under the Social Welfare Scheme, while insurance companies paid close to £70 million,
95 per cent. of the claims being settled out of court.

The Social Welfare Scheme covers all employees, but not the self-
employed, and is based on the principle of employers' liability for
accidents to employees arising out of and in the course of employment. It is in its essentials a "no-fault" scheme. It appears to be concerned exclusively with compensation, it does not contribute to a

policy of prevention, and it appears to have developed very much in isolation from the schemes of the Department of Labour.

In the case of actions in tort, court awards are often large and unpredictable, there is often considerable delay in reaching settlements, and the premiums required by insurance companies have been increasing rapidly. The procedures are costly from the point of view of the individual, and in regard to public policy, the tort system not only does not contribute to prevention but may in certain circumstances hamper improvement. More important, however, is that employers' liability insurance is not compulsory in Ireland although it has been so in the United Kingdom since 1969.

THE COMMISSION'S RECOMMENDATION

In regard to all these matters, the recently published report of the Commission of Inquiry on Safety Health and Welfare at Work recommends a framework Act which on the one hand would require a general duty of care, and on the other, would establish a highly participative system largely of self-regulation. In the light of the present pressure for productivity and technical innovation, it is difficult to assess what its impact will be.

6 Sex Discrimination

INTRODUCTION

The results of the 1981 census show that females make up almost exactly half of the population of the Republic of Ireland.[1] At the same time, in 1981, only about 28·4 per cent. of the total workforce were women,[2] a relatively small proportion compared with some other Western European countries. To what extent this low participation in the labour market is caused or aggravated by sex discrimination is hard to gauge, but it has traditionally been felt that such discrimination is at the very least a contributing factor.

The difficulty does not of course end there. Even within employment women are frequently victims of attitudes and practice which result in low pay, lack of opportunity and inferior status. In December 1982, women's weekly earnings in manufacturing industry were on average only about 60 per cent. of male earnings. This figure represents a closing of the gap by about 7 per cent. since 1975 (the year in which a statutory entitlement to equal pay became operative), an improvement which is hardly dramatic. At the same time women are still concentrated in specific areas of work considered to be peculiarly "female," which have little opportunity for advancement. Women constitute the majority of clerical employees, service workers and shop assistants, while the number of women working as managers, farmers and farm workers, and production workers is proportionally very small; furthermore, just under 30 per cent. of all working women are employed in the "professional services," mainly as nurses, nuns and teachers (see *Equality for Women*, 1980, Discussion Paper by Irish Transport and General Workers' Union, p. 7).

[1] The figures, as supplied by the Central Statistics Office, are as follows. Male: 1,729,354. Female: 1,714,051. Total 3,443,405.
[2] The figures, based on the Census, are: Male: 905,700. Female: 358,800. Total: 1,264,500. This is an estimate based on a 5 per cent. sample of the population.

This employment pattern is clearly unsatisfactory. At the same time there is no obvious or immediate remedy, since the causes are deep-rooted and not amenable to instant solutions. In 1972 the Commission on the Status of Women pointed out that the problem of sex inequality involved an area of discrimination consisting of factors such as "the stereotyped role that is assigned to women" and "the inculcation of attitudes in both boys and girls in their formative years . . . that a woman's life pattern must be predominantly home-centered while the man's life pattern will be predominantly centered on employment" (1972, Prl. 2760, at p. 12). The idea that the primary contribution by women to society is made by working at home is to some extent reinforced in Article 41.2.1 of the Irish Constitution, which declares that "the State recognises that by her life within the home, woman gives to the State a support without which the common good cannot be achieved." The pressure for change and the re-appraisal of sex roles which, to varying degrees, have affected other European countries are perhaps not yet so much in evidence in Ireland. In the absence of widespread contraception, maternity still tends to be a long drawn-out period of a woman's life, at the end of which her entry into the labour market is neither easy nor attractive.

All these factors represent significant obstacles to sex equality in employment. In recent years it has been increasingly accepted that the law should be used to deal with the problem of inequality. It would be a mistake, however, to think that the law has a primary function in this field. Attitudes, prejudices and long-standing practices cannot be swept away overnight by legislation. But within certain limits the legal system can deal with some of the symptoms, and in particular, it can tackle some of the more blatant forms of discrimination which occur. It is in that context that the law can play a useful if limited role.

THE GENERAL LEGAL FRAMEWORK

(1) The Constitution

The Irish Constitution of 1937 provides in Article 40 that "all citizens shall, as human persons, be held equal before the law"; but the Article goes on to emphasise that the State may "in its enactments have due regard to differences of capacity, physical and moral, and of social function." If one reads this in conjunction with the "recognition" which the Constitution extends to women's "life within the home" in Article 41 it must seem at least possible that due regard given to "differences of social function" would permit some forms of legislative differentiation between men and women in the employment relationship. This conclusion can be drawn from the Supreme Court decision in *Murphy* v. *Attorney-General* (1980), in which Kenny J. expressed the view that discrimination against married couples in the income tax scheme could be justified under Article 40 (though not under Article 41, dealing with the family) because of the "social function of married couples living together"; similar arguments might be constructed in relation to discrimination against working women, and in particular married women at work.

At the same time discrimination in respect of pay and other conditions of employment, if based solely on sex, is probably unconstitutional. This would follow from the very clear statement by Walsh J. in the case of *De Burca* v. *Attorney-General* (1975) that a measure which "is undisguisedly discriminatory on the ground of sex only" would be repugnant to the Constitution. In the earlier case of *Murtagh Properties Ltd.* v. *Cleary* (1972), Kenny J. had also decided that women have a constitutional right to equal access to employment, so that an employer who objects in principle to taking on women as such is acting unconstitutionally.

(2) Pre-1974 legislation

Prior to 1974 there were no legal provisions in Irish law specifically relating to sex discrimination in employment. The only statutes which dealt with the employment of women were, apart from some regulations relating to health and safety, the Conditions of Employment Acts 1936 and 1944, already mentioned in Chapter 4. The Acts, which remain in force at the time of writing, prohibit the employment of female workers between the hours of 10p.m. and 8a.m., and stipulate a minimum interval of 11 hours between periods of work. These measures are broadly in line with Convention No. 89 of the International Labour Organisation, which Ireland has ratified. Nevertheless, they have attracted widespread criticism. The Employment Equality Agency (the functions of which are explained below), asked by the Minister of Labour to review the legislation, declared in 1978 that the ban on night work effectively deprived women of job opportunities, additional income and experience relevant to training and promotion (*Annual Report*, 1978, p. 36). The Agency thus recommended a relaxing of the rules in so far as this could be made compatible with the Convention, and further advised the Government to denounce the Convention at the earliest opportunity. This approach had the approval of the Federated Union of Employers, but the Irish Congress of Trade Unions felt that the Government should await the review of Convention No. 89 to be carried out by the ILO itself before taking unilateral action (*Annual Report*, 1980, pp. 109–110). The Government eventually denounced the Convention in March 1982, with effect from February 1983, but no statutory amendment has been announced or implemented.

(3) The 1974 and 1977 Acts

In the discussion on employment equality the main focus has in recent years been on the provision of the Anti-Discrimination (Pay) Act 1974, the Employment Equality Act 1977, and more recently the Maternity Protection of Employees Act 1981. The 1974 and 1977 Acts are, under section 56(2) of the 1977 Act, to be "construed together as one Act," a point which could be significant for the purposes of interpretation. These Acts are supplemented by the "Code of Practice for the Elimination of Sex and Marital Status Discrimination and the Promotion of Equality of Opportunity in Employment," drawn up by the Employment Equality Agency under section 37 of the 1977 Act to "provide guidelines and advice for employers, workers, trade unions and employment agencies to help them to eliminate unlawful discrimination and to avoid its recurrence" (para. 1.1). The Code was issued in February 1984.

In international law the principle of non-discrimination is of fairly long standing. In 1951, for example, the International Labour Organisation passed Convention No. 100 which envisaged the implementation of equal pay. However, in a more direct sense the Irish legislation was prompted by Ireland's entry into the European Economic Community in 1973. The Treaty of Rome itself provides:

> Each Member State shall . . . maintain the application of the principle that men and women should receive equal pay for equal work.

In the case of *Defrenne* v. *Sabena* (1976) the European Court of Justice held that Article 119 has direct effect in the domestic law of member States, so that an employee could rely on it directly in a court action. This was re-affirmed by the Court in the cases of *Macarthys Ltd.* v. *Smith* (1980) and *Garland* v. *British Rail Engineering Ltd.* (1982).

In addition there are also EEC Directives which impose upon member States the obligation to introduce measures to achieve employment equality. These are Council Directive 75/117, which requires the introduction of measures to implement equal pay, and Directive 76/207, which obliges member States to introduce measures prohibiting other forms of sex discrimination in employment in such areas as recruitment, promotion, training and conditions of employment. These Directives prompted the 1974 and 1977 Acts respectively.

The importance of European Community law was illustrated in developments occurring after the enactment of the 1974 Act, when the Minister for Labour attempted to postpone the implementation of equal pay and was prevented from doing so by the Community's Social Affairs Commissioner, Dr. Patrick Hillery (himself a former Irish Minister for Labour).

At the same time it would not be true to say that all the impetus had come from abroad. In 1965, following the submission of a memorandum prepared by the Public Services Industrial Committee of the Irish Congress of Trade Unions, the Executive Council of Congress decided to set up an Equal Pay Committee to prepare a report on the matter (see ICTU *Annual Report*, 1965, p. 65). This marked the beginning of a fairly intensive campaign by the ICTU to secure equal pay for women.

Following this, in 1970, the Government established the Commission on the Status of Women, which was instructed in its terms of reference to recommend on "the steps necessary to ensure the participation of women on equal terms with men in the political, social, cultural and economic life of the country" (*op. cit.*, p. 7). When the Commission reported two years later it recommended, *inter alia*, the enactment of legislation to achieve equal pay for women and to abolish certain other forms of sex discrimination.

THE 1974 ACT

The Anti-Discrimination (Pay) Act 1974 came into force on December 31, 1975. The scheme of the Act is explained in section 2(1), which provides:

> "Subject to this Act, it shall be a term of the contract under which a woman is employed in any place that she shall be entitled to the same rate of remuneration as a man who is employed in that place by the same employer (or by an associated employer . . .) if both are employed on like work."

Although the Act refers to equal pay for "women" throughout, it is made clear in section 11 that the same rules apply to equal pay for men where that is an issue.

(1) Waiver of equal pay entitlement

The method used by the Act is one of automatic contractual modification. Under section 4 every contract of employment is deemed to have written into it "an implied term giving effect to [section 2]," and where the implied equality clause conflicts with any express term of the contract it will override it. Furthermore, section 5 states that a provision in a collective agreement or similar instrument (such as an employment regulation order of a Joint Labour Committee, or a registered employment agreement: see Chap. 4) in which "differences in rates of remuneration are based on or related to the sex of employees" are "null and void."

Despite these provisions the question has arisen on a number of occasions whether the entitlement to equal pay can be waived or signed away. The Employment Equality Agency's Code of Practice is very clear on the point, stating that "a worker cannot contract out of this entitlement to equal pay nor can the entitlement be waived by agreement between the employer and the trade union representing the employee" (para. 14.2). This was broadly the view of the Labour Court in the case of *Data Products (Dublin) Memories Ltd.* v. *Simpson* (1979). Having made an equal pay claim the employee had left her employment before the claim could be fully processed. She accepted a severance payment "in final settlement of all remuneration claims on the company," but the Labour Court found that because of section 4 this could not be construed as a waiver of the right to pursue the equal pay claim. The significant point here is that section 4 as worded seems to refer to contracts of employment only, but the case did not actually concern an employment contract in the strict sense. The decision of the Labour Court would therefore seem to imply that conflicting terms not only in employment contracts, but also in severance agreements and possibly in other contracts, are overriden by the equality clause.

The same general question has also been considered by the High Court and the Supreme Court. In the case of *PMPA Insurance Co. Ltd.* v. *Keenan* (1983) the applicants were 15 female insurance officials who, prior to 1978, had been on a separate female grade and had thus been denied equal pay. In 1978 a collective agreement was concluded between the company and the employees' trade union under which a new unisex salary scale was implemented as from

January of that year. The applicants then sought equal pay for the period between December 31, 1975 (the date on which the 1974 Act came into force) and December 31, 1977. The company refused this, stating that the benefits (including some benefits in addition to the new salary scale) conferred by the 1978 collective agreement had been offered, and accepted, expressly on the understanding that they were "in full and final settlement of all claims"; this agreement, in the company's view, was binding on the union and on the affected employees.

On appeal the Labour Court accepted in principle that the collective agreement was enforceable (see Chap. 1). However, the Court found that "an agreement not to pursue an equal pay claim through the procedures laid down by the Oireachtas even if the agreement forms part of an individual's contract of employment should be regarded as void to that extent on the grounds that it is contrary to public policy." On appeal in the High Court, Carroll J. took the different view that a claim for arrears of equal pay could be waived if the agreement were "supported by consideration." However, she upheld the Labour Court's decision on the grounds that no waiver of the right to claim arrears was necessarily implied in the agreement under consideration.

The case was then taken to the Supreme Court, which, however, did not discuss the legal principles. Henchy J. merely doubted whether a point of law suitable for an appeal from the Labour Court had actually been raised by the employers. It is therefore not clear whether the view offered by the Labour Court stands, or whether a waiver of the kind suggested by Carroll J. is permissible. Overall the inference can perhaps be drawn that under the provisions of sections 2, 4 and 5 a person cannot waive, or be deprived of, her entitlement to equal pay under the 1974 Act in all but the most remote circumstances. The *PMPA* case was somewhat complex in that it concerned arrears only, the current entitlement to equal pay not being an issue.

(2) Establishing the equal pay entitlement

In order to be able to lodge a claim for equal pay, a woman must establish comparability under the Act with a suitable man. In the comparison she will have to show that four requirements are satisfied:

(a) Both she and the man must be "employed," which section 1(1) of the Act explains as "employed under a contract of service or apprenticeship or a contract personally to execute any work or labour." For example, it was decided in the case of *Department of Public Service* v. *Robinson* (1978) that a member of the National Parliament, the Oireachtas is "employed" for the purposes of the Act, while in *P.C. Moore & Co.* v. *Flanagan* (1978) it was held that a partner in a firm is not. The European Court of Justice has held that a woman may, under Article 119 of the Treaty of Rome, compare herself with an immediate predecessor in the post, but not with an "hypothetical" man doing like work: *Macarthys Ltd.* v. *Smith* (1980). The latter point is reinforced by the Equality Officer's decision in *Ostlanna Iompair Eireann* v. *Nine Female Employees* (1981); she stressed that the applicant must claim equal pay with a named individual, not "the same rate somebody else might be receiving if they were doing his job."

(b) They must work in the same "place," which under section 1(1) includes "a city, town or locality." Therefore it has been held that local authority employees working at swimming pools in different parts of Dublin are all employed in the same "place": *Dublin Corporation* v. *Sixteen Female Baths Attendants* (1980). Furthermore in the case of *PMPA* v. *Three Women Insurance Officials* (1981) the Equality Officer held that where employees working in different localities for the same employer have their remuneration fixed centrally they are, for the purposes of the Act, working in the "same place"; therefore women in the company's office in Waterford were found to be working in the "same place" as men in the company's Kilkenny office. However, in the case of *ITGWU* v. *Twenty-three Female Employees* (1983) the Equality Officer accepted the respondent trade union's argument that its employees in Castlebar, Athlone and Dublin were not working in the "same place," although the rates of pay were centrally negotiated. This case is, at the time of writing, currently being appealed.

(c) The claimant and the comparable man must both be employed by the same employer, or by an associated employer (provided that the employees of both employers in general work under the same terms and conditions of employment). Under section 2(2), employers are "associated" if one is a body corporate of which the other has control or if both are bodies corporate of which a third person has control. Employers cannot in other words be "associated"

unless at least one is a body corporate. In more practical
terms, for example, a father and son who are employers in
their personal capacities are not "associated" for the purposes of the Act. A case however in which the requirement
was fulfilled was where a woman worked in a different hospital than the man with whom she was claiming comparability,
but where both hospitals were run by the same Health
Board: *Clonskeagh Hospital* v. *Two Telephonists* (1979).

(d) The man and woman must be "employed on like work."

(3) Like work

The interpretation of this requirement has proved to be the most
difficult feature of the Act. Section 3 of the Act provides that "like
work" covers the following situations: (a) where the work is identical
or interchangeable; (b) where the work is "of a similar nature," with
differences occurring only "infrequently" or being "of small importance"; and (c) where the work is "equal in value . . . in terms of the
demands it makes in relation to such matters as skill, physical or
mental effort, responsibility and working conditions."

It is worth noting that the comparison relates to the work as it is
actually performed, so that theoretical differences in the job description which are not reflected in work practice are disregarded. The
Code of Practice puts it as follows (para. 14.4):

"An employer cannot avoid equal pay by using different job
descriptions or by imposing different work responsibilities as
between jobs done by men and those done by women . . . . It is
the actual work performed by a person which must be assessed
and not the work which an employee might be capable of or
liable to perform."

In the case of *Department of Posts and Telegraphs* v. *Kennefick* (1980)
the applicant, a post office clerk, was seeking equal pay with male
clerks. The Department refused, arguing that the male workers had
in their contract of employment an "attendance liability and range
of duties" which did not apply to the applicant. However, the Equality Officer and the Labour Court found that in practice she performed substantially the same work as the male clerks so that she
was entitled to receive equal pay.

The concept of work "equal in value" is both the most important
and the most difficult of the categories, and few general conclusions

can be drawn from the case law on it. However, it is intended to be a flexible concept, allowing for the weighing and balancing of various attributes attaching to a job. This is illustrated by the recommendation contained in para. 14.8 of the Code of Practice that in equal value claims "a fair and just evaluation" should be given to each factor, and that "it is important . . . to carefully balance the level of skill and mental and physical effort required."

Examples of work "equal in value" include the case of *Linson Ltd.* v. *Two Female Group Leaders (Stomahesive)* (1981), in which "paperwork" was equated with an "onerous supervisory function." In another case, *Youghall Carpet Yarns Ltd.* v. *ITGWU* (1981), the Equality Officer found that although the applicants, who were female operatives, were doing different work than the male operatives, roughly "the same amount of physical effort had to be expended by all," so that they were entitled to equal pay. In *Coombe Lying-In Hospital* v. *Bracken* (1980) the Equality Officer found that the fact that the applicant had to use "a somewhat higher degree of mental effort" than her male counterpart compensated for the fact that his work "involved more sustained physical effort."

Formal job evaluation schemes are not commonly used in these cases, and as a result few of them could realistically be considered to be precedents for future decisions. The decisions are, to use the terminology of the Code of Practice, based on "rule of thumb methods" rather than on "formal and systematic procedures" (para. 14.6). In fact, the services of the Irish Productivity Centre are available to the parties in such cases, and have on occasion been used; however, this has been controversial, particularly in procedural terms. (See Chapter 9.)

The resulting somewhat unstructured approach has presented a number of problems, not least being the uncertainty as to the relative importance of the relevant criteria mentioned in section 3(c). In so far as one can generalise, the most difficult argument an applicant may have to face is that her work is of a less "responsible" nature than that of the comparable male. The alleged, and not always objectively recognisable, "responsibility" attaching to a post (usually a male post) seems to have been elevated to a level of some importance, as witnessed for example in the Equality Officer's statement in *Blood Transfusion Service Board* v. *O'Sullivan* (1981) that "responsibility is more important than physical effort." As a result of these and other factors, the trend appears to be that the success rate in applications based on section 3(c) is diminishing. This is of particular significance, since section 3(c) is the provision of the Act

on which further improvements in comparative pay between men
and women must increasingly depend.

(4) Lower pay for work of higher value

Another disturbing development is represented by the determination of the Labour Court in *Arthur Guinness Son & Co. (Dublin) Ltd.*
v. *Federated Workers' Union of Ireland* (1983). The applicant, Mrs. Rita
Murtagh, was a waitress in the company's coffee bar, and she
claimed equal pay with the male employee working in a "tea kiosk."
The Equality Officer in her recommendation found that the applicant was not doing "like work" since "the work performed by Mrs.
Murtagh is higher in value than that performed by the male"; she
was thus not entitled to equal pay. This was confirmed by the
Labour Court on appeal, and the Court reached the same conclusion in the recent case of *An Bord Telecom* v. *Irish Women Workers'
Union* (1984). The outcome of these decisions is that an employer
can justify *lower* pay for a woman with the *higher* value of her work,
which may be correct on a strict interpretation of the Act but is
hardly acceptable on policy or commonsense grounds. It will also
need to be investigated whether it is acceptable under EEC law.

The justification of the decision by the Equality Officer and the
Labour Court would presumably be that the Act does not provide
for equal pay for work which is *at least* of equal value, or indeed more
generally for fair pay as between men and women. As was stated by
the Equality Officer in another similar case, *Department of Posts and
Telegraphs* v. *Twenty-nine Female Post Office Factory Workers* (1983), "the
equality officer has no power to recommend equal pay where a like
work situation does not exist"; and work of higher value is apparently not "like work" for the purposes of the Act. But if this is so an
amendment should be considered. In the meantime the Equality
Officers and the Labour Court should perhaps adopt a more flexible
evaluation process, as suggested by the English Employment Appeal
Tribunal in *Waddington* v. *Leicester Council for Voluntary Services* (1977).

(5) Unequal pay not based on sex

The case law has established that even where there are some differences in the work duties these will not prejudice the entitlement to
equal pay if the differences are imposed purely on the basis of the
workers' sex and do not have any independent foundation or justification. On the other hand, section 2(3) provides that "nothing in
this Act shall prevent an employer from paying . . . different rates of

remuneration on grounds other than sex." What this means is that if
an employer can show that differences in pay are based on grounds
which are not caused by or in any way connected with the sex of the
employees he will not be in breach of the Act.

It has to be remembered that the purpose of the 1974 Act was to
prohibit discrimination in remuneration based on sex, and it does
not therefore affect other forms of or motives for pay discrimination
or differentiation. In the case of *Department of Public Service* v. *Association of Higher Civil Servants* (1979) the Labour Court put it as follows:

> "The Oireachtas has given powers to the Court to prohibit the
> continuance of one traditionally accepted pay differential, *i.e.*
> differential between the pay of men and women. The Oireach-
> tas has not given the Court any power to prohibit by law the use
> of any other criteria whether justified or not."

One category of cases which is relatively straightforward concerns
pay differentials based on the personal characteristics of the individuals compared with each other. So, for example, a male employee's
greater age, experience or educational qualifications would be a
non-sex based ground: see, *e.g. Department of Agriculture* v. *Instructors*
(1979). Furthermore, genuine additional duties or work liabilities
may justify higher pay. Other examples would include the so-called
"red circle" cases, where an employee is paid a "personal" rate of
pay, frequently on compassionate grounds, which other employees
do not enjoy. This could occur, for example, where a male employee
is moved from a more responsible position but still retains his former
salary: *Coras Iompair Eireann* v. *Six Female Carriage Cleaners* (1980);
Central Bank of Ireland v. *One Female Cleaner* (1980); *ITGWU* v. *Twenty-
three Female Employees* (1983). In all cases, however, section 2(3) will
not apply unless the ground put forward by the employer is the
genuine reason for the differential and not just an excuse for sex-
based pay discrimination. Furthermore, grounds which apply to
members of one sex only cannot be used under section 2(3); so an
Equality Officer held in *Shield Insurance Co. Ltd.* v. *Two Female
Employees* (1984) that the exclusion of "disablement arising from
pregnancy or childbirth" from the employers' "Income Continuance Plan" was illegal since it applied to females only.

However, once one leaves the "personal" level in pay differentials
the matter is much more complex. The question here is whether the
Act prohibits discrimination in pay applied on economic or structural grounds. Lord Denning M.R. in the English Court of Appeal,
in the case of *Clay Cross (Quarry Service) Ltd.* v. *Fletcher* (1979) held

that it was only permissible "to have regard . . . to the personal equation of the woman as compared to that of the man, irrespective of any extrinsic forces which led to the variation in pay" (p. 477). There is in fact a difference in the wording between the relevant provisions of the British Equal Pay Act 1970 and the Irish 1974 Act, but we shall assume that that is not material, particularly since Lawson L.J. in the same case felt that the decision was in line with European Community law (see p. 481), which is the basis of both Acts.

The real point here is that if section 2(3) permits extrinsic grounds of an economic or structural nature it will have opened the door to indirect pay discrimination, which the 1974 Act, unlike the 1977 Act in matters other than pay, does not expressly prohibit. This was discussed in the English case of *Jenkins* v. *Kingsgate (Clothing Productions) Ltd.* (1981), which was referred to the European Court of Justice. The applicant, a female part-time worker, had been paid a lower hourly rate than the equivalent full-time male employees, and the Court found that this violated Article 119 if the percentage of women able to work full-time was "considerably smaller" than that of men; that of course is essentially a definition of indirect discrimination.

The judgment of the Employment Appeal Tribunal, to which the case was referred back, extends this idea. The Tribunal held that indirect discrimination covers "cases where, because a class of persons consists wholly or mainly of women, a difference drawn between that class and other persons operates in fact in a manner which is discriminatory against women" (p. 723). It can be "intentional"—*i.e.* where discrimination is the intended, if hidden, effect—and in that case it is always illegal; or it can be "unintentional," that is "where the employer has no intention of discriminating against women on the ground of sex but intends to achieve some different purpose, such as the greater utilisation of his machinery." In the latter case, according to the E.A.T., the discrimination is also illegal unless the employer can "show that the pay differential actually achieved that different objective" (p. 724).

(6) Section 2(3) and the development of equal pay

The above British cases must be treated with some care because, as already noted, the Equal Pay Act 1970 does not have a wording identical to that of the 1974 Act in this context. However, they show an approach which demonstrates an attempt to come to grips with the problem of indirect pay discrimination in a way not yet evident in Ireland. The absence of clarity in this country can be witnessed in what we may call the "grading" cases. These arise where an employer argues that unequal pay as between a man and a woman is not on grounds of sex, but because the man and woman are employed in different grades subject to different pay scales.

The response by Equality Officers to such arguments has been inconsistent. In the case of *Ostlanna Iompair Eireann* v. *Nine Female Employees* (1981) the company argued that the wage rates were "based on grading systems and not on the sex of the job holders." The Equality Officer did not entirely accept this defence:

> "The males are in the higher paid grades and the females are in the lower paid grades. Consequently, if a like work situation exists between the males and females it would be difficult to sustain an argument that the differences in their rates of pay are not related to their sex."

Such a conclusion would of course have particular force if, as is frequently the case, the historical origin of the grades arose out of a deliberate segregation of men and women.

On the other hand, in the case of *Coras Iompair Eireann* v. *Four Female Clerks* (1981) another Equality Officer came to the conclusion that section 2(3) applies where "the claimants are in receipt of lower remuneration than the males in question, not because of their sex, but because they are in a different grade than the males." Put this way the conclusion is most unsatisfactory, since it would almost appear to allow employers to operate separate *de facto* female grades with lower pay, at any rate as long as they do nothing that can be proved to be illegal under the 1977 Act. The Equality Officer's decision was all the more remarkable since she conceded that in fact the applicants did "like work" with two of the three males named by them.

More recently in the case of *ITGWU* v. *Twenty-three Female Employees* (1983) the Equality Officer put the position as follows:

> "Where significant blocks of work in a lower grade were found to be like work with that performed by people in a higher grade and where workers have argued that a [grading] structure has been introduced unilaterally, equality officers were inclined to accept the arguments made on behalf of claimants that the gradings were faulty."

Whether that is a correct description of current practice may perhaps be doubted, but it certainly is a correct statement of how the Act should be applied.

The importance of these cases and of the questions they raise is that they determine the extent to which the 1974 Act can continue to be a useful piece of legislation. Section 3(*c*) as worded at least potentially prohibits indirect discrimination, although it is weakened by the lack of a consistent evaluation process. But if section 2(3) can be used to justify extrinsic grounds for pay discrimination, then section 3(*c*) becomes to all intents and purposes a dead letter. If therefore this connection between the two provisions is not properly recognised by the Labour Court or the Equality Officers that may prove to be fatal to the further effectiveness of the 1974 Act.

The most recent decision by an Equality Officer on this point, in the case of *St. Patrick's College, Maynooth* v. *Nineteen Female Employees* (1984), the above problems were fully recognised and a satisfactory conclusion was reached. The case concerned the refusal by the College to pay permanent female part-time staff the same *pro rata* pay as their permanent male full-time equivalents. The College argued that this was not illegal discrimination, since it was based on the different status of part-time employees (who all, coincidentally, happened to be female) rather than on sex. The Equality Officer found that since, under section 56(2) of the Employment Equality Act 1977, both the 1974 Act and the 1977 Act are to be construed as one Act indirect discrimination on the basis of sex is prohibited under both statutes. On the facts he concluded:

" . . . The Equality Officer considers that a requirement to work full-time in order to qualify for a higher rate of pay . . . could possibly constitute indirect discrimination on the basis of sex having regard to the reasonably assumed fact that a substantially greater proportion of men than of women is in practice able to work full-time because of difficulties encountered by women with children, and not generally by men, in arranging to work on that basis."

Since the method of payment was not "objectively justifiable on grounds which do not discriminate in any way on the basis of sex" the Equality Officer found that there had been a violation of the 1974 Act. It is to be hoped that this decision will be followed by other Equality Officers and by the Labour Court.

(7) Remuneration

Where the four requirements mentioned above are satisfied, the woman is entitled to "the same rate of remuneration" as the man.

Section 1 of the Act provides that "remuneration" includes "any consideration, whether in cash or in kind, which an employee receives, directly or indirectly, in respect of his employment from his employer." In *Linson Ltd.* v. *ASTMS* (1977) the Equality Officer explained that the statutory definition includes "all benefits, including pension benefits, or allowances based on the wage or salary received by an employee." It can thus be said that "remuneration" is a broad concept which can cover a variety of benefits. Some examples of what has been held to be "remuneration" for the purposes of the equal pay entitlement include the following.

(a) *Bonus payments*

In *Plunder and Pollack* v. *ATGWU* (1979) the employers claimed that the men's additional earnings consisted solely of "rest allowances" which could not be described as "remuneration." However, the Labour Court held that the latter term covered "equal basic rates and equal bonus earnings for equal levels of output."

(b) *Pensions*

These were held to be included in the cases of *Department of Public Service* v. *Robinson* (1978) and in the *Linson* case. Furthermore in the case of *University College Dublin* v. *Irish Federation of University Teachers* (1979) it was held by the Labour Court that not only pension benefits, but also the entitlement to contribute to a voluntary pension scheme were covered by the 1974 Act. The European Court of Justice has also held that contributions to a pension scheme made by the employer in the name of the employee are also covered: *Worringham* v. *Lloyds Bank Ltd.* (1981).

(c) *Gratuities and preferential loans*

In the *PMPA* case (see above) the Labour Court determined that both a marriage gratuity paid only to female employees and a house purchase loan scheme at preferential rates available only to male employees were "remuneration."

(d) *Payments in kind and other benefits*

In the case of *Garland* v. *British Rail Engineering Ltd.* (1982) the European Court of Justice held that, in this case, travel concessions for British Rail employees and their families, even on an *ex gratia* basis and even where they applied beyond retirement, were "pay" for the purposes of Article 119 of the Treaty of Rome. While the case itself concerned the interpretation of the British Sex Discrimination

Act 1975 (in most respects the equivalent of the Employment Equality Act 1977), the Court's finding in respect of Article 119 suggests that it would apply in Ireland to the 1974 Act, as well as to actions based directly on the Article. The equal pay entitlement would therefore probably apply to any concessionary benefit for employees and their families, whether or not provided for under the contracts of employment.

(e) *Redundancy and severance payments*

In the case of *Kiernan* v. *Grant, Barnett & Co. Ltd.* (1983) the applicant claimed that she had been paid a lower *pro rata* redundancy payment than the comparable male employees. However, she brought the case under the 1977 Act, and the Equality Officer found that the claim under the 1974 Act would have been appropriate (a doubtful conclusion, perhaps, in view of the fact that both are to be construed as one Act). The case has been appealed to the Labour Court.

THE 1977 ACT

While the Anti-Discrimination (Pay) Act is designed to tackle sex discrimination in relation to remuneration, the Employment Equality Act 1977 deals with other matters arising out of the employment relationship. The purpose of the Act is to combat discrimination based on a person's sex or marital status, and under section 2 a number of practices are prohibited, which for shorthand purposes may be referred to as (a) direct discrimination, (b) indirect discrimination, and (c) victimisation. The last of these is covered by section 2(*d*) and occurs where a person is penalised for opposing any form of sex discrimination prohibited by the 1974 and 1977 Acts, or for bringing proceedings under the Acts, or for giving evidence in such proceedings brought by someone else, or for giving notice of an intention to do any of these things. Under section 26 a dismissal for any of the reasons taken under the heading of "victimisation" is a criminal offence, and in the event of a prosecution the employer has the onus of proving that the "sole or principal reason" for the dismissal was something else; if no prosecution is brought, the aggrieved employee may bring a claim to the Labour Court under section 27.

An employer may not discriminate, directly or indirectly, against female employees (and equally, of course, against male employees) or married persons in the decisions he makes or practices he applies in relation to "access to employment, conditions of employment . . . training or experience for or in relation to employment, promotion or re-grading in employment or classification of posts in employment" (section 3(1)).

(1) "Direct" and "indirect" discrimination

"Direct" discrimination takes place where one person is treated less favourably than another person of the other sex, or of the same sex but a different marital status. An example of this was where a woman applying for the job of national school teacher was turned down because "the Board of Management wanted a man for the post": *Management of Fyborough National School* v. *A Worker* (1981).

The main difficulty in such cases is frequently that of proving the intention on the part of the employer to discriminate, and that this intention was put into effect. This was evident in the case of *Board of Management of Ballindine National School* v. *A Worker* (1983), in which the Labour Court decided to disregard a fair amount of evidence that the employers had decided in principle to employ a male. Indeed the Court did not think the admitted prejudice in favour of a male applicant to be relevant unless it could be proved that it was this prejudice which had crucially determined the outcome of the selection. It is submitted that this decision is wrong, for the onus which it places on applicants is almost incapable of being discharged. The very well thought out observations of the Equality Officer in this case about stereo-typed assumptions (see below) amount to a rather more useful assessment of the situation.

Discrimination is "indirect" where a person is obliged to comply with a requirement or condition of employment nominally applicable to all employees which is not however essential to the job and with which a substantially higher proportion of persons of the other sex or a differential marital status is able to comply. It is not relevant whether the employer actually imposed the condition with the intention of discriminating; once the effect can be shown to be discriminatory the condition of employment is illegal. An example of indirect discrimination is the imposition of unnecessary maximum age limits since these could discriminate against women, and married women in particular. In *Eastern Health Board* v. *Local Government and Public Services Union* (1981) the employers had imposed a maximum age limit of 27 for the appointment to permanent clerk-typist posts, as a result of which the 42-year-old applicant was ineligible. Her claim succeeded and the Labour Court found that "the operation of an entry age limit generally would appear to be discriminatory against married women as the proportion of that group who can comply is evidently smaller than the proportion of married or single persons of either sex."

A more difficult case perhaps was that of *An Foras Forbartha* v. *A Worker* (1982). The applicant, Mrs. Geraghty-Williams, applied for and was offered the post of biological technician by the employers, subject to her furnishing a "satisfactory medical report." Her doctor's report subsequently disclosed that she was pregnant but "otherwise . . . in good health." When the respondents received this report the offer of employment was withdrawn. The question that arose was whether discrimination based on an employee's pregnancy is sex discrimination. A previous decision of the British Employment Appeal Tribunal, *Turley* v. *Allders Department Stores Ltd.* (1979), had concluded that it was not illegal discrimination because a pregnant woman has no male equivalent. However, the Labour Court declined to follow this and determined that it was a case of indirect discrimination because the requirement that an employee should not be pregnant could be complied with by 100 per cent. of male employees, a "substantially higher" proportion than that of female employees who could comply. The case may thus have established that the difference in percentage points between males who can satisfy a job requirement and females who cannot (or *vice versa*) does not have to be enormous to make the requirement illegal. It has since also been held by an Equality Officer in the case of *Southern Health Board* v. *Cronin* (1984) that the exclusion of pregnancy-related illness from a sick leave scheme is discriminatory and thus illegal under the 1977 Act.

Another difficult case involving an allegation of indirect discrimination was *Kelly* v. *Jervis Street Hospital* (1981), in which the applicant claimed that she was not selected because she had a young child. This, she argued, was indirect discrimination against married persons, since the proportion of single persons able to comply would be substantially higher. She failed, and the Equality Officer took the rather startling view that there is a distinction between "discrimination" against, and "hesitation in regard to employing," women with young children. This, it is submitted, is wrong; it may well be that some individual women with children are unsuitable for certain posts, but to elevate that to a general criterion, even if it is not the only one, is precisely the sort of conclusion which the legislation was designed to prohibit. The approach of the English E.A.T., enunciated in the case of *Hurley* v. *Mustoe* (1981), is much more satisfactory. It is worth quoting the following extract from the judgment of Browne-Wilkinson J.:

> "[We] suggest that industrial tribunals should look with care at the unsupported evidence of a respondent that a particular class of persons lacks desirable features that others possess especially when such evidence leads to discriminatory practices . . . . We are not deciding whether or not women with children as a class are less reliable employees. Parliament has legislated that they are not to be treated as a class but as individuals. No employer is bound to employ unreliable employees, whether men or women. But he must investigate each case, and not simply apply what some would call a rule of convenience and others a prejudice to exclude a whole class of women or married persons because some members of that class are not suitable employees" (pp. 495–6).

(2) Recruitment and selection

In view of the position of women in the labour market which we noted above, the operation of the 1977 Act in relation to access to employment is of particular importance. Under section 3(3) it is unlawful for an employer to discriminate against a prospective employee in relation to access to employment on the grounds of sex or marital status. It can of course be very difficult to establish the reason for non-selection, but some applicants do succeed in such cases. In *Bradley* v. *Eastern Health Board* (1981) Mr. Bradley was unsuccessful in his application for the job of laundry worker in an hospital. He had applied by telephone, and was allegedly told by the head laundress that, *inter alia*, "this work is not suitable for men," and "it is a rule that men are not employed for the position." The Equality Officer found that a case of unlawful discrimination had been established.

There may be unlawful discrimination at the selection stage even if it can be shown that the most suitable candidate for the job was in fact appointed. In the case of *Carey* v. *McCarthy Daly Stapleton* (1981) the applicant was, together with 10 other candidates, interviewed for the post of dictaphone typist. Apparently the interview was extremely brief and touched only on her marital status. She was not put on the final short list, nor indeed was the only other married candidate (who also, independently, brought an action). The Equality Officer found that this was a case of unlawful discrimination, despite the fact that the employers produced some evidence that the successful applicant was in fact highly suitable for the post. He found that where discrimination was one factor, even if it was not the only one or did not affect the final outcome, the applicant had a good case. This finding was not disturbed by the Labour Court.

However, the mere fact that a woman who, on the basis of some criteria but not of others, is suitable for the post is not selected, is not of itself evidence of discrimination. The applicant will have to show that her sex or marital status was a factor in the process leading to her non-selection: *Hewitt* v. *Aer Lingus Teoranta* (1983).

In fact, the Act does not only tackle discriminatory selection for employment, but also deals with related matters which might have a bearing on the suitability of women for particular jobs or their readiness to offer themselves for available posts. Under section 3(7) an employer is prohibited from classifying posts by reference to sex and section 8 prohibits discriminatory advertising. In *Bradley* v. *Quinnsworth Power Supermarkets Ltd.* (1981) an advertisement which read "Lady required for canteen work" was found to be unlawful by the Equality Officer. Where an advertisement uses a name for a post which implies a particular sex, such as "foreman" or "waitress," the employer must under section 8(2) insert a specific clause stating that the job is open to men and women. Finally, section 8(3) provides that where an employer places a non-discriminatory advertisement when in fact he intends to discriminate unlawfully he is guilty of a criminal offence.

In relation to advertisements, the Employment Equality Agency's Code of Practice recommends in para. 4.4(*f*) that "advertisements should be placed in publications that are likely to reach both sexes." Furthermore, the code stresses that other sources of recruitment should be used with care so that they do not "exclude or reduce by a significant proportion the number of applicants of a particular sex or marital status" (para. 4.5). For example, it points out that recruitment through single-sex schools should be conducted in such a way that school leavers of both sexes are approached, and that "recruitment solely or primarily by word of mouth in a workforce of predominantly one sex should be avoided" (para. 4.6).

The Code also contains detailed recommendations on how job applications should be processed and interviews conducted. In relation to interviews a particular problem is the tendency to ask questions about marriage plans, home and family commitments and so forth of women only, and the Code (para. 5.6), as well as the Equality Officer in the case of *Chaney* v. *University College Dublin* (1983), state that such questions, if deemed absolutely necessary, must be asked equally of male and female candidates and the answers must be evaluated in the same manner in each case. Where a disproportionate amount of time is spent at an interview on questions relating to marital status, children and family commitments, this will tend to amount to illegal discrimination: *O'Connor* v. *Southern Health Board* (1984).

Access to employment is of course frequently gained through employment agencies. Section 7(1) of the Act provides that an agency may not discriminate unlawfully in the way in which it does or does not offer or provide its services. It escapes liability however under section 7(4) if it can show that it acted "in reliance on a statement made to it by the employer concerned" to the effect that nothing unlawful was being proposed, if "it was reasonable for it to rely on the statement." If in fact it turns out that the employer's statement was deliberately false or misleading the latter is guilty of a criminal offence.

(3) Career development

Section 3(5) of the Act makes it unlawful to discriminate on the grounds of sex or marital status in relation to "training or experience." An employer must not therefore refuse "to offer or afford to [the] employee the same opportunities or facilities for employment counselling, training (whether on or off the job) and work experience" as are available to employees of the other sex or a different marital status in similar circumstances. Section 6 further prohibits discrimination in respect of vocational training courses.

Section 3(6) prohibits discrimination in relation to "access to opportunities for promotion." In this area there is again a danger of indirect discrimination, and the Code of Practice lists requirements such as unbroken service or age limits as criteria which "may in practice lead to indirect discrimination" (para. 6.2).

In many respects the criteria acceptable in decisions to promote or not to promote are similar to those acceptable in the selection process. But there are additional factors. For example, it is unlawful to calculate seniority in a discriminatory way. In the case of *Department of Posts and Telegraphs* v. *35 Women Telephonists* (1982) the applicants had been compelled to resign from their jobs on marriage prior to 1973 when the marriage bar for women still applied across the public service. This rule was rescinded in 1973, and the applicants were all eventually re-employed. However, their service prior to 1973 was not counted for seniority purposes. The Labour Court found that this was unlawful discrimination and held that "the continuing effects of past discrimination should be corrected," so that the telephonists should in effect be treated as if their employment had not been broken. This has been followed in subsequent cases: see, *e.g. North-Eastern Health Board* v. *Conlan* (1983).

(4) Terms and conditions of employment

Under section 3(4) of the Act employers may not discriminate "in relation to conditions of employment"; this includes "terms of employment" (other than pay, since that is covered by the 1974 Act), "working conditions," and "treatment in relation to overtime, shift work, short time, transfers, lay-offs, redundancies, dismissals . . . and disciplinary measures." An example of discriminatory conditions was the refusal of an insurance company to allow female staff members to wear trousers during working hours "as it considered that the appropriate dress for female staff in line with the image it wished to project to be either dresses or skirts and blouses." The Equality Officer, while stressing that some regulation of minimum standards of dress was quite reasonable, found that this particular condition was discriminatory: *Female Clerical Workers* v. *Norwich Union Insurance Group* (1981). Similarly, in *South Eastern Health Board* v. *Mulhall* (1984) the Equality Officer found that the refusal of a Carlow hospital to allow female nurses to work overtime—while overtime was available to male nurses—amounted to illegal discrimination.

Section 4 of the Act also introduces into each contract of employment an automatic modification in the form of an "equality clause." This has the effect of modifying the terms of, or adding terms to, a person's contract of employment to bring it into line with the contract of a person of the other sex employed to do work which "is not materially different," unless the variation in terms is due to a material difference other than sex. This means that discrimination in respect of terms and conditions of employment may not merely be a violation of the Act, but could also be a straightforward breach of contract for which the employee affected could sue the employer. To complete the contractual modification, section 10(2) of the Act provides that discriminatory terms in the contact of employment are "null and void."

Section 10(1) of the 1977 Act, as the equivalent of section 5 of the 1974 Act, further provides that any provisions in collective agreements, registered employment agreements or employment regulation orders which constitute discrimination are equally "null and void." This may not actually be very significant since many collective agreements are not enforceable anyway (see Chap. 1) and most agreements do not rely on their legal status for their practical effectiveness. Additional safeguards might therefore be useful. In Britain, for example, the parties to a collective agreement or the Secretary of State for Employment can, under section 3 of the Equal Pay Act 1970, refer the agreement to the Central Arbitration Committee, which can amend it to make it non-discriminatory (*e.g.* by raising the lower female pay rate to the male rate). The Labour Court could be given a similar function.

(5) Dismissals

Section 3(4), as has been noted, prohibits discriminatory dismissals, but in fact not very many dismissed employees are making use of this. As it happens, an employee who feels that her dismissal was on the grounds of sex or marital status could equally bring a claim to the Employment Appeals Tribunal under the Unfair Dismissals Act 1977; this may in some circumstances be the better way of proceeding as the employer has, under the latter Act, the onus of proving that the dismissal was fair, whereas under the Employment Equality Act the burden of proof generally lies with the applicant.

However, there have been some cases under the Employment Equality Act. In *O'Neill* v. *Hunting Lodges Ltd.* (1980) the applicant was dismissed, being told by the employers that they wished to employ a man instead. The company later argued that they had told her this so as to soften the blow, and that the real reason was the shortcoming in her general deportment and hygiene. This kind of retrospective change of reasons was not however accepted by the Equality Officer or the Labour Court.

Section 27 of the Employment Equality Act, read in conjunction with section 26, sets out the procedure to be followed by the Labour Court and the civil courts (as enforcement agencies) in dismissal cases. As under the Unfair Dismissals Act, a successful applicant can be awarded re-instatement, re-engagement or compensation of up to 104 weeks' pay. Non-compliance by an employer with Labour Court order may lead to a criminal prosecution.

A dismissed employee may claim either under the Employment Equality Act (or, if it applies, the 1974 Act) or under the Unfair Dismissals Act, but she "shall not be entitled to accept redress" under both sets of legislation. This is a curious wording which implies that an *unsuccessful* applicant under the Unfair Dismissals Act could claim again under the Employment Equality Act, and *vice versa*.

Indirect discrimination is also possible in respect of dismissals. For example, the Code of Practice points out that a "last in, first out" arrangement in the case of redundancies may be discriminatory if members of one sex tend to have shorter service because of previous discrimination in relation to access to employment or promotion (para. 9.5). This would in fact be an analogous situation to that of the telephonists of the Department of Posts and Telegraphs referred to above.

However, in the case of *Kelly* v. *Food Products (Donegal) Ltd.* (1982) the Equality Officer found that where an employer has to consider which employees he will retain in a redundancy situation he may choose those most suitable; if the job involves "heavy physical work" he may choose to keep the men rather than the women. Nevertheless, it is hard to see why this should be acceptable in cases where the employer could not have *selected* employees on the basis of sex for the same kind of work. It might be noted in this context that the Code of Practice holds that "strength and stamina" are not good grounds for choosing men rather than women" (para. 7.3). It should be noted that the Act does not apply to voluntary retirement schemes in that different retirement ages for men and women are not unlawful. This was determined by the European Court of Justice in *Burton* v. *British Railways Board* (1982), but the Court did point out that redundancy or retirement schemes could be covered by the equal treatment principle in other respects.

(6) Exemptions

The protection afforded by the Act is however subject to some exceptions and qualifications. It might be noted that section 11 originally provided that it was not unlawful under the Act "to give access to training or employment as a midwife or a public health nurse to persons of a particular sex." As a result however of a 1981 Reasoned Opinion by the European Commission the Minister for Labour repealed this provision in the European Communities (Employment Equality) Regulations 1982.

Under section 12 certain other employments are excluded from the statutory protection, these being the Defence Forces, the Garda Siochana, the prison service, and employment in a private residence or by a close relative. Section 12(3) also somewhat curiously excludes "appointments to an office or position" by the Local

Appointments Commissioners or the Civil Service Commissioners
from some of the individual remedies provided by the Act. However,
while the effect of this is to debar the employees, or prospective
employees, concerned from initiating Labour Court proceedings in
the usual way, it does not prevent other measures, such as prosecutions or actions under section 25 and 26 relating to dismissal or court
actions for breach of the contractual equality clause, nor does it
relieve the respective Commissioners of the substantive obligations
imposed by the Act. All these exclusions apply to the 1977 Act only,
and do not affect any entitlements under the 1974 Act.

Section 13 of the 1977 Act withdraws protection from employees
who "will not undertake the duties attached to [a] position or who
will not accept the conditions under which these duties are performed." An employer is not therefore obliged to employ or retain in
employment persons who will not or do not carry out their normal
duties. However, this has to be read in conjunction with the rest of
the Act, and in particular the prohibition of indirect discrimination,
so that an employer may not impose non-essential duties which he
knows members of one sex will find difficult to undertake. Furthermore, section 13 does not create a positive right of employers, so that
actions under, say, contract law, the Constitution or the Unfair Dismissals Act 1977 are not excluded by it.

(7) Protective legislation

Section 14 of the Act provides that where an employer acts in
compliance with the requirements of the Conditions of Employment
Act 1936, the Shops (Conditions of Employment) Act 1938, the Factories Act 1955, or the Mines and Quarries Act 1965, this will not
"constitute discrimination in contravention of [the 1977] Act." The
reason for this exemption is that the above statutes to some extent all
require specific protective standards for women, in areas such as lifting of weights, hours of work, and so forth, which if implemented
could lead employers to fail to select women for some jobs, or to offer
different conditions of employment.

As section 14 is worded, it might appear that anything done by an
employer so as to comply with these statutes is not unlawful discrimination. However, the Employment Equality Agency (the functions of which will be discussed below) has taken a view which
suggests that one should assess the employer's behaviour by asking
whether he could have adopted other, non-discriminatory methods
of complying with the statutes. In a review of the weight-lifting

restrictions for women under the Factories Act 1955 (Manual Labour) (Maximum Weights and Transport) Regulations 1972 the Agency pointed out that the restrictions should not deny women access to jobs or promotional opportunities; instead, employers could use, for example, mechanical aids or teamwork to overcome the weight-lifting problems. The legislation as framed, the Agency pointed out, "does not in itself constitute grounds for discrimination against women in employment or in opportunities for employment" (*Report to the Minister*, 1981, p. 8). The Code of Practice similarly states that "the above Acts should not be used as an excuse to discriminate" (para. 13.1).

This point perhaps also raises the more general question of how one should evaluate a claim by an employer that his contested actions or practices were in fact required under some other statute. That indeed was one of the submissions of the Department of Posts and Telegraphs in the case of the *35 Women Telephonists* (1982); the Department contended that it was obliged by virtue of the legislation governing civil service employment not to count for seniority purposes previous periods of employment before a resignation. The reaction to this of the Labour Court was to state that if this were really true "the statutory provisions should be changed." In other words, since the Court did not accept a defence based on the requirements of the civil service legislation it must be taken to have held that in cases of conflict the 1977 Act takes precedence over other statutes. A similar conclusion was reached by the Equality Officer in the case of *An Bord Altranais* v. *Black* (1984), in which it had been argued that discriminatory procedures for electing members of the Nursing Board were required under the Nurses Act 1950, a defence which was not accepted.

Whether such an interpretation of the law would find support in the High Court or Supreme Court is hard to say. It would certainly be correct to say that domestic law statutes should, if there is any ambiguity, be interpreted so as to comply with Ireland's international obligations (in this case the Treaty of Rome and the Directives); that was stressed by Lord Diplock in the English House of Lords in *Garland* v. *British Rail* (1982). In any case, all of this should prompt employers to hesitate to use other Acts, in the words of the Code of Practice, as an "excuse to discriminate."

(8) "Positive action"

The main purpose of the Act is to bring about an end to sex discrimination. Whether this can be achieved entirely by a string of prohibitions or whether it requires a measure of corrective action is a much debated point, and incidentally one, it might be added, on which the authors of this book disagree with each other. The Employment Equality Code of Practice puts the case for positive action as follows:

> [The legislation] will not . . . adequately eliminate all forms of discrimination as between men and women in the labour market unless parallel measures are taken to counteract or compensate for the impact of existing employment structures on individual behaviour or to redress the effects of previous unequal opportunities. (para. 15.1)

However, it all depends of course on how far one wishes to go, and the term "positive action" embraces a number of possibilities ranging from better education to outright reverse discrimination. It must also be borne in mind that there may be a constitutional question involved, the precise effect of which must however be uncertain in this context: see J.M. Kelly, *The Irish Constitution*, 1984, pp. 446–466.

In the event the 1977 Act does allow some positive action, but of a fairly limited kind. Section 15 provides that the Act does not prevent employers from encouraging job applications from, or arranging special training for, "persons of a particular sex in a type, form or category of work in which either no, or an insignificant number of, persons of that sex had been engaged" during the previous 12 months. It must be emphasised that section 15 does *not* permit positive discrimination at the selection stage, although it does probably allow, for example, recruitment for jobs to which the section applies through single sex schools, or advertisements in periodicals read largely by members of one sex. The Code of Practice also outlines other measures which employers could undertake in a "positive action programme" (paras. 15.3 to 15.5).

Finally, section 16 of the Act allows "special treatment" for women "in connection with pregnancy or childbirth." In the *Foras Forbartha* (*Geraghty-Williams*) case the view was canvassed by the employers that this section would permit the dismissal or non-employment of pregnant women, but that was rejected by the Labour Court. The purpose clearly is to permit favourable treatment, not to encourage discrimination *against* pregnant women.

(9) Sex as an "occupational qualification"

Discrimination is permissible under section 17 of the Act where the sex of the employee is "an occupational qualification," that is, where it is genuinely necessary that the job should be carried out by a man rather than a woman (or *vice versa*). Section 17(2) spells out the circumstances where this exception applies; they include cases where there are "grounds of physiology" or grounds of "authenticity for the purpose of a form of entertainment"; where persons of both sexes are required for "personal services"; where it is "unreasonable" or "impracticable" for an employer to provide separate sleeping or sanitary accommodation; or where work takes place outside the State in countries where only members of one sex will be able to carry out the duties. It should however be noted that an employer may not lawfully discriminate on the grounds of sex or marital status where he is being pressurised into so discriminating; for example, industrial action by male employees taken to compel the employer to discriminate against female employees is illegal (section 9 of the 1977 Act) and it does not provide an excuse for the employer: *South Eastern Health Board* v. *Mulhall* (1984).

It may seem then that the qualification of the non-discrimination principle introduced by the wording of section 17 is relatively wide. This, indeed, largely prompted the European Commission to issue a Reasoned Opinion in 1981 criticising the 1977 Act. The Commission found that the "breadth of the exceptions" in section 17(2) "goes beyond the strict and objective limits of [Directive 76/207]," which permits exceptions only where a person's sex "constitutes a sufficiently strict and objective determining factor by reason of the nature of the occupational activity." The Minister for Labour has since in fact repealed two paragraphs of section 17(2)—which were in addition to those quoted above—in the European Communities (Employment Equality) Regulations 1982.

The Employment Equality Agency's Code of Practice also presents a more narrow view than section 17 of what amounts to an "occupational qualification." It points out that "an employer must in such cases be able to show that sex is a genuine and bona fide occupational qualification" in an objective sense (para. 7.1), and adds that "there are very few jobs the essential nature of which only one sex can perform" (para. 7.2). Only "purposes of authenticity" are mentioned, while various other grounds are rejected, such as a refusal to recruit because of the "preference or prejudices of co-workers, clients or customers" or a "stereotyped characterisation of the sexes" (para. 7.3).

Presumptions of prejudices of the above kind are very deep-rooted, and it must be stressed that they do not justify unequal treatment. In the recent British case of *Horsey* v. *Dyfed County Council*

(1982), for example, the employers sought to justify the discrimination alleged by the applicant by arguing that a married women is
likely to join her husband at his place of residence or work (which in
this case was elsewhere). The E.A.T. held that while it would be
quite acceptable to discriminate against a woman who actually
declares an intention to move away or who does in fact move, it was
unlawful to do so on the mere stereo-typed assumption as to what
women are likely to do. Similarly, in *Skyrail Oceanic Ltd.* v. *Coleman*
(1981) the E.A.T. held that the assumption made by the employer in
dismissing the applicant that "the husband presumably was the
breadwinner" was discriminatory and unacceptable.

Some of these prejudices appear to have played a part in the *Ballindine National School* case (1983, see above). The Equality Officer in
his recommendation pin-pointed, for example, the "generalised discriminatory assumptions regarding the reasonableness and the ability of female teachers" (including their ability to "maintain pupil
discipline") and the assumption that some women "only remain
working for short periods before resigning." If the 1977 Act is to
have any serious effect on recruitment and selection patterns, then
such assumptions must be dealt with by its provisions. The failure of
the Labour Court to uphold the Equality Officer's recommendation—although it did not in fact deny the existence of prejudice in
the case—is thus a serious cause for concern.

The Code further notes that in some cases the worker's sex may be
an occupational qualification for some, but not all, of the duties, and
where that is so "a restriction upon access to a job would not be justified where there are sufficient existing employees to carry out the
duties concerned without undue inconvenience" (para. 7.6).

ENFORCEMENT OF THE LEGISLATION

The procedures under which the remedies available under the 1974
and 1977 Acts can be enforced, though not identical, are broadly
similar. Claims under both statutes are processed by the Labour
Court and officials of the Court known as "Equality Officers." The
Labour Court was in fact set up for a rather different purpose, the
investigation and resolution of industrial conflict, and in retrospect
it must seem surprising that the interpretation of individual statutory rights should have gone to this body. The exact procedures to
be followed in sex discrimination cases are outlined in Chapter 9.

Section 34 of the 1977 Act also set up a body known as the
Employment Equality Agency, whose task it is, under section 35, to

"work towards the elimination of discrimination in relation to employment," to "promote equality of opportunity between men and women in relation to employment," and to keep the two Acts (and other relevant legislation) under review. In particular, the Agency can conduct investigations (s.39), can, subject to appeal to the Labour Court, issue "non-discrimination notices" with mandatory effect (s.44), and can assist claimants under the Acts (s.48). While the Agency has in many ways been a very effective monitoring and enforcement body, it is perhaps arguable that it could make greater use of some of its functions, particularly in conducting investigations.

THE 1981 ACT

The Maternity Protection of Employees Act 1981 is the most recent legislation in the field of women's rights in employment. Under Part II of the Act female employees are entitled to a period of maternity leave of at least 14 weeks, if notice is given to the employer at least four weeks before the expected confinement, together with a medical certificate establishing the fact of pregnancy. The exact dates of the maternity leave can be chosen by the employee, but the period must cover the four weeks before and the four weeks after the confinement; it can be extended if the birth is delayed.

During the period of maternity leave the employment relationship is suspended, and there is no break in the continuity of service. In Part II it is also provided that the employee is entitled to return to her job after the birth, to the same employer and on the same terms as before. The right to return to work is, under section 22, subject to the employee notifying the employer in writing at least four weeks before the envisaged date of return of her intention; this must be confirmed again in writing at a date between four and two weeks prior to the expected return to work. Strict compliance with these requirements is essential, since, as the Employment Appeals Tribunal has determined, the failure to issue the required notification will deprive the employee of her statutory right to return to work: see *Murphy* v. *Clarkes of Ranelagh Ltd.* (1983); and *Doyle* v. *Connolly* (1983).

Where for technical reasons the employer cannot comply with this (as, for instance, where he could not keep the precise job vacant during the maternity leave), then under section 21(1) he must offer the employee "suitable alternative employment." Subsection (2) specifies that such alternative work must be "suitable" and "appropriate," and that in particular the terms and conditions of her new contract of employment must not be "substantially less favourable to her" than those of the old contract. For example, the E.A.T. has held that a switch from part-time to full-time employment is not "suitable" in the circumstances: *Leech* v. *PMPA Insurance Co. Ltd.* (1983). Interestingly, disputes under the Act go not to the Labour Court but to the Employment Appeals Tribunal, which now hears the majority of cases involving individual employment rights, other than under the employment equality legislation.

EVALUATION AND CONCLUSIONS

As indicated earlier, it would clearly be a mistake to expect the legislation to bring about instant employment equality. It could not fulfil—and, of course, it has not fulfilled—that role. Inequality of pay has decreased slightly, but only slightly, and there has been some evidence of employer resistance to the principle of equal pay, particularly in the public sector. Although the 1974 Act provided for the complete implementation of equal pay as from December 31, 1975, employees of the State did not get its benefit until December 31, 1977, and then only because of vigorous trade union protests.

There have also been some other problems connected with the 1974 Act. On some occasions employers conceded equal pay claims, only to find themselves faced with a demand for the restoration of differentials by the comparable male employees. A further problem existed in the manufacturing industries in which, as a result of the employment patterns referred to above, women rarely did the same work as men so that there tended to be no basis for a direct comparison for equal pay purposes. It is generally recognised that further progress can now only come through a development of the criterion of work "equal in value" and the use of better job evaluation schemes. However, this may not be possible if section 2(3) of the Act is interpreted too widely.

In relation to both the 1974 and 1977 Act there are other unsatisfactory features. The Acts appear to be seen primarily as instruments giving remedies to individuals in cases of individual grievances. The fact that discrimination must ultimately also be tackled at the macro level appears to some extent to have been overlooked. This has a number of consequences. For example, employers do not on the whole appear to take note of the decisions of the Equality Officers or the Labour Court awarded against other employers, for there is a fair amount of repetitiveness in the forms of discrimination being challenged. Furthermore some employers, and in particular public sector employers including the State, appear at times to ignore the statutory requirements altogether. There are alarming examples of certain employers apparently refusing to implement determinations awarded against them, or at any rate dragging their heels so much that it amounts to refusal. Particular problems in this context were for example experienced with the former Department of Posts and Telegraphs. It therefore appears that these employers have approached the legislation with a negative attitude, seeing it as a challenge to be resisted.

Finally, because of the various procedural problems (to be discussed in Chapter 9), including delays, the difficulty of satisfying the burden of proof, and the often poorly argued decisions of the Labour Court and the Equality Officers, actions by individuals can be costly in terms of both financial resources and emotional strain. There is still therefore far to go before sex discrimination in employment has been eradicated.

7 Minimum Notice and Unfair Dismissal

MINIMUM NOTICE

Prior to the passing of the Minimum Notice and Terms of Employment Act 1973 the giving of notice was regulated under the contract of employment, the terms of which would govern both the period of notice required and the rights and duties of both parties in relation to the notice. The common law principles involved are discussed in Chapter 3. As a general rule, where the period of notice was not specified in the contract a "reasonable" period, based primarily on the status of the employee, would be implied; in the case of manual workers the period tended to be one week.

The position was changed substantially by the 1973 Act, which has provided for a series of rights in relation to the giving of notice. In particular, the Act has set out minimum periods of notice based on the length of service of the employee, and has provided for redress in the event of non-compliance by the employer.

(1) Application of the Act

Under section 4(1) of the Act, the entitlement to the statutory minimum notice is held by any "employee who has been in [the employer's] continuous service for a period of thirteen weeks or more." Under section 1 an "employee" is "an individual who has entered into or works under a contract with an employer, whether the contract be for manual labour, clerical work or otherwise, whether it be expressed or implied, oral or in writing, and whether it be a contract of service or of apprenticeship or otherwise." This definition thus goes beyond the common law concept of a "servant," and indeed beyond the definition of "employee" under the Unfair Dismissals Act 1977 (see below). The Employment Appeals Tribunal (E.A.T.) has held that the 1973 Act's definition covers directors of companies—*Parry* v. *Limegrove Fabrics Ltd.* (1978)—and that a person whose pay is in the form of irregular lump sums may still be an "employee"—*Coleman* v. *Corry* (1978). However, a person who is hired to do certain work using his own equipment and without the usual employment terms is not an "employee' and thus not covered: *Sinnott* v. *New Ross U.D.C.* (1978).

Certain categories of employment are excluded under section 3(1), these being: (a) employees who are "normally expected to work for the same employer for less than twenty-one hours in a week"; (b) persons employed by close relatives where they are members of the employer's household and work in a private dwellinghouse or on a farm; (c) persons employed in the civil service; (d) members of the Defence Forces; (e) members of the Garda Siochana; and (f) persons employed "under an employment agreement pursuant to Part II or Part IV of the Merchant Shipping Act 1894." The Minister for Labour is further empowered to add to these categories, or to apply the Act specifically to any classes of employment including the above excluded categories, by statutory instrument.

Section 8 provides that the Act does not affect "the right of any employer or employee to terminate a contract of employment without notice because of misconduct by the other party." This is a reference to common law contractual rules, including those relating to summary dismissal; in line with this the E.A.T. has held that only "severe misconduct" can justify the application of section 8: *Hughes* v. *T.Q. Shoes Ltd.* (1979). More recently the Tribunal has held that the misconduct, to come within the section, must be of a "deliberate or positive kind," so that mere neglect or, as in the case itself, falling asleep on the job are not sufficient: *Kelly* v. *Sanser* (1983). An example of misconduct to which section 8 applies was supplied in *Hilliard* v. *Johnston McInerney Ltd.* (1978), in which the applicant had been summarily dismissed for using a company van without permission, having previously been warned not to do so.

Finally, section 7 of the Act permits both parties to an employment relationship to waive the minimum notice entitlements, but Costello J. has held in *Industrial Yarns Ltd.* v. *Greene* (1983) that a waiver, to be effective, must be "clear and unambiguous" (p. 23).

(2) The periods of minimum notice

Section 4(2) of the Act sets out the periods of minimum notice to which employees covered by the Acts are entitled. These periods are as follows:

Continuous service of employee	*Minimum notice*
Less than two years	1 week
More than two years, less than five years	2 weeks
More than five years, less than ten years	4 weeks
More than ten years, less than fifteen years	6 weeks
Fifteen years or more	8 weeks

It must be emphasised that these are *minimum* periods of notice. Therefore, if the contract of employment gives, expressly or through an implied term, an entitlement to a longer period, then that longer period will apply. Indeed, it appears that this can be enforced through the 1973 Act, in that the E.A.T. has held that where the employee is entitled under his contract to a longer notice than the statutory minimum, the statutory notice "should occupy the last appropriate number of weeks of the contractual notice": *Jameson* v. *M.C.W. Ltd.* (1983). Where on the other hand the contract specifies a period which is *shorter* than the statutory minimum, section 4(5) provides for an automatic modification of the contract to bring the notice up to the statutory period.

Under section 6 the employer is in turn entitled to a period of notice of not less than one week from an employee who has been in continuous employment for 13 weeks or more. This period does not increase in line with length of service, and there is not therefore under the Act a principle of reciprocity as between the parties to the employment relationship.

In all this it is important to determine the period of continuous employment of the employee, and this is done in accordance with the provisions of the 1973 Act's first Schedule, as amended by section 20 of the Unfair Dismissals Act 1977. Paragraph 1 of the Schedule provides that service is continuous unless terminated by the employee's dismissal or resignation, and the paragraphs following list a number of events which do not bring about a break in continuity; these include lock-outs, strikes, dismissals followed by immediate re-employment, and transfers of the "trade, business or undertaking" in which the employee was employed. Under paragraph 5 (as amended) an employee who claims and receives a redundancy payment in respect of lay-off or short time (see Chap. 8) is deemed to have voluntarily left his employment, but Costello J. has held in *Industrial Yarns Ltd.* v. *Greene* (1983) that if the lay-off or short time itself is such as to repudiate the contract of employment it will amount to a dismissal allowing the employee to claim his rights under the 1973 Act. Paragraphs 8 to 13 of the Schedule also list periods which are or are not counted in computing a period of service; for example, an absence of up to 26 weeks due to a lay-off, or sickness, or by agreement with the employer, is counted as a period of service (paragraph 10), while any week during which the employee was absent because he was on strike is not (paragraph 11).

(3) The meaning of notice

What is meant by the term "notice" is not explained anywhere in the Act. However, the E.A.T. has developed certain principles which must be noted here. Above all, the notice given must be sufficiently certain and precise to admit of no ambiguity if it is to fulfil the statutory requirements. As the E.A.T. put it in the case of *McCauley* v. *McGee* (1983), "the notice contemplated by the Act must have absolute certainty about it." It must in particular specify the precise expiry date. Where therefore an employee is entitled to eight weeks notice, but is only given one week, then the fact that the termination of employment does not follow for some weeks does not mean that the employer has in fact given a longer notice than the initially announced one week, but rather that he has given none at all, since the original notice will be deemed to have lapsed: *Mullen* v. *Coras Iompair Eireann* (1980). Similarly the E.A.T. held in *Murtagh* v. *Ennis Morgan International Ltd.* (1981) that a general "protective notice" which specifies no expiry date is not sufficient.

Finally, the E.A.T. has held that the notice requirements of the 1973 Act are fulfilled only if the notice is given directly to the employee. Giving it to somebody else, for example the employee's trade union, does not discharge the statutory obligation: *McHugh* v. *Killeen Paper Mills* (1979).

(4) Rights during the period of notice

Under section 5, read with the second Schedule of the Act, employees to whom the notice provisions apply are entitled to the same rights during the minimum notice period as they would enjoy but for the notice. In other words, they are entitled to the normal pay (including, where an employee is normally expected to do overtime, the normal overtime pay), and all other contractual and statutory benefits such as holidays, sick pay, and so forth. Where there are no normal working hours or where pay is not calculated wholly by reference to working hours, the employee is during each week of the notice period entitled to a sum equal to the average weekly pay for the preceding 13 weeks. The Act does not require the employer to provide work during the notice period, so that a payment in lieu of notice calculated as set out above is acceptable. On the other hand, the employee cannot refuse to do his normal work, since if he does he loses his contractual entitlement to be paid: *Bunn* v. *Campbell* (1980, E.A.T.).

(5) Remedies

Under section 11 of the 1973 Act disputes arising out of the Act's provisions can be referred to the Employment Appeals Tribunal. Section 12(1) provides that where an employer fails to give the statutory minimum notice or to observe his obligations during the period of notice, "the employee may refer the matter to the Tribunal for arbitration and the Tribunal may award to the employee compensation for any loss sustained by him by reason of the default of the employer." It is not entirely clear why the E.A.T.'s role is described as "arbitration" rather than "adjudication"; the former term might be thought to imply that a recommendation is made on the factual merits of the particular case, rather than a determination on the application of statutory rights. In practice however what the E.A.T. does is more properly described as adjudication.

The remedy which the Tribunal can award is compensation, but only compensation for "loss" sustained by the employee. What happens therefore is that the E.A.T. considers the financial position of the employee during the minimum notice period. If the employee was able to obtain alternative employment the income is deducted from the pay to which he was under the Act entitled from his original employer. In *Hogan* v. *Van Hool McArdle Ltd.* (1980) the E.A.T. put it as follows:

> "If an employee finds a new job and starts the next day without any drop in wages, then he suffered no loss, and in the course of our arbitration we would measure the loss at nil. If the wages in that new job were less we would measure his loss at the difference in wages over the weeks when he should have had notice."

On the other hand the E.A.T. has held that income other than employment-related income obtained during the notice period is not deducted so that, for example, social welfare payments do not affect the level of compensation: *White* v. *Smyth & Co. Ltd.* (1980).

Similarly, since compensation is based on the employee's "loss," nothing is awarded for any period during which the employee would not have been entitled to be paid. So for example in *Sampson* v. *Micade Ltd.* (1979) the applicant, who had been dismissed while on sick leave, was held not to be entitled to compensation because, even if she had been given the proper notice, she would have been unable to work; she had therefore suffered no loss.

The effect of the above decisions is that the Act gives an employee the right to receive compensation in case of loss, but it does not as a matter of principle penalise employers who are in breach of its provisions. This is all the more evident in the fact that the E.A.T. will apparently only award compensation to the extent that the aggrieved employee endeavoured to mitigate his loss, as stated in *Bunn* v. *Campbell* (1980); there is in fact no basis in the statute for this E.A.T.-imposed requirement.

UNFAIR DISMISSAL

The concept of unfair dismissal was first put forward in Recommendation 119 of the International Labour Organisation in 1963; this has now been superseded by the I.L.O. Convention Concerning Termination of Employment at the Initiative of the Employer (Convention No. 158, 1982). In these islands, protection against unfair dismissal was first introduced in the otherwise very controversial Industrial Relations Act 1971 in Britain. Section 22 of that Act, following, in part at any rate, the recommendations of the Donovan Commission (*Royal Commission on Trade Unions and Employers' Associations*, 1968, Cmnd. 3623, Chapter IX), provided that "every employee shall have the right not to be unfairly dismissed by his employer." The relevant provisions in Britain are currently contained in Part V of the Employment Protection (Consolidation) Act 1978 (E.P.C.A.).

The Irish legislation is the Unfair Dismissals Act 1977 (U.D.A.); in most of its general principles it is based on the British legislation, but with some significant differences which, as we shall see, are not always sufficiently recognised. One important difference is that what the U.D.A. gives to all employees to which it applies is an entitlement to redress in the case of an unfair dismissal; this way of putting it is important, for the Act does *not* give a right not to be unfairly dismissed (and thus imposes no duty not to dismiss unfairly), but only a right to be given redress of a particular—and in some cases very limited—kind. This has particular consequences when one comes to consider the remedies (see below).

In a general sense the U.D.A. puts an onus on employers to prove the fairness of each dismissal (see below), but before that stage can be reached a number of other matters may need to be established, these being in particular (a) the application of the Act to the employee or to his employment, and (b) the fact of dismissal. In relation to these matters the burden of proof is generally thought to be on the applicant, although the E.A.T. has held in one case, *O'Sullivan* v. *Western Health Board* (1979), that the employer must establish that the applicant belongs to an excluded category where this is an issue. While it is clearly desirable that the onus should in such matters be on the employer, it is not at all clear how this can be read into the Act as presently in force.

APPLICATION OF THE ACT

(1) Excluded categories

Sections 2 to 4, and some other provisions, of the U.D.A. exclude a number of employments from the protection of the Act. These excluded categories are as follows:

(a) Employees with less than one year's continuous service with the same employer are excluded, but this does not apply where the dismissal has resulted wholly or mainly from pregnancy or where the employee can, in line with section 6(7), establish that the dismissal has resulted wholly or mainly from trade union membership or activities (see below). The question whether an applicant's employment has been "continuous" is determined in accordance with the first Schedule of the Minimum Notice and Terms of Employment Act 1973 (as amended). The period of employment used for these purposes includes any period of notice to which the employee is entitled under the 1973 Act or under his contract: see *Fitzgerald* v. *Topps Ireland Ltd.* (1981). The dismissal can furthermore only become operative when the employee is informed of it and given the required notice; the fact that the decision to dismiss was taken earlier is irrelevant: *Hatton* v. *Darton Distributors Ltd.* (1983).

(b) Employees who on the date of dismissal have reached the "normal retiring age" or the cut-off retiring age applicable under the Redundancy Payments Acts (currently 66, see Chapter 8) are excluded. What is meant by the term "normal retiring age" has recently been considered by the British House of Lords in *Waite* v. *Government Communications Headquarters* (1983), with Lord Fraser of Tullybelton explaining that it is determined by reference to "what would be the reasonable expectation or understanding of the employees holding that position at the relevant time" (p. 344). This exclusion does also not apply where the applicant can establish that his dismissal resulted wholly or mainly from trade union membership or activities.

(c) Close relatives of the employer who are members of his household and work in a private dwellinghouse or on a farm where the employer and the employee reside are excluded.

(d) Members of the Defence Forces or the Garda Siochana are excluded.

(e) Persons who are being trained by or under An Chomhairle Oiliuna (AnCO) or who are AnCO apprentices are excluded.

(f) Persons employed "by or under the State" are excluded. The E.A.T. has held in *Hayes* v. *B. & I. Line* (1980) that the test is whether the employee is a civil servant as defined in the High Court case of *O'Loughlin* v. *Minister for Social Welfare* (1958); an employee of a State-owned company is not therefore excluded, while in the case of *Watson* v. *Department of Posts and Telegraphs* (1979) a porter in a government department was held not to be covered by the Act. Persons "standing designated for the time being under section 17 of the Industrial Relations Act 1969" are not excluded.

(g) Officers of a local authority, a health board, a vocational education committee or a committee of agriculture are excluded. In cases arising under this heading the crucial question tends to be whether the applicant is an "officer" rather than an employee (see chap. 3), and the factors to be taken into account in this have been considered by the E.A.T. in *O'Sullivan* v. *Western Health Board* (1979), by Judge Gleeson in the Circuit Court in *Ponnampalam* v. *Mid-Western Health Board* (1981), and by Barrington J. in the High Court in *Western Health Board* v. *Quigley* (1982).

(h) Persons working under fixed-term contracts are in some cases excluded. Section 2(2) of the U.D.A. provides that the non-renewal of an expired fixed-term contract made before September 16, 1976 cannot be challenged under the Act; the non-renewal of other (*i.e.* post-1976) fixed-term contracts or contracts for a specified purpose of limited duration cannot be challenged if the contract was in writing and provided expressly that the Act should not apply "to a dismissal consisting only of the expiry or cesser." Where however there is no such provision in the contract, a non-renewal may be an unfair dismissal and must be justified under the Act by the employer. The fact that the employment was entered into on a temporary basis may not be a sufficient justification, as was pointed out by the E.A.T. in *Fitzgerald* v. *St. Patrick's College, Maynooth* (1979). On the other hand, the argument was canvassed by the respondents in the case of *Western Health Board* v. *Quigley* (1982) that the applicant's employment under a series of consecutive three-month contracts brought her outside the protection of the U.D.A.; the report of the case does not disclose whether these fixed-term contracts contained clauses excluding the U.D.A., but Barrington J. appeared to have accepted the respondents' argument in this regard, which in the absence of such clauses would be a highly doubtful conclusion. It might incidentally be noted that in Britain, under the E.P.C.A., employees with fixed-term contracts can be excluded from unfair dismissal protection only if the contracts are for one year or more, which would make impossible the kind of arrangement which was perhaps used in the *Quigley* case.

(i) Persons who under their contracts "ordinarily worked outside the State" are excluded. The Act does apply however where such an employee was "ordinarily resident in the State during the term of the contract," or was domiciled in the State while the employer was resident, or if a company had its principal place of business, in the State.

(j) Persons on probation or undergoing training are excluded if the period of probation or training is one year or less and is so specified in a written contract of employment; once the period is longer than one year the employee is not excluded, as in *Quinn* v. *Ken David Ltd.* (1979, E.A.T.). Also the Act does not apply to persons undergoing training for certain professions, including in particular professions associated with the health services (such as nurses, pharmacists, health inspectors, and so forth) and social work, nor does it apply to persons employed under a statutory apprenticeship if the dismissal takes place within certain time limits. In all these cases the applicants are not excluded if they can establish that their dismissal resulted wholly or mainly from trade union membership or activities.

(k) Under section 6(5) of the U.D.A. the dismissal of civilians employed with the Defence Forces is "deemed for the purposes of [the U.D.A.] not to be an unfair dismissal if it is shown that the dismissal was for the purpose of safeguarding national security." The latter purpose is established through a certificate signed by the Minister for Defence.

(l) The Act's protection applies only to "employees," so that a person who does not come within the definition of "employee" contained in section 1 is excluded. Sub-contractors or persons working under a "contract for services" (see Chap. 3) are therefore not covered: see *e.g. O'Friel* v. *St. Michael's Hospital* (1980, E.A.T.); and *Evans* v. *Calor Gas (Ireland) Ltd.* (1982, E.A.T.). The general factors determining whether a person was or was not an employee were considered by the E.A.T. in *O'Riain* v. *Independent Newspapers Ltd.* (1978).

(m) Under the first Schedule of the 1973 Act, which governs the question of continuity of employment for the purposes of the U.D.A., a week in which the employee "is not normally expected to work for at least twenty-one hours or more" is not counted for computing a period of service. In effect this means that part-time employees working for less than 21 hours per week are excluded: see *Garrett* v. *Concord Services Ltd.* (1983).

(n) Employees who fail to bring a claim to the Rights Commissioner or the E.A.T. within six months of the date of dismissal are excluded under section 8 of the Act (see Chap. 9).

As can be seen, the excluded categories are extensive, and it has been estimated by Redmond (*Dismissal Law in the Republic of Ireland*, 1982, p. 132)—conservatively in our view—that "approximately one-fifth of the working population in Ireland" do not enjoy the protection of the Act. Some of these categories have available to them alternative procedures, but it is hard to avoid the conclusion that the range of exclusions is far too wide, with the reasons for some of them being far from clear. It should however be noted that workers cannot be excluded from the protection of the U.D.A. through clauses in their contracts of employment or in collective agreements. Section 13 provides that "a provision in an agreement . . . shall be void in so far as it purports to exclude or limit the application of, or is inconsistent with, any provision of this Act." Such an exclusion can only be effected in a fixed-term contract fulfilling the requirements of section 2(2), as discussed above.

(2) Illegal contracts of employment

In some recent cases the E.A.T. has held that persons working under illegal contracts of employment cannot claim the protection of the U.D.A. In *Lewis* v. *Squash Ireland Ltd.* (1983) the applicant had had part of his salary paid as an "expense," thus illegally evading some of his income tax liability. The E.A.T. found that the contract was as a result "wholly tainted with the illegality" and stated:

> "It is public policy that the courts and this Tribunal should not lend themselves to the enforcement of contracts either illegal on their face or in which the intended performance of obligations thereunder was illegal to the knowledge of the party seeking to enforce the contract" (p. 369).

The E.A.T. considered at some length previous British decisions in similar cases, in particular *Tomlinson* v. *Dick Evans 'U' Drive Ltd.* (1978) and *Newland* v. *Simons and Willer (Hairdressers) Ltd.* (1981), which had reached similar conclusions. Drawing on these the Tribunal found that the contract was unenforceable, thus depriving the applicant of the status of "employee" necessary to bring him within the ambit of the U.D.A. This decision has been applied in subsequent E.A.T. determinations, as for example in *Magee* v. *Campbell* (1983).

The attitude of the Irish and British tribunals to the question of illegal contracts of employment cannot wholly be welcomed. The view of the British E.A.T., supported in the *Lewis* case, that statutory unfair dismissal is based entirely on contract and that anything which affects the contract also affects the statutory rights has wider implications which re-surface in other contexts; it has, at any rate arguably, helped to undermine the effectiveness of the statutory protection. Furthermore, one cannot help wondering whether the public policy issues have been properly thought through. As noted by Mogridge ("Illegal Employment Contracts," *Industrial Law Journal*, 1981, Vol. 10, p. 23) and Kerr ("Labour Law 1982/83," *Journal of the Irish Society for Labour Law*, 1983, pp. 61, 82) there are other remedies for tax evasion, and it is hard to see why the employer should be entitled to benefit from an illegality to which he too was a party.

ESTABLISHING THE FACT OF DISMISSAL

Section 6(6) of the U.D.A. provides that the burden of proving that a dismissal is fair rests with the employer. However, there is nothing in the Act to suggest that he can be required to prove anything else. If therefore a dispute arises on any other matter, the onus is on the applicant. This applies in particular to the question of whether he has in fact been dismissed.

(1) "Dismissal" under the 1977 Act

That it is for the employee to prove the fact of dismissal has been clearly stated by the E.A.T., for example in the case of *Sherlock* v. *Irish Rubber Ltd.* (1978). An applicant must therefore be familiar with the Act's definition of "dismissal," which can be found in section 1. This provides that "dismissal" means:

> "(a) the termination by his employer of the employee's contract of employment with the employer, whether prior notice of the termination was or was not given to the employee,
>
> (b) the termination by the employee of his contract of employment with his employer, whether prior notice of the termination was or was not given to the employer, in circumstances in which, because of the conduct of the employer, the employee was or would have been entitled, or it was or would have been reasonable for the employee, to terminate the contract of employment without giving prior notice of the termination to the employer, or
>
> (c) the expiration of a contract of employment for a fixed term without its being renewed under the same contract or, in the case of a contract for a specified purpose . . . , the cesser of the purpose."

Leaving aside fixed term contracts (which have been dealt with above), it can be seen that there are under the Act two forms of dismissal, which for the sake of convenience we can term "actual" and "constructive." The difference between them is that in the case of an actual dismissal it is the employer who terminates the contract, while in the case of constructive dismissal it is technically the employee who terminates the contract, albeit with justification.

It should be noted here that the draftsman of the 1977 Act chose to follow the wording of the relevant British legislation, at present contained in the E.P.C.A., in defining a dismissal as a termination of an "employee's contract of employment" rather than, say, a termination of an "employment relationship." That is not a semantic point, since it may have contributed to the development of the contractual approach to dismissal outlined below.

The important thing to note in dismissal cases is that the description given to the occurrence by either party may be wrong, and that the appearance of acts by employers or employees may not be the legal reality. Therefore, the fact that an employer has told an employee to leave, or that he has refused to let the employee stay at work or (as the case may be) return to work, or that he has handed him his cards, is not necessarily evidence that he has, in legal terms, dismissed him. For example, in the recent British case of *Martin* v. *Yeomen Aggregates Ltd.* (1982) the E.A.T. held that even where an employer uses clear words which "standing alone would indicate a dismissal," they can "lose that effect if one looks at the surrounding circumstances" (p. 51); in the case itself the employer withdrew the words of dismissal almost immediately after issuing them, but the applicant insisted on bringing an unfair dismissal claim (which failed). This also means that particular care must be taken with ambiguous statements made by employers, statements which might or might not amount to dismissal. In *O'Connor* v. *Ryan* (1983) the E.A.T. held that the employer's comments about "having to let staff go," coupled with the statement that the applicant could "take it for what it means," did not amount to dismissal.

(2) Frustration

In some cases an employer may argue that there was no dismissal but that rather the contract of employment has been "frustrated." In contract law "frustration" occurs where events take place which make the performance of a contract illegal, impossible or in some other way fundamentally different from what the parties had initially envisaged. In dismissal cases this is most likely to be argued where the employee is ill or has been incapacitated. The British E.A.T., in the case of *Egg Stores (Stamford Hill) Ltd.* v. *Leibovici* (1977), held that a contract is frustrated either if there is an event which is "so dramatic and shattering" that everyone knows immediately that the contract must be regarded as being at an end, or if after an initial uncertain outcome it gradually becomes clear that the contract is no longer subsisting.

This was the case in *O'Flynn* v. *Eamonn P. O'Sullivan Ltd.* (1981). The employee had sustained a back injury and left work. Just over three years later he informed the employer, who had in fact ceased trading in the interim, that he was returning to work. While the E.A.T. did not actually mention the doctrine of frustration, it did hold that the employment contract could not be seen as having survived the lengthy break; there was therefore no dismissal. A similar conclusion was reached in the case of *Lawlor* v. *Patrick McCormack Ltd.* (1982).

However, frustration can only occur if both parties are innocent in relation to the frustrating event. If therefore the event was actually caused by either side, it will not amount to frustration. In a recent case the British E.A.T. has therefore held that imprisonment for a criminal offence, since it is caused by the employee committing an offence, cannot frustrate the employment contract: *Norris* v. *Southampton City Council* (1982). The E.A.T. did however allow that such behaviour might be taken as a repudiation by the employee of his contract.

(3) Repudiation

Repudiation, therefore, is the second contractual doctrine which may be used in this context. In general terms, a contract is repudiated where a party behaves in such a way as to show that he no longer intends to be bound by the fundamental terms. Applied to dismissal law the argument would be that the conduct of either the employer or the employee can, if sufficiently serious, amount to a repudiation of the contract of employment, resulting in the termination of the contract. Arguments of this kind perhaps made some sense under the British Industrial Relations Act 1971, which did not provide for constructive dismissal; an employee who had resigned could therefore only argue in contractual terms, *i.e.* that the employer had, by his repudiatory conduct, terminated the contract of employment and thus effected a dismissal. This form of reasoning was accepted by the National Industrial Relations Court: see *e.g.* *Sutcliffe* v. *Hawker Siddeley Aviation Ltd.* (1973).

However, by using repudiation as a method of getting round a deficiency of the 1971 Act the N.I.R.C. opened up a line of argument which has had serious repercussions. First, it has opened up a somewhat legalistic argument as to the effect of a repudiation of a contract of employment, and whether such repudiation must be accepted by the innocent party in order to become effective (see Chapter 3 and Redmond, *op. cit.*, pp. 135–40).

Secondly, it has allowed employers to argue that if there is in unfair dismissals law a recognition of the doctrine of repudiation it can of course apply to employees as much as to employers. Therefore, if an employee is guilty of serious misconduct the employer, rather than just dismissing him, might be tempted to argue that the employee had repudiated the contract and thus terminated it himself; there would then be no dismissal and thus no remedy under the U.D.A. To put it another way, the employer would in effect be arguing that in such cases it is the employee who, by his conduct, has "dismissed himself."

In fact, this kind of reasoning has been adopted in a number of cases, starting in Britain with the decision of the E.A.T. in *Gannon* v. *Firth* (1976). It has equally been accepted by the Irish E.A.T., as in the case of *McGuigan* v. *Dix Transport Ltd.* (1979). In the latter case the applicant was a long distance lorry driver based in Dublin. Having made deliveries in Cork he was asked, unexpectedly, by the respondents to stay in Cork for another night to await the arrival of a perishable cargo. He refused, and was told over the telephone by a director of the company that "if he did not comply with the request he would be leaving his job." He refused to stay in Cork, and on arriving in Dublin he was paid off. The E.A.T. found that the applicant had not discharged the burden of proving that he was dismissed. In another case, *Skelly* v. *Dublin Corporation* (1979), the applicant refused to move from one kind of work to another and was told as a result to "leave the yard." The E.A.T. found that this did not amount to a dismissal, since the applicant had known that he could be moved from one kind of work to another under his contract; he was therefore taken to have resigned.

(4) Resignation or dismissal

The effect of the cases outlined above is that the line separating dismissal from resignation has been badly blurred. If for example one were to take the *Skelly* case, it would be hard to explain why such facts amount to resignation (or "repudiation," or "self-dismissal") rather than dismissal for misconduct. But the consequences of classifying them under the former heading are serious, mainly for two reasons: first, if an employee has resigned, the question of the reasonableness or fairness of the employer's conduct becomes irrelevant, since there is no dismissal for the purposes of the Act; and secondly, where there is a dispute about the fact of dismissal the onus of proof is, as explained at the outset, on the applicant, so that the employer need only raise a doubt about whether the applicant was dismissed and can then sit back to see how the latter acquits himself. The cumulative effect of this approach is therefore to allow employers to avoid the rigours of the 1977 Act by a simple technical device which requires nothing other than the making of an allegation, however unreasonable it might seem to neutral observers.

In many ways the position is not made any easier by the fact that the E.A.T. demonstrates no consistency in these matters, and indeed offers little explanation of the rationale underlying its decisions. This can be demonstrated by comparing a couple of cases. In *Williams* v. *Gleeson* (1979) the respondent, who was anxious to prevent the unionisation of his workforce, told his employees (who had applied to join a trade union) that it was "either the union or their jobs." They chose to remain in the union, and the employer subsequently argued that by doing so they had resigned. This was rejected by the E.A.T. On the other hand, in the recent case of *Rutherford* v. *P. Mulrine & Sons Ltd.* (1983) there was some evidence that the employers had put pressure on the applicant to resign, but the E.A.T. rejected the submission that this amounted to dismissal. It held:

> "If [the employee's] resignation had followed an ultimatum 'either resign or you will be dismissed' there would clearly have been a dismissal. Where the resignation was brought about, not by an ultimatum, but by other factors, such as the offer of financial benefits, there is no dismissal."

On the other hand again, in the case of *Durnin* v. *O'Kane* (1983), the claimant was told by the employer that "it would be better for both of them if they parted company," and this was held to be a dismissal.

It may well be that there are rational grounds for distinguishing between the facts in those cases which the E.A.T. finds amount to dismissal and those which amount to resignation, but if there are they have not as yet been explained by the Tribunal. Furthermore, in some of these cases one might have expected an analysis of whether there was a constructive, as distinct from an actual, dismissal.

(5) Constructive dismissal

In the case of constructive dismissal we are again faced with the intrusion of contractual doctrine. When this concept was first introduced under the relevant British legislation there was some debate as to whether the correct criterion of constructive dismissal was the general unreasonableness of the employer's conduct or, from the other perspective, the reasonableness of the employee's decision to quit, or whether it was a contractual test in line with the doctrine of repudiation. What eventually proved decisive was the definition of constructive dismissal under what is now section 55(2)(*c*) of the E.P.C.A.; this declared that it occurred where the employee was "entitled to terminate [the contract] without notice by reason of the employer's conduct." The courts and tribunals found that this was a definition rooted in the law of contract, so that constructive dismissal depended on the employer having behaved in such a way as to amount to repudiation of his contractual obligations. This was summed up in the judgment of Lord Denning in the case of *Western Excavating (ECC) Ltd.* v. *Sharp* (1978):

> "If the employer is guilty of conduct which is a significant breach going to the root of the contract of employment, or which shows that the employer no longer intends to be bound by one or more of the essential terms of the contract, then the employee is entitled to treat himself as discharged from any further performance . . . " (p.226).

In Ireland the criteria for constructive dismissal are something of a mystery. For a start, it must be pointed out that our statutory definition is not the same as that in Britain, in that a constructive dismissal may, apart from the test of contractual entitlement, be found where it is "reasonable for the employee to terminate the contract of employment" because of the employer's conduct. In other words, section 1 of the Unfair Dismissals Act admits of *both* the contractual approach *and* the "reasonableness" approach.

However, the decisions of the E.A.T. constitute yet again a somewhat curious jumble. In the case of *McKeon* v. *Murphy Plastics (Dublin) Ltd.* (1980) the E.A.T. declared that

> "The test of constructive dismissal has now been established for some time as that laid down by Lord Denning MR in *Western Excavating (ECC) Ltd.* v. *Sharp.*"

A similar conclusion was reached in the case of *Higgins* v. *Donnelly Mirrors Ltd.* (1980). The Tribunal therefore did not appear to have been at all aware that the 1977 Act's definition not only allowed, but actually required a wider view. In *McKeon's* case it did not in substance matter, since the E.A.T. found on the facts that there had been a constructive dismissal, but in a subsequent case, *Conway* v. *Ulster Bank Ltd.* (1982), the matter became crucial when the Tribunal rejected the claim of constructive dismissal since there had in its view been no contractual repudiation by the employer.

On the other hand, in the earlier case of *Sherlock* v. *Irish Rubber Ltd.* (1978) the E.A.T. had held that the criterion to be applied was "whether it was reasonable in the particular circumstances of the case and in the context of good industrial relations" for the employer to act in the way he did. This kind of reasoning appears to have been followed in some more recent cases like *Maddock* v. *Rosroyal Co. Ltd.* (1983).

However, there have also been a number of cases in which the criteria used by the E.A.T. are not clear at all. For example, in *Long* v. *Reuters Restaurant* (1982) the Tribunal found that there had been a constructive dismissal when the employer insisted on the applicant working a seven day week. The E.A.T. did not explain its decision, but the facts as disclosed do not appear to rule out that the employer's requirement, though patently unreasonable, was quite in line with the applicant's contract of employment. In some other cases a finding of constructive dismissal was reached despite the fact that there appeared to have been a fairly obvious *actual* dismissal, in so far as there was a dismissal at all. In *Traynor* v. *Killiney Golf Club* (1980), for example, there was a straightforward conflict of evidence as to whether the claimant had been told that he was sacked; the E.A.T. side-stepped this by finding that there had been a constructive dismissal which, on the facts as disclosed, was about the only conclusion which made no sense at all.

In a row of other cases the E.A.T. has decided that where the employer behaves in such a way as to show a lack of mutual respect and confidence in the employment relationship there will be a constructive dismissal: see, *e.g. Newman* v. *Brady* (1980); and *Colgan* v. *Hire Here Ltd.* (1981). This kind of conclusion has also been reached in some more recent English cases based on the contractual approach, but it is probably possible to base it on either the contractual or the reasonableness test. In the *Colgan* case the E.A.T. explained that an employee was entitled to resign from (in this case) her employment "when the reasonable confidence which she was entitled to have in her position was undermined."

(6) Evaluation

It is clear from the above review that the Unfair Dismissals Act 1977 is being prejudiced in its effectiveness as a result of the legal ambiguity which surrounds the fact of dismissal. In these circumstances it is obviously advisable for an employer to attempt, in all cases, simply to argue that there has not been a dismissal, and indeed the evidence suggests that some employers are doing this in an almost frivolous way. An obviously desirable amendment of the 1977 Act is therefore to impose the burden of proof on the employer at this stage as well. If it is socially desirable to make the employer argue the justifiability of a dismissal, then it would seem to be equally socially desirable to make him establish, if he wishes to do so, that there has been no dismissal at all.

Finally, it would be highly desirable to rid the U.D.A. of the contractual connection. It would be much preferable to have "dismissal" as a separate statutory concept, to be interpreted in accordance with industrial relations commonsense, rather than having it as a contractual concept which, in the nature of these things, will encourage employers to apply legalistic arguments in support of their case.

ESTABLISHING THE REASON FOR DISMISSAL

As has already been noted, the onus of proving the fairness of a dismissal, once the fact of dismissal and the eligibility of the employee to claim under the Act have been established, rests with the employer. More precisely, section 6(1) of the Act provides that every dismissal is prima facie—*i.e.* in the absence of evidence to the contrary—an unfair dismissal. The exact wording is as follows:

> "Subject to the provisions of this section, the dismissal of an employee shall be deemed, for the purposes of this Act, to be an unfair dismissal unless, having regard to the circumstances, there were substantial grounds justifying the dismissal."

The section then goes on to enumerate, in each case "without prejudice to the generality of subsection (1)," grounds for dismissal which are to be deemed unfair or not unfair, as the case may be, and then to provide in subsection (6):

> "In determining for the purposes of this Act whether the dismissal of an employee was an unfair dismissal or not, it shall be for the employer to show that the dismissal resulted wholly or mainly from one or more of the matters specified in subsection (4) [grounds which are deemed not unfair] or that there were other substantial grounds justifying the dismissal . . . ."

Section 6 of the Act thus establishes a general presumption of unfairness, specific categories of unfair and not unfair grounds for dismissal, and an onus to be discharged by the employer that the dismissal has not resulted from an unfair ground but rather has resulted from one of the specified grounds deemed to be not unfair (which we shall call the "fair" grounds) or from "other substantial grounds justifying the dismissal." Furthermore, section 14(4) obliges the employer to furnish the employee with "particulars in writing of the grounds for the dismissal" within 14 days of the employee having requested them.

The first thing to be noted, therefore, is that the Act requires of a respondent employer that he should establish what the real ground for dismissal was. As it was put by Donaldson L.J. in the English Court of Appeal in *Union of Construction, Allied Trades and Technicians* v. *Brain* (1981), "this is no great burden upon the employer. He must, after all, know why he dismissed the employee" (p. 549). It is not however enough for the employer to nominate a ground which is disputed as the real ground by the dismissed employee unless he can back it up with some evidence. According to Ellis J. in the High Court case of *McCabe* v. *Lisney & Son* (1981), the employer has the onus of proving the grounds for dismissal "on the balance of probabilities," which is of course the normal standard of proof in non-criminal cases.

An illustration of the onus on the employer is provided in the recent British case of *Maund* v. *Penwith District Council* (1982), in which the applicant was ostensibly dismissed for redundancy. He claimed however that the respondent council had deliberately engineered the redundancy situation in order to be able to dismiss him, and that the real underlying reason was the council's disapproval of his trade union activities. This was rejected by the industrial tribunal, which held that in such cases it was for the applicant to provide evidence to disprove the stated reason for dismissal. On appeal, however, the Employment Appeal Tribunal held that no such onus rested with the applicant, and that in all cases the burden of proof is on the employer both to establish the reason for dismissal and to prove, where necessary, that the stated reason was not merely a "device."

It is not in fact clear whether the Irish E.A.T. is always sufficiently aware of the Act's requirements in relation to the burden of proof. According to the Tribunal's reports it occasionally happens that neither party appears or is represented at a hearing, and in such cases the E.A.T. invariably strikes out the unfair dismissal claim. A recent example was the case of *Smyth* v. *Wong* (1983), in which the E.A.T. decided that "because both parties failed to attend the hear-

received giving a reason for the fail-
smiss the claim, subject to a stay of
However, it is at least arguable that in the
he pre-hearing documentation that the fact
plicant's eligibility to claim are in dispute the
ply find that the respondent has not discharged
e a determination in favour of the applicant.

so be noted that what the employer must establish is
ason for the dismissal at the time of dismissal. In other
there are good grounds for dismissal these cannot be used
as ication by the employer at a hearing if he was unaware of
them when he dismissed the employee. There must therefore not
only be a valid reason for dismissing the employee, but also that
reason must be the one which actually motivated the employer at
the time. This was decided by the British House of Lords in the case
of *W. Devis & Sons Ltd.* v. *Atkins* (1977), with Viscount Dilhorne
explaining the point as follows:

> "Without doing very great violence to the language I cannot
> construe [section 57 of the E.P.C.A.] as enabling the tribunal to
> have regard to matters of which the employer was unaware at
> the time of dismissal and which therefore cannot have formed
> part of his reason or reasons for dismissing an employee," (p.
> 46).

The principle underlying the decision in *Devis* v. *Atkins* has also
been adopted by the Irish E.A.T. This might seem surprising in that
section 14(4) of the U.D.A. provides that, apart from the grounds for
dismissal actually given to the employee, "any other grounds which
are substantial grounds and which would have justified the dismissal" may be taken into account. However, the "other grounds" must
apparently still be ones which were known to the employer at the
time, for in *Kenna* v. *Non-Ferrous Metals Ltd.* (1983) the Tribunal held
that a decision to dismiss taken before the facts which would justify
the dismissal are known is unfair, even if a subsequent investigation
reveals a good ground. However, it must also be noted that in a
recent case, *O'Malley* v. *Finan* (1983), the E.A.T. found that while a
ground not known by the employer could not make the dismissal
fair, it could nevertheless be used by the Tribunal to lower the compensation awarded to nil. It is submitted that this is wrong, since it
makes the principle of *Devis* v. *Atkins* completely ineffective.

Although the fairness of a decision to dismiss can only be assessed on the basis of the employer's knowledge at the time of dismissal, it has been held by the Northern Ireland Court of Appeal that a reason for dismissal not disclosed at the time by the employer can nevertheless justify his decision subsequently, and that indeed would be the position under section 14(4) of the U.D.A. In *McCrory* v. *Magee* (1983) the Court held that an industrial tribunal could consider whether the employer's real reason, as distinct from his stated reason, justified the dismissal, although the tribunal could not substitute a reason which was "neither given nor entertained by the employer" (p. 416).

REASONABLENESS OF THE DECISION TO DISMISS

For the purposes of assessing the E.A.T. case law on the U.D.A. it is necessary at this stage to point out that the equivalent legislation in Britain—*i.e.* sections 54 to 80 of the E.P.C.A.—provides for a somewhat different method of establishing the fairness or unfairness of a dismissal. Under section 57(1) the employer must show what was the reason or principal reason for the dismissal and that it was one of the four reasons permitted under section 57(2) (similar to those listed in s. 6(4) of the U.D.A., see below) or "some other substantial reason." But even where the employer has established that the reason for dismissal was potentially fair, the industrial tribunal must go on to consider, under section 57(3) as amended in 1980, "whether in the circumstances . . . the employer acted reasonably or unreasonably in treating it as a sufficient reason for dismissing the employee"; this question is to be determined "in accordance with equity and the substantial merits of the case." In other words, under the E.P.C.A. the employer must not only have a good reason for dismissing the employee, he must also act "reasonably" in deciding to use that reason in order to dismiss.

Under the U.D.A. in Ireland there is no equivalent "second stage," and the Act merely requires that the employer establish a fair ground. However, the E.A.T. in its decisions has followed what in effect is the scheme of the E.P.C.A. and has demanded of employers not only a fair ground but also reasonable behaviour in treating that ground as a reason for dismissal. In the recent case of *St. Laurence's Hospital* v. *Grant* (1983), for example, the Tribunal declared that the test to be applied was whether "the respondent acted unreasonably in the light of the evidence before it at the time of dismissal." There is also a whole string of cases on disciplinary procedures and "natural justice" (discussed below) which make

sense only if the E.A.T. has incorporated the second stage of the
E.P.C.A.'s scheme into Irish Law. In one of these cases, *Mogan* v.
Donegal Co-operative Fisheries Ltd. (1983), the Tribunal concluded its
determination as follows:

> "The respondents have not satisfied the Tribunal in the cir-
> cumstances (having regard to equity and the substantial merits
> of the case) that they acted reasonably in treating the claim-
> ant's [conduct] . . . as sufficient reason for dismissal."

This not only adopts the E.P.C.A.'s general scheme, but also its precise wording which is neither copied nor mirrored anywhere in the
U.D.A.

The reason for this application of British unfair dismissals law is
probably connected with the tendency to follow British case law.
Many of the British unfair dismissal cases now tend to focus on section 57(3) of the E.P.C.A., and this has perhaps prompted the Irish
E.A.T. to apply principles from these cases which do not however
arise obviously out of the Irish Act. However, if one wanted to rationalise the Irish case law one could possibly also suggest that section
6(1) of the U.D.A., in requiring the E.A.T. to have "regard to all the
circumstances" of a dismissal case, allows the reasonableness of the
employer's decision to be a factor in the assessment of the dismissal's
fairness or unfairness. This is the conclusion suggested, albeit without much analysis, by Redmond (*op.cit.*, pp. 158–169). The E.A.T.
has not, to our knowledge, itself actually explained its policy in any
such way, but it would at least be a possible explanation. What it
would mean in practice is that there are no "automatically fair"
grounds for dismissal under the U.D.A., and the "fair" grounds to
be discussed below provide, in the parlance of the E.A.T. in *Durnin*
v. *Building and Engineering Co. Ltd.* (1978), "at best only a prima facie
justification." Overall, whatever misgivings one may have about its
explanation, it must be accepted that the reasonableness test—*i.e.*
the second stage of section 57 of the E.P.C.A.—has become part of
Irish law. It would however be preferable if this could be expressly
incorporated into the Act in any amending legislation.

"FAIR" GROUNDS FOR DISMISSAL

As already noted, section 6(6) of the U.D.A. requires the employer
to show that the dismissal "resulted wholly or mainly from one or
more of the matters specified in subsection (4) or that there were

other substantial grounds justifying the dismissal." Subsection (4) specifies four "fair" grounds, so that, also taking the additional category of "other substantial grounds," the employer has five headings under which his decision may be justified. He must however be able to fit the dismissal under at least one of these headings if he is to succeed in his defence. It is appropriate at this point to analyse each of the categories.

(1) Capability, competence or qualifications

Section 6(4)(a) of the U.D.A. provides that the first fair ground for dismissal relates to "the capability, competence or qualifications of the employee for performing work of the kind which he was employed by the employer to do." Section 57 of the E.P.C.A. in Britain uses identical wording, but unlike the U.D.A. goes on to define "capability" as "capability assessed by reference to skill, aptitude, health or any other physical or mental quality," and "qualifications" as "any degree, diploma or other academic, technical or professional qualification relevant to the position which the employee held"; these definitions are useful in that they broadly reflect Irish case law as well. In general one might say that this first category relates to the inherent suitability for the job of the employee, as distinct from "conduct" (see below), which relates to his deliberate behaviour while employed.

"Capability" was in one case held by the E.A.T. to apply where the employee was "not able" for the job, or "unable to cope": *Delaney* v. *Sanbra Fyffe Ltd.* (1981). More usually however capability is thought to relate to dismissals arising out of illness, injury or similar incapacity. In *Farrell* v. *Rotunda Hospital* (1978), for example, the applicant was dismissed because of his frequent absences due to illness and domestic responsibilities, and the E.A.T. held that this was a fair dismissal because of the employee's lack of capability. A similar decision was reached in *Matthew* v. *Roof Sealers Ltd.* (1981), in which the applicant was dismissed when he was unable to continue as a roofer due to a broken leg. The British E.A.T. has also held that a dismissal of an employee who occasionally had epileptic fits was not unfair since he was from time to time a danger to fellow employees: *Harper* v. *National Coal Board* (1980). It has been stressed by the Irish Tribunal that the question whether the employee was or was not to blame for the illness or incapacity is irrelevant: *Mooney* v. *Rowntree Mackintosh Ltd.* (1981); *Barbour* v. *Irish Glass Bottle Co. Ltd.* (1983). As the E.A.T. put it in *Molloy* v. *Irish Glass Bottle Co. Ltd.*

(1984), the crucial question is "whether the respondent was reasonable in thinking that he could not rely on the claimant's continuing attendance at work in the future."

However, the employer's discretion to dismiss in these circumstances is qualified in a number of ways. First, the E.A.T. has held that where an employee who is incapacitated due to injury or illness could have been given lighter work which he would have been able to perform the dismissal is unfair: *Farrell* v. *Fiat (Ireland) Ltd.* (1981); the Tribunal declared that the employer is in such cases under an obligation to "respond," if he can, to attempts by the employee to return to work or continue working, and this decision was subsequently upheld by Judge Ryan in the Circuit Court. Secondly, where an employee is absent it is up to the employer to try to find out why; he cannot merely assume without further investigation that the absence is due to illness of a kind which might justify dismissal: *Irwin* v. *Smith* (1982, E.A.T.). Finally, the British E.A.T. has held that where an employee's incapability actually results in part from the employer's failure to carry out his common law duties—such as the duty to make the place of work safe—then the dismissal is unfair: *Jagdeo* v. *Smith Industries Ltd.* (1982).

"Competence" is a factor in cases in which an employee is alleged to demonstrate a poor work performance: see, *e.g. Hickey* v. *National Agro-Chemical Co. Ltd.* (1982, E.A.T.). So for example, the failure by an employee to meet reasonable targets set by the employer is a good ground for dismissal: *Kearns* v. *Levi Strauss (Ireland)* (1982, E.A.T.). At the same time, the employer must not set unreasonable targets; in one case the E.A.T. held that an employer who suddenly and without warning raised the sales target by two and a half times could not fairly dismiss a salesman who failed to achieve it: *Hanlon* v. *Smiths (Dolphin's Barn) Ltd.* (1983). Furthermore, a poor performance in the absence of guidance and targets as well as general assistance from the employer cannot fairly be used as a ground for dismissal: *McGinley* v. *Disable Aid Ltd.* (1984).

The term "qualifications" refers, as the E.P.C.A. definition suggests, primarily to the absence of formal requirements, such as degrees, licences and so forth, which are essential to the job. In the case of *Ryder and Byrne* v. *Commissioners of Irish Lights* (1980), for example, Costello J. held that a dismissal for failure to pass a required test was not unfair. Similarly, in *Flynn* v. *Coras Iompair Eireann* (1980) the employee was dismissed as a road freight driver when he was disqualified from driving for 12 months for a road traffic violation; the E.A.T. accepted this as a good ground for dismissal, and the principle was re-affirmed in *Kavanagh* v. *Walden Motor Co. Ltd.* (1981).

(2) Conduct

Under section 6(4)(*b*) a dismissal relating to the conduct of the employee is not unfair. In fact, a large proportion of dismissals are defended by employers under this heading, and there is substantial case law on this category. As already noted, conduct relates to the employee's deliberate behaviour while employed. An employer may therefore dismiss for conduct such as an assault on a fellow employee: *Queenan* v. *J. Payen (Ireland) Ltd.* (1982); the refusal to do the full range of duties (without reasonable cause): *Waters* v. *Kentredder (Ireland) Ltd.* (1977); the refusal to obey reasonable instructions: *Doyle* v. *Liebig International Ltd.* (1980); an unjustified absence from work: *Evans* v. *Coras Iompair Eireann* (1982); a breach of the employer's rules (but only if these are contained in the contract of employment): *Caulfield* v. *Pantry Franchise (Ireland) Ltd.* (1981); the unauthorised use of the employer's property: *Smith* v. *Coleman Signs* (1979); "off-duty conduct which embarrasses or has undesirable repercussions for employers": *Flynn* v. *Sisters of the Holy Faith* (1984); and so forth.

It is in the misconduct cases that the significance of the "reasonableness" test becomes particularly clear. There are in fact many kinds of conduct of which an employer is clearly entitled to disapprove and which are therefore potentially fair reasons for dismissal, but again and again the E.A.T. has gone beyond that to inquire whether dismissal was an appropriate or reasonable response to the particular circumstances in which the misconduct occurred. So the Tribunal has decided that in misconduct cases the employer must, before taking the decision to dismiss, consider whether there were mitigating circumstances: *Moore* v. *Irish Glass Bottle Co. Ltd.* (1983); more generally the position was put by the E.A.T. in *Snia Ireland Ltd.* v. *Connolly* (1983) as follows:

> "Misconduct must be measured in the context of the employee's act, not just its consequences or potential consequences to the employer. The reasons for the act have to be evaluated and put into the context of his employment and responsibility. An act of an employee can cause damage or risk to the employer but it need not be misconduct. An act, minor in one situation, can be gross misconduct in another."

In the *Connolly* case itself the applicant, a security man, had left his plant unsecured when he received a telephone call from his wife telling him that his daughter had been injured. The E.A.T. held that in the circumstances the employers' decision to dismiss was unfair. The Tribunal similarly pointed out in *Killean* v. *Carr* (1979) that misconduct is not a good ground for dismissal if it was wholly or partly due to the inadequate supervision and training provided by the employer; in *Kelleher* v. *Murrays Europcar Ltd.* (1982) it held that abusive language was a good ground only in certain circumstances and that (in this case) calling the manager a "brat" was not sufficient for dismissal, although stronger abusive language, at any rate if unprovoked, may make a subsequent dismissal fair: *Lyons* v. *Johnson* (1984).

Apart from reviewing the general circumstances, an employer must also ask himself whether dismissal is not too harsh a penalty in the particular case; we discuss this in more detail below.

Particular problems have arisen in cases in which an employee was dismissed for conduct of which it was subsequently found that he was innocent, or where the guilt was never actually established. In *Coras Iompair Eireann* v. *Bennett* (1982) the E.A.T. held that the "innocence" or "guilt" of the employee is not the decisive factor:

> "The question of guilt or innocence of the [employee] does not arise. What the Tribunal has to decide is if the employer had a reasonable belief, founded on the result of a reasonable investigation, that it (sic) could no longer place total confidence in the [employee's] integrity."

Therefore, the fact that the employee in the case itself was acquitted in criminal proceedings of the theft for which he was dismissed did not necessarily render the dismissal unfair.

A similar view was expressed by the E.A.T. in the cases of *Reilly* v. *P.W. Shaw & Co. Ltd.* (1981) and *Stewart's Hospital* v. *Falconer* (1982). In this context it has however also been stressed by the English Court of Appeal in *W. Weddell & Co. Ltd.* v. *Tepper* (1980) that an honest belief by the employer in the employee's guilt is not of itself sufficient, in that the employer must have reasonable grounds for his belief and must act reasonably.

Similar issues arise where an employee is dismissed as a result of his having been convicted of a criminal offence. A number of employers operate rules under which an conviction will automatically lead to the employee's dismissal. In an early case, *Clarke* v.

Coras Iompair Eireann (1978) the E.A.T. held that such a rule is not compatible with the U.D.A.:

" . . . We feel that a blanket policy of dismissal upon conviction of an offence unconnected with employment is at variance with the wider public good. Each case must be decided on its own facts and on its own merits."

The Tribunal reached a different conclusion in the later case of *Thompson* v. *Aer Lingus* (1980) in which it found that the employers' policy of dismissing "for any violation of the criminal law" did not produce unfair dismissals if acted upon. In the case of *Kavanagh* v. *Cooney Jennings Ltd.* (1983) the E.A.T. also held that the conviction of an offence unconnected with the job could be a good ground for dismissal if the employers thought that the continued employment of the employee would harm their reputation with their customers. Despite these decisions, it is submitted that the approach adopted in the *Clarke* case is correct, and that a dismissal for conviction of a criminal offence can only be fair if each case is evaluated separately by the employer.

(3) Redundancy

Section 6(4)(c) of the Act provides that a dismissal resulting from "the redundancy of the employee" is not unfair. "Redundancy" is defined in section 1 by a cross-reference to section 7(2) of the Redundancy Payments Act 1967 (as amended), which is discussed in more detail in Chapter 8. Broadly, what it means is that a dismissal caused by the fact that the employer has ceased his business or that he no longer requires the particular kind of work carried on by the employee or that he is reducing the size of his workforce is not an unfair dismissal. Because of the identity of definition between the U.D.A. and the Redundancy Payments Acts it follows that in the ordinary course of events an employee fairly dismissed for redundancy will be entitled to claim a redundancy payment; this need not however always apply, since for example the qualifying period for eligibility to claim under the Redundancy Payments Acts is longer than under the U.D.A.

An example of a dismissal for redundancy is provided by the case of *Farrell* v. *Deerpark Ltd.* (1982), in which the employer was able to show that his business had declined and, moreover, that a redundancy payment had been given to and accepted by the applicant. On the other hand, the E.A.T. has also stressed that an employer cannot simply claim that there was a redundancy; he must back up his claim with some evidence. In *Hogan* v. *Keadeen (Carlow) Ltd.* (1982) an employee who had taken legal action against the employers was dismissed, allegedly for redundancy. In fact all the signs were that the employer's business was improving and that he was expanding it, so that his reason for dismissal was not accepted by the E.A.T. The Tribunal has also held in *Smythe* v. *Radio Telefís Eireann* (1981) that an employer cannot "starve" an employee of work and then purport to dismiss him for redundancy, a conclusion which was also reached by the British E.A.T. in *Maund* v. *Penwith District Council* (1982). In all such cases, as was emphasised by Ellis J. in the case of *McCabe* v. *Lisney & Son* (1981), the onus of proving the existence of a redundancy situation is on the employer.

Even where there is a genuine redundancy situation not all dismissals will necessarily be fair. The U.D.A. has additional provisions dealing with selection for redundancy in circumstances in which not all employees are being dismissed. In *Williams* v. *Compair Maxam Ltd.* (1982) Browne-Wilkinson J. of the British E.A.T. explained the purpose of the equivalent provision of the E.P.C.A. as follows:

> " . . . If the circumstances of the employer make it inevitable that some employee must be dismissed, it is still necessary to consider the means whereby the applicant was selected to be the employee to be dismissed and the reasonableness of the steps taken by the employer to choose the applicant, rather than some other employee, for dismissal" (p. 161).

The relevant provision in the U.D.A. is section 6(3), and this provides that if the "circumstances constituting the redundancy applied equally to one or more other employees in similar employment with the same employer who have not been dismissed," then the dismissal is unfair *if either* the dismissed employee was selected for an additional, unfair, ground (say, his trade union membership) *or* he was selected in contravention of a procedure which had been agreed between the employer and the employee or his trade union or which was established by custom and practice, and there were "no special reasons justifying a departure from that procedure."

The first of these two categories refers to the possible existence of an ulterior motive on the part of the employer in selecting the employee; if there is such an ulterior motive and it amounts to an unfair ground, then the dismissal is unfair even if there is a genuine redundancy: see *e.g. Quilty* v. *Cassin Air Transport (Dublin) Ltd.*

[section 6(1)]," so that the list is not exhaustive, and other reasons may also be unfair.

It could be asked whether a dismissal for one of these grounds is automatically unfair or merely potentially unfair. It has been argued that if the grounds under section 6(4) are merely *potentially* fair grounds and if the reasonableness of the employer's decision falls to be considered as well, then by analogy it could be said that section 6(2) merely outlines *potentially* unfair grounds (see Kerr, "Labour Law 1981/82," *Journal of the Irish Society for Labour Law*, 1982, p. 36). It could however equally be argued that in view of the qualifications to the protection provided by section 6(2)(*a*) and (*f*), as discussed below, and in view of the difficulty an employer would have in establishing under section 6(6) that a dismissal resulting "wholly or mainly" from an unfair ground also resulted "wholly or mainly" from a fair ground, section 6(2) establishes *automatically* unfair grounds.

Again, we shall briefly consider each of the categories listed in the subsection.

(1) Trade union membership and activities

Under section 6(2)(*a*) a dismissal is unfair if it results wholly or mainly from

"the employee's membership, or proposal that he or another person become a member, of, or his engaging in activities on behalf of, a trade union or excepted body under the Trade Union Acts, 1941 and 1971, where the times at which he engages in such activities are outside his hours of work or are times during his hours of work in which he is permitted pursuant to the contract of employment . . . so to engage."

[Se]ction 1 defines "trade union" for the purposes of the Act as "a [tra]de union which is the holder of a negotiation licence granted [un]der the Trade Union Acts, 1941 and 1971" (see Chap. 1). This [me]ans that the subsection only refers to membership and activities [con]nected with so-called "authorised" trade unions, or excepted [bod]ies, and does not therefore give protection against dismissals for, [or] activities designed to set up or support new or breakaway trade [unio]ns; such dismissals could of course still be unfair, but not under [secti]on 6(2)(*a*).

[Th]e actual or proposed membership of a trade union (as defined

(1983), in which the E.A.T. found that the selection of the applicant for redundancy while she was on maternity leave was an unfair selection; or *Dillon* v. *Wexford Steamless Aluminium Gutters Ltd.* (1983), in which it was held that the selection of the only employee who was a union member—and who at the time was in dispute with the employer—was unfair.

The second category refers to a question of fact: was there in fact an agreed or customary procedure, and if so, was the dismissal in accordance with it? If it was not, were there "special reasons" for the departure? It is clear from the case law that once the employer can establish both the existence of a procedure and compliance with it the dismissal is fair. In other words, the fact that the dismissed employee does not like the substance of the procedure is irrelevant: see *Grehan* v. *G. & T. Crampton Ltd.* (1982, E.A.T.); *Valor Newhome Ltd.* v. *Hampson* (1982, British E.A.T.). A frequently applicable customary procedure is the "last in, first out" rule, and in *Hayden* v. *McCormick McNaughton Ltd.* (1981) the E.A.T. accepted this as a proper procedure. The other side of the coin is that deviation from an agreed or customary procedure will, in the absence of very special circumstances, almost always render a selection for redundancy unfair: see *Tilgate Pallets Ltd.* v. *Barras* (1983).

The general approach in these cases has been that employers should, in so far as that is possible, be prevented from applying arbitrary criteria in selecting for redundancy. In *Hayden* v. *McCormick McNaughton Ltd.* the E.A.T. held that all aspects of the employer's conduct will be considered, including his observance of statutory obligations such as those under the Protection of Employment Act 1977 (see Chap. 8); the Tribunal concluded that "chance such as the toss of a coin would not be fairly considered until all other logical methods [of selection] have been exhausted." This is broadly in line with the British case of *Williams* v. *Compair Maxam Ltd.*, in which the E.A.T. held that redundancy selection should be evaluated in accordance with "the principles of good industrial relations practice": employers would normally be expected to give warning of impending redundancies, consult the trade unions whose members would be effected and use objective, rather than subjective, criteria for selection. These principles are not, as Browne-Wilkinson J. put it, "immutable," but they have broadly been followed in *Grundy (Teddington) Ltd.* v. *Plummer* (1983) and (by the Northern Ireland Court of Appeal) in *Robinson* v. *Carrickfergus Borough Council* (1983). These United Kingdom cases again rely heavily on section 57(3) of the E.P.C.A. (or the Northern Ireland equivalent), but their approach appears through cases like *Hayden* to have been incorporated into the standards required in Ireland by the U.D.A. Finally, the E.A.T. has held that an employer must not only apply proper criteria, but that these criteria must not be "unfairly applied": *Overseas Publications Ltd.* v. *Leavy* (1983).

(4) Illegality of employee's work

Under section 6(4)(*d*) a dismissal resulting wholly or mainly from "the employee being unable to work or continue to work in the position which he held without contravention . . . of a duty or restriction imposed by or under any statute or instrument made under statute" is not unfair. For example, in *Ponnampalam* v. *Mid-Western Health Board* (1981) the applicant's continued employment as a consultant surgeon required the sanction of a statutory body, Bord na n'Ospideal, under the Health Act 1970; since this was not forthcoming, his employment became illegal under the Act and his dismissal was thus held by Judge Gleeson of the Circuit Court to be fair. Another example might include a dismissal following on the revocation of a licence legally required for carrying out the job.

(5) Other substantial grounds

Section 6(4) of the U.D.A., which enumerates the "fair" grounds for dismissal, is expressed to be "without prejudice to the generality of subsection (1)," which in turn provides that a dismissal is unfair unless there are "substantial grounds" justifying it. Section 6(6) further provides that the employer must show that the dismissal resulted from one of the "fair" headings or from "other substantial grounds." All this means that the four categories of section 6(4) are not exhaustive, and an employer may on occasion be able to succeed even if his reason does not fall within the subsection's grounds. Another way of putting it would be to say that there is a fifth category, that is to say, "other substantial grounds."

The decisions of the E.A.T. have not painted a very clear picture of the kind of cases subsumed under this fifth heading. In many cases the Tribunal declares that an employer has shown a "substantial ground justifying the dismissal," where on a closer inspection it is clear that the reason was more properly one of the four grounds listed in section 6(4). This was the case, for example, in *Coleman* v. *Lilly Industries Ltd.* (1980), in which the applicant was dismissed for his poor work performance in the aftermath of several warnings; the

proper reason for dismissal here should clearly have been classifi as either "competence" or "conduct," rather than as merely a "s stantial ground." It has been suggested by Redmond that "dis tion or bad example among fellow employees" can be "ano substantial ground" (*op.cit*, p. 153), but again it is difficult t why this should not be treated simply as misconduct.

The E.P.C.A. in Britain provides in section 57(1)(*b*) that a d sal for "some other substantial reason" is not unfair, and the courts and tribunals have held that this relates primarily to sals prompted by the general business needs of the employe review of the British position, see John Bowers and Andrew "Unfair Dismissal and Managerial Prerogative," *Industrial L nal*, 1981, Vol. 10, p. 34). In the case of *R.S. Components* (1973), for example, the employers required all their emp agree to a new contract of employment containing a restri enant designed to deal with a particular problem which causing them losses. They dismissed those who refused t the N.I.R.C. held that this amounted to a fair dismissa other substantial reason." A similar decision was reach by the British E.A.T. in *Chubb Fire Security Ltd.* v. *Harp* which it held that if it was reasonable for the employer t reorganisation of his business, then a dismissal for th refusal to accept it would be fair even if the employer' amounted to a unilateral contractual variation. One be somewhat uneasy about these decisions, since if, a the unfair dismissals legislation is based on contract, have thought that an attempt by an employer to bre of employment (in this case by unilaterally varying i statutory protection for the employee. It is perhaps employers to plead "other substantial grounds" in missals arise out of their legitimate business needs, broad nature of the grounds under section 6(4) th rare indeed.

UNFAIR GROUNDS FOR DISMI

As already noted, the onus of proving the fairne the employer, and to discharge it he must bring one of the five categories just discussed. Anythi gories is an unfair dismissal. However, the A section 6(2) five reasons for dismissal which a to be unfair. However, this is "without preju

above) is clearly an unfair ground for dismissal. In the case of *Williams* v. *Gleeson* (1978) the applicants, who had become members of the Federated Workers' Union of Ireland, were told that it was "either the union or their job"; the subsequent dismissals were held by the E.A.T. to be unfair.

The protection under the U.D.A. of trade union activities is not quite so straightforward, in that it is qualified in two respects. First, the activities must be "on behalf of" a trade union, thus implying that the worker must in some sense be acting as an agent for the union. There are no Irish cases directly on this, but British case law has tended to stress the need for some formal involvement of a trade union: see *e.g. Chant* v. *Aquaboats Ltd.* (1978). The activities of individual trade unionists which are neither authorised nor supported by their trade union may thus be unprotected.

Secondly, a dismissal for trade union activity is only unfair under section 6(2)(a) if either the activity takes place outside working hours or, if during working hours, it is "permitted pursuant to the contract of employment." The British courts have held that a flexible approach should be adopted to the question of whether a period is "during" or "outside" working hours. In *Post Office* v. *Union of Post Office Workers* (1974), for example, the House of Lords held that "periods when in accordance with his contract of employment the worker is on his employer's premises but not actually working" are outside working hours; examples would include time spent at the place of work just before or just after official working hours, or during authorised meal breaks. During working hours trade union activities are protected only if authorised under the contract of employment, which would include activities authorised under a collective agreement which has been incorporated into the contract (see Chap. 3).

An example of an unfair dismissal for protected trade union activities is the case of *Gordon* v. *Dealgan Amusement Enterprises Ltd.* (1981). The applicant had a grievance with his employers, and he told the personnel manager that he would "consult a solicitor or a trade union." He consulted a trade union official and shortly afterwards he was dismissed, allegedly for his poor work performance. Since there was some evidence of the employers' hostility to trade unions, the E.A.T. found that this was an unfair dismissal for trade union activities.

In a more general vein, the E.A.T. has held that where an employer dismisses a union member or activist for misconduct or poor performance, the dismissal will be unfair if the same conduct or performance is tolerated in the case of other employees who are non-unionists: see *McElhinney* v. *Neil Sheridan & Sons (Creeslough) Ltd.* (1980). On the other hand, the Tribunal has also held that the fact that a dismissed employee is a union member is not of itself evidence of an unfair dismissal under section 6(2)(*a*): *A la Francaise* v. *Monaghan* (1978).

(2) Religious or political opinions

Under section 6(2)(*b*) a dismissal resulting wholly or mainly from "the religious or political opinions of the employee" is unfair. There have at the time of writing apparently not been any decided cases under this heading.

(3) Involvement in legal proceedings

Paragraphs (*c*) and (*d*) of section 6(2) render dismissals resulting wholly or mainly from the employee's involvement in, respectively, civil and criminal proceedings affecting the employer unfair. This applies to where the employee threatens civil proceedings against the employer or is a party to or witness in such proceedings, or where he initiates or is a witness in criminal proceedings against the employer. In the case of *Milchem Incorporated* v. *White* (1980) the applicant's mother was threatening legal proceedings against the employer, and the E.A.T. found that the likelihood of the applicant appearing as a witness had substantially caused the dismissal, which as a result was unfair.

(4) Race or colour

Under section 6(2)(*e*) a dismissal resulting wholly or mainly from "the race or colour of the employee" is unfair. To date no applicant has been successful in a claim based on this heading, but there have been two interesting cases. In *Ponnampalam* v. *Mid-Western Health Board* (1981) the applicant failed in his claim that he had been dismissed as a result of racial prejudice as he was ineligible, as a health board officer, to claim under the 1977 Act (see above). But Judge Gleeson in the Circuit Court did point out that a strong case had been made by the applicant which, in other employments, might have allowed him to succeed in his claim.

In *Cunningham* v. *Isle of Man Tourist Board* (1983) the applicant, the respondents' Irish representative, was dismissed since the Board had decided to replace him with a salesman based on the Isle of

Man. His claim that this preference for an island-based representative implied that he had been dismissed for reasons of "race" was rejected by the E.A.T., although the Tribunal did not explain this further.

(5) Pregnancy

Under section 6(2)(*f*) of the U.D.A. a dismissal which results wholly or mainly from "the pregnancy of the employee or matters connected therewith" is unfair, but this is subject to a qualification. If because of the pregnancy the employee was unable "to do adequately the work for which she was employed" or to continue to work without a breach of a statute or statutory instrument by her or her employer, and if there was no suitable alternative work for her or an offer of such suitable alternative work was turned down by her, then the protection of section 6(2)(*f*) does not apply. The alternative work must be "employment on terms and conditions corresponding to those of the employment to which the dismissal related."

An example of the above qualification was provided in the case of *Corcoran* v. *Weatherglaze Ltd.* (1981), in which the applicant was dismissed when her pregnancy caused her to be frequently absent from work. The E.A.T. found that these absences resulted in her being unable to do the job for which she was employed and that her dismissal was not therefore unfair. Similarly, in *Matthews* v. *Ophardt Product Ltd.* (1983) the dismissal of the applicant because, during her pregnancy, she was unable to do the agreed overtime was held by the E.A.T. to be not unfair. In neither of these cases, however, does there appear to have been any inquiry into whether the employers could have provided alternative work.

In cases where the pregnancy does not affect the employee's work performance or render it illegal a dismissal will generally be unfair. In *Mullins* v. *Standard Shoe Co. Ltd.* (1979), for example, the applicant was dismissed when she informed her employers that she was pregnant. The employers explained in a memorandum that "she was employed on the basis of not expecting pregnancy as we employ staff on a long-term basis," and that the reason for her dismissal was not her pregnancy but her failure to state at the time of her appointment that she was or would be pregnant (which in fact she did not know at the time). The E.A.T. found that the dismissal was unfair and that, however it was put, the employers' argument amounted to no more than that she was dismissed because of her pregnancy. Equally in *McNamara* v. *Nihill* (1981) the dismissal of the applicant because the employer "believed the continuance in his employment of a pregnant unmarried mother would lead to awkward questions from his children" was held by the E.A.T. to be unfair.

However, in the recent case of *Flynn* v. *Sisters of the Holy Faith* (1984) the E.A.T. held that where a pregnancy—in this case of an unmarried woman—is part of a general conduct which is inconsistent with a "certain code of behaviour and standards" required by the job—in this case that of a school teacher—then the employer is entitled to dismiss. The tribunal chairman in this case, Mr. Barry Hickson, dissented from the majority determination, holding that the dismissal is unfair once the pregnancy is "a factor" in the dismissal. On appeal to the Circuit Court, Judge Ryan upheld the determination of the majority in the E.A.T., offering the somewhat gratuitous comment that "in other places women are being condemned to death for this sort of offence" (*Irish Times*, July 5, 1984). In general this decision could only be applied to a relatively narrow range of jobs and professions in which moral standards are relevant in this way, but in any case the present authors would tend to favour the E.A.T. chairman's dissenting view.

Finally it should be noted that there is a connection between section 6(2)(*f*) of the U.D.A. and the Maternity Protection of Employees Act 1981 (see Chap. 6). The latter Act gives to pregnant employees an entitlement to a period of maternity leave; this being so, a dismissal because the employer thinks that a period of 14 weeks' maternity leave is excessive—even where that is a reasonable conclusion from the point of view of the employer's business requirements—is unfair: *Litton* v. *J.K. Smith Foy & Co.* (1983, E.A.T.). On the other hand, if the employee does not adhere to the procedural requirements of the 1981 Act in relation to her return to work, this may terminate the contract of employment. The E.A.T. has held that in such cases an unfair dismissal claim cannot be entertained, since there is technically no dismissal: *Murphy* v. *Clarkes of Ranelagh Ltd.* (1983); and *Doran* v. *N.E.P.S. Ltd.* (1984).

INDUSTRIAL ACTION AND UNFAIR DISMISSAL

Section 5 of the U.D.A. deals with the fairness of dismissals during a time of industrial action. The effect of this section is far from clear and must be considered with some care. First, section 5(1) provides that the "dismissal of an employee by way of a lock-out" is not unfair "if the employee is offered reinstatement or re-engagement as from the date of resumption of work." The re-employment can under section 5(4) be "by the original employer or by a successor of that employer or by an associated employer."

Section 5(2) then provides that "the dismissal of an employee for taking part in a strike or other industrial action" is unfair if any employee or employees of the same employer who took part in the strike or industrial action were either not dismissed or were subsequently, unlike the dismissed employee, offered reinstatement or re-engagement.

The terms "strike" and "industrial action" are further defined in section 1 of the Act, whereby it should be noted that "industrial action" must be "lawful," while a "strike" apparently need not be; it is not entirely clear what are either the reasons for or the implications of that distinction. In both cases however the strike or other action must relate to a dispute with an employer or with employees and must be taken with a view to compelling that employer or those employees to meet the demands of those taking the action.

What is clear from the wording of section 5 is that a lock-out ending with the re-employment, on suitable terms, of all locked-out employees does not amount to an unfair dismissal, and that a discriminatory dismissal of some (as distinct from all) employees taking part in a strike or other industrial action *does* amount to an unfair dismissal. So for example in *Duffy* v. *Tara Mines Ltd.* (1980) the dismissal of the applicant for mounting a one-man picket was held by the E.A.T. to be unfair because the employees who refused to pass the picket were not also dismissed. Equally, it is clearly unfair for an employer to dismiss an employee who incited industrial action without dismissing those who eventually joined in it with him, however unreasonable the employee's action may have been: *Butler* v. *M.B. Ireland* (1983, E.A.T.). Furthermore, the British House of Lords has held, in *Stock* v. *Frank Jones (Tipton) Ltd.* (1978), that the failure to dismiss strikers who, at the date of the dismissal of the remaining strikers, had returned to work, rendered the dismissal of the remaining strikers unfair.

Difficulties however arise if an employer re-employs only *some* employees he had previously locked out, or if he does in fact dismiss *all* employees taking part in a strike or other industrial action. It is frequently assumed that the intention of the draftsman of section 5 of the U.D.A. was to produce the same effect as that of the equivalent British provision, now section 62 of the E.P.C.A. This provides that an industrial tribunal "shall not determine whether the dismissal was fair or unfair" where the dismissal takes place during a lock-out, strike or other industrial action, *unless* one or more of the employees affected were not dismissed or were subsequently re-employed. In other words, a non-discriminatory dismissal of *all* relevant employees cannot be challenged under the E.P.C.A. It might therefore be argued that section 5 of the U.D.A. is intended to have the same effect.

However, section 5 of the U.D.A. is worded differently in a crucial way. The section must be seen in conjunction with the rest of the Act, and in particular with the duty of the employer under section 6(1) to show that, "having regard to all the circumstances, there were substantial grounds justifying the dismissal." Although therefore the provisions of section 5(2) do not directly apply to a dismissed employee who took part in a strike or other industrial action where all others who participated in the action were also dismissed, it is submitted that the employer must still discharge the onus of proving that he had a fair ground under one of the five headings listed above, and if he cannot do so the dismissal will be unfair, as it was in the case of *Power* v. *National Corrugated Products Ltd.* (1981).

DISCIPLINARY PROCEDURES

Section 14(1) of the U.D.A. provides that an employer must, within 28 days of taking on an employee, give him "a notice in writing setting out the procedure which the employer will observe before and for the purpose of dismissing the employee." Such procedures must be contained in a collective agreement or have been established by custom and practice.

Furthermore, we have already noted that the E.A.T. has applied a "reasonableness" test to the question of fairness in dismissal cases, despite the questionable statutory basis of such an approach. This has in particular led the Tribunal to require of employers that, before dismissing employees for misconduct or poor performance (and possibly for other reasons), they apply an adequate disciplinary procedure. This requirement was made by the British courts and tribunals from an early stage. In *Earl* v. *Slater and Wheeler (Airlyne) Ltd.* (1972) Sir John Donaldson, in the National Industrial Relations Court, declared that "good industrial relations depend upon management not only acting fairly but being manifestly seen to act fairly." In that case the employee had been dismissed for a number of alleged shortcomings in his work performance, but had been given no opportunity to make representations in his defence. The N.I.R.C. held that this rendered the dismissal unfair because the employer had not acted reasonably, and this general principle has been followed in a number of subsequent cases.

In Ireland under the U.D.A. the same general approach has been adopted. The basis for such an approach is, as noted above, unclear, but the water has further been muddied by the E.A.T.'s use of the term "natural justice" in some cases to explain its decisions. It is generally thought that the administrative law concept of natural justice does not apply to an ordinary employment relationship, but rather only to office holders: see *e.g. Garvey* v. *Ireland* (1979, S.C.); and *National Engineering and Electrical Trade Union* v. *McConnell* (1983, H.C.). Nevertheless the E.A.T. has on several occasions, as for example in the case of *Bunyan* v. *U.D.T.* (1981), held that employers must, in order to establish fairness under the U.D.A., show that they "observed the rules of natural justice" (p. 413). It would perhaps be possible to explain such an approach; for example, it could simply be asserted that the old common law principle that natural justice does not apply to the termination of employment is relevant only in the context of wrongful dismissal (see Chap. 3) and does relate to the modern statutory concept of unfair dismissal, or indeed that "constitutional justice," developed in cases such as *East Donegal Co-Operative Livestock Mart Ltd.* v. *Attorney-General* (1970), is not tied to the restrictions imposed upon natural justice. However, the E.A.T. has not made any such attempt to rationalise and explain its decisions.

The substance of the procedural obligations imposed on employers in this context was explained by the E.A.T. in the case of *Behan* v. *Autoglass Replacements Ltd.* (1983) as follows:

"The Unfair Dismissals Act and perhaps other influences place on the employer [a] duty to act fairly towards an employee when contemplating his dismissal. To discharge this duty an employer is advised to take all reasonable steps to investigate the allegation and assess the information upon which he will make his decision. In doing so he is directed towards any disciplinary procedure which might exist in his employment and in any event is required by natural justice to acquaint his employee of [*sic*] any allegations and the nature of same to give to the employee the right to defend himself. On the basis of the amassed information the employer is charged with reaching a fair or reasonable conclusion and if the allegation is so 'proven' to impose a penalty which must be reasonable as proportionate to the offence."

From the case law it can be concluded that there are four basic obligations which an employer must observe; they can be summarised as: (1) investigation; (2) hearing; (3) warnings; and (4) proportionate penalties. It should further be noted that where a collective agreement prescribes a particular form of disciplinary procedure, a departure from it will almost always tend to render the dismissal unfair: see *Condron* v. *Rowntree Mackintosh Ltd.* (1980).

(1) Investigation

The E.A.T. has held that an employer must conduct an adequate investigation of the circumstances before deciding to dismiss so that the dismissal is not based on incorrect or incomplete information. For example, in *Crilly* v. *Rucon Ltd.* (1979) the applicant was dismissed because of his apparently unexplained long-term absence from work. In fact he had sent in medical certificates which had been lost due to the employers' inadequate filing system, and the dismissal was therefore held to be unfair for lack of a proper investigation. In *Dunne* v. *Harrington* (1979) the E.A.T. held that a proper investigation must involve an attempt to obtain all relevant evidence, including (where appropriate) the testimony of witnesses, the disclosure of this evidence to the employee, and a "fair and reasonable" analysis of the evidence; similar criteria were set out in *Hennessy* v. *Read and Write Shop Ltd.* (1979).

(2) Hearing

It has been held repeatedly by the E.A.T., for example in *Bunyan* v. *U.D.T.* (1981), that it is necessary for an employer to give the employee "an opportunity to state his case" before he is dismissed (p. 412). So for example it was held in *Behan* v. *Autoglass* (1983) to be unfair for an employer to dismiss an employee on the basis of complaints made against him, when he had not acquainted the employee with the substance of the complaints or given him an opportunity to rebut them. What this means is that the employer—in practice usually the member of management who will actually take the decision to dismiss—must put the full position to the employee and give the latter every opportunity to react to all the points made against him. The E.A.T. has further held that it is unfair to dismiss an employee if the employer did not permit trade union representation at the hearing: *Devlin* v. *Player & Wills (Ireland) Ltd.* (1978); and *Mount Brandon Hotel* v. *Lee* (1982).

(3) Warnings

It has been held that as a rule an employer must, before deciding to dismiss because of misconduct or poor performance, give the employee at least one warning. The object of this is, as a British industrial tribunal put it in *Sharma* v. *Inland Revenue* (1980), "to make sure that the employee concerned realises that unless he improves he will be dismissed; so that he cannot say afterwards, 'Well, I could have done better, if I had realised my job was at risk.' "

Apart from giving the warning, the employer must also subsequently facilitate the desired improvement in conduct or performance. In *Richardson* v. *H. Williams Ltd.* (1979) the E.A.T. held that where a warning has been issued the employee must be given: (a) a "reasonable time" within which to effect the improvement; (b) a "reasonable work situation" within which to do so; and (c) a "fair and reasonable" process of monitoring his progress and reaction. The first of the above points implies that in most cases there must be a fairly substantial interval between the first warning and the eventual dismissal; in the case of *McDowell* v. *Wagstaff & Wilson Ltd.* (1980) the E.A.T. held that four weeks were insufficient, although of course the exact period of time required will depend on the circumstances.

(4) Proportionate penalties

In the case of *Dunne* v. *Harrington* (1979) the E.A.T. held that where an employee is dismissed, the dismissal as a penalty should "relate reasonably to the 'offence.' " Even if therefore the employer has established a fair ground under the U.D.A., the dismissal may be unfair if it amounts to an over-reaction to the circumstances, and in particular if a lesser penalty could have been applied more appropriately: see *Connor* v. *Aloby Ltd.* (1984, E.A.T.). So for example in the case of *Mullen* v. *Coras Iompair Eireann* (1980) Judge Ryan in the Circuit Court held that a dismissal for working for a competitor of the employer during holidays was, in the circumstances, too harsh a penalty.

(5) Necessity of disciplinary procedures

One question which has been considered on a number of occasions by the British E.A.T. is whether a dismissal is rendered unfair, where the above procedural requirements have not been satisfied, even if the employer is able to argue convincingly that, had he carried out all the requirements, his decision would in the end still have been the same. In *British Labour Pump Ltd.* v. *Byrne* (1979) the E.A.T. held that in such circumstances, if the employer with hindsight can show "on the balance of probabilities" that with or without proper procedures he would have taken the same decision, the dismissal is not unfair. However in recent cases, such as *Dunn* v. *Pochin (Contractors) Ltd.* (1982) and *Murray MacKinnon* v. *Formo* (1983), the E.A.T. has imposed a relatively severe burden of proof on the employer in such a situation, so that a mere assertion that it would have made no difference will not suffice. There appear to be no Irish cases directly on this point, but it is submitted that if a procedural requirement of reasonable conduct is to be imposed on employers on public policy grounds, it should be imposed regardless of the necessity of such conduct in specific cases. The *British Labour Pump* decision should not therefore, in our view, be followed.

REMEDIES

Section 7 of the U.D.A. makes available three alternative remedies to an unfairly dismissed applicant, to be awarded in accordance with what the Rights Commissioner, the E.A.T. or the Circuit Court (each of which may hear unfair dismissal cases, as is outlined in Chap. 9) "considers appropriate having regard to all the circumstances." The remedies are reinstatement, re-engagement and compensation. It should be noted that section 15 of the U.D.A. provides that an applicant cannot recover damages at common law or redress under the Anti-Discrimination (Pay) Act 1974 (or the Employment Equality Act 1977, under s. 27(3) of that Act) and at the same time get redress under the U.D.A. in respect of the same dismissal.

(1) Reinstatement

Section 7(1)(*a*) of the U.D.A. provides that a successful applicant may be awarded

> "re-instatement by the employer of the employee in the position which he held immediately before his dismissal on the terms and conditions on which he was employed immediately before his dismissal together with a term that the re-instatement shall be deemed to have commenced on the day of the dismissal . . .
> ."

What this means in practice is that the employee, to use the slightly different definition of section 69(2) of the British E.P.C.A., is treated "in all respects as if he had not been dismissed." The effect of reinstatement under the U.D.A. was explained by the E.A.T. in the case of *Groves* v. *Aer Lingus Teo* (1980) as follows:

> "The reinstatement of the claimant shall be deemed to have commenced on the day of the dismissal. The respondent shall pay to the claimant any arrears of salary from the date of dismissal to the date of implementation of this order, less any Social Welfare Benefits received by the claimant. The term 'salary' shall include any benefits, including any salary increases, which the claimant might reasonably have expected to have had but for the dismissal. The claimant shall have restored to him any rights and privileges, including seniority and pension rights (if applicable) which he might reasonably expected to have had but for his dismissal."

While the applicant is entitled to back pay, it has been held by Judge Ryan in the Circuit Court in *Farrell* v. *Fiat (Ireland) Ltd.* (1981) that a reinstated employee is not entitled to pay for any period between the dismissal and the order during which he would have been unfit for work and thus ineligible to be paid. Finally in some cases, as for example in *Smythe* v. *Radio Telefís Eireann* (1981), the E.A.T. has held that social welfare payments should be repaid, rather than be deducted from the arrears of salary.

(2) Re-engagement

Under section 7(1)(*b*) of the U.D.A. an employee may be awarded

> "re-engagement by the employer of the employee either in the position which he held immediately before his dismissal or in a different position which would be reasonably suitable for him on such terms and conditions as are reasonable having regard to all the circumstances."

This allows a fair measure of flexibility with regard to the terms of an order of re-engagement. For example, re-engagement can be awarded as from the date of dismissal, as in *Harrison* v. *Gateaux Ltd.* (1981), or can be subject to a prior period of suspension, as in *Healy* v. *O'Neill* (1982).

(3) Compensation

The third remedy, under section 7(1)(*c*), is

"payment by the employer to the employee of such compensation (not exceeding in amount 104 weeks remuneration . . .) in respect of any financial loss incurred by him and attributable to the dismissal as is just and equitable having regard to all the circumstances."

"Financial loss" is defined in section 7(3) as including "any actual loss and any estimated prospective loss of income attributable to the dismissal," as well as loss or diminution of rights under the Redundancy Payments Acts or in relation to superannuation. The kind of losses which can be included in the calculation were illustrated in the case of *Ogden* v. *Harp Textiles Ltd.* (1980), in which the E.A.T. allowed compensation for the loss of rights under a pension scheme, the use of a company house and a company car, the Voluntary Health Insurance premium paid by the employers, and the expense incurred in moving house (necessitated by the dismissal) together with the cost of temporary accommodation.

The calculation of compensation is based on the dismissed employee's remuneration, and "remuneration" is described in section 7(3) as including "allowances in the nature of pay and benefits in lieu of or in addition to pay." More specific provisions are contained in the Unfair Dismissals (Calculation of Weekly Remuneration) Regulations 1977; these provide in particular for a means of calculating the weekly remuneration of employees whose pay actually varies from week to week (because of overtime, piece rates, bonuses and suchlike); broadly this is done by taking average figures for a period of 26 weeks ending 13 weeks before the date of dismissal. In general, all payments which formed part of the remuneration are counted, as for example bonus payments, dividends and so forth: see *e.g. Kilcullen* v. *Holland Automation Ireland Ltd.* (1981, E.A.T.). If the employer was actually paying the employee less than he was bound to pay—for instance if he was not observing the terms of the contract of employment or, perhaps, an Employment Regulation Order (see Chap. 4)—then the full amount that should have been paid will be used for the calculation: see *Kinsella* v. *Banagher Concrete Ltd.* (1981, E.A.T.); and *Sheridan* v. *Walker & Co.* (1982, E.A.T.).

The award may not exceed 104 weeks remuneration, but if deductions are made (see below) these must be from the total loss and not from an already reduced 104 weeks maximum: see Ellis J. in *McCabe* v. *Lisney & Son* (1981).

The definition of "financial loss" requires that both past and future loss be taken into account. The case law of the E.A.T. indicates that the Tribunal has found it most difficult to apply the calculation of future loss, calling it a calculation which is "full of imponderables"—*Kearns* v. *Chesterton International B.V.* (1979)—and "highly speculative"—*Groarke* v. *Hygiene Distributors Ltd.* (1980). Most of the decisions simply state that compensation for future loss is being allowed for a specified period, recently of generally between three and eight months, and no further explanation is offered. In one case, *Keenan* v. *Raheny and District Credit Union Ltd.* (1980), the E.A.T. took into account the combined factors of the applicant's comparatively high age and of the worsening recession to allow compensation for a rather longer period of future loss, but there is no evidence of a systematic approach of this kind. Finally, in *O'Donovan* v. *O'Donoghue* (1982) the E.A.T. held that no future loss (or indeed past loss) could be awarded beyond a date on which the respondent has closed down his business, if that has occurred by the date of the hearing, since from that date the applicant would have been made redundant anyway.

In the *O'Donovan* case the E.A.T. awarded no compensation beyond the date, three weeks after the dismissal, on which the employer closed down his business. Had the employee had the required length of service of two years to qualify for a redundancy payment (see Chap. 8), then under section 7(3) of the U.D.A. the Tribunal would have had to award compensation for employee's loss of rights under the Redundancy Payments Acts, as was done in *Kelly* v. *Gazelle Ltd.* (1983). In such a case the loss of a redundancy payment arising from the dismissal is clearly measurable. In most cases however it is not, because while the employee will have lost accrued rights under the Acts, it is not easy to predict the likelihood of this loss becoming actually relevant in a redundancy situation. In the case law the E.A.T. has tended to suggest a percentage risk of a future dismissal for redundancy and to calculate the compensation by applying that percentage to the total accrued redundancy lump sum entitlement: see *e.g. Richardson* v. *H. Williams Ltd.* (1979); and *Keenan* v. *Ferrans Stud Ltd.* (1979).

(4) Deductions from compensation

When the applicant's "financial loss" has been calculated, certain deductions can still be made from this basic figure under section 7(2) of the U.D.A.; this provides that "regard shall be had" to certain factors "in determining the amount of compensation." More specifically, what must be taken into account is whether the finan-

cial loss of the employee is "attributable to an act, omission or conduct" by either the employer or the employee, whether the employee
has or has not adopted measures to "mitigate the loss," and whether
the parties have complied with agreed procedures and with codes of
practice. In fact, the E.A.T. also makes some other deductions from
time to time, such as social welfare payments which the applicant
has received since the dismissal, or indeed has not, but could have,
received—*Bunyan* v. *U.D.T.* (1981)—or income tax rebates received
by the applicant—*Milchem Inc.* v. *White* (1980). Why such deductions are made is not altogether clear; what it actually means is that
the State pays part of the compensation, which hardly makes much
sense. In any case, there is no statutory basis for these particular
deductions, and it would be much preferable to adopt the approach
of the British E.A.T. as expressed, for example, in *M.B.S. Ltd.* v.
Calo (1983).

In practice the two main headings for deductions are contributory
fault and failure to mitigate the loss. The former is most frequently
applied where an employer has dismissed the applicant without
applying proper disciplinary procedures, but where there was nevertheless a good ground for dismissal. So for example in *McAnaspie* v.
Athlon Golf (Ireland) Ltd. (1981) the applicant's dismissal for her
absence from work was held by the E.A.T. to be unfair because the
employers refused to allow her to explain her position in private;
however, she was also held to have contributed to her dismissal and
had her compensation reduced by 50 per cent. In certain cases, such
as *Condron* v. *Rowntree Mackintosh Ltd.* (1980) and *Tunney* v. *Coras Iompair Eireann* (1983), the E.A.T. has applied deductions of 100 per
cent., leaving a nil award. It also appears that compensation can be
reduced as a result of conduct by the applicant which has nothing to
do with the actual ground for dismissal—see Ellis J. in *McCabe* v.
Lisney & Son (1981). For example, previous bad conduct unconnected with the dismissal in issue can be used in this way: *O'Conchub-
huir* v. *Securicor (Ireland) Ltd.* (1982, E.A.T.). All this does not appear
to be the case in Britain under the E.P.C.A.: see *Nelson* v. *B.B.C. (No.
2)* (1979).

The other main basis for a reduction of compensation is the applicant's failure to mitigate his loss. As the British E.A.T. put it in the
case of *Gardiner-Hill* v. *Roland Berger Technics Ltd.* (1982), "the duty
on a claimant is to take such steps as in all the circumstances are
reasonable to reduce the loss he suffers from the respondent's wrongful act" (p. 500, per Browne-Wilkinson J.). Usually this duty is not
discharged if the applicant makes insufficient efforts to find new

employment or income. So for example in *Fitzgerald* v. *Craft Cleaners Ltd.* (1981) the E.A.T. held that because the applicant had, after his dismissal, mounted a one-man picket on the employers' premises he would have found it difficult effectively to look for other work at the same time, and accordingly it reduced his compensation. However, the mere fact that the applicant did not look for employment is not necessarily indicative of a failure to mitigate his loss if he attempted other ways of securing an income, for example by starting his own business: *Bunyan* v. *U.D.T.* (1981).

On the whole, the E.A.T. tends not to explain in its decisions exactly in what way the applicant whose compensation is being reduced has failed to mitigate his loss. Also, from the reports the calculation of the deduction is apparently made pretty much on a rule-of-thumb basis, sometimes expressed merely in percentage terms. This contrasts with the approach of the British E.A.T. in *Gardiner-Hill* (above), in which Browne-Wilkinson J. held that the calculation must be precise, reached by identifying the exact time or event at which the failure to mitigate occurred and by deducting an appropriate amount from that point onwards, in precisely calculated amounts rather than in percentage or rule-of-thumb terms. If that is the approach of the Irish E.A.T. it is not generally explained in this (or indeed any other) way.

(5) Choice of redress

The main thing to be noted in relation to the remedies available under the U.D.A. is that the vast majority of successful applicants are awarded compensation rather than reinstatement or re-engagement. The most recent annual report of the E.A.T. states that in 1982, of the 240 applicants who succeeded in obtaining a determination of unfair dismissal, 218 were awarded compensation (which in 48 cases was nil), while only eight were awarded reinstatement and 14 re-engagement (E.A.T., *Fifteenth Annual Report,* 1982, p. 2). This has been the general practice throughout recent years, and indeed it appears that in Britain an even smaller proportion of applicants succeed in securing re-employment (see Dickens *et al.*, "Re-employment of Unfairly Dismissed Workers: The Lost Remedy," *Industrial Law Journal,* 1981, Vol. 10, p. 160).

The U.D.A. itself does not give any express priority to any particular remedy, but it does specify the re-employment remedies first, reflecting the preference implicit in I.L.O. Recommendation 119 and now expressed in I.L.O. Convention 158 (Art. 10). The form which applicants must complete when bringing a claim asks them to indicate the "redress sought," but on the other hand this does not seem to be in any way crucial in determining the remedy awarded by the E.A.T.

Exactly why the E.A.T. gives such priority to compensation is not clear, but one can speculate on some possible reasons. First, there are now generally substantial delays between a dismissal and an E.A.T. hearing, so that re-employment becomes less practicable. Secondly, it is thought that to compel the resumption of an employment relationship after legal proceedings which may well have been acrimonious is generally not sensible. This means that re-employment tends in particular not to be awarded when the employer raises objections to it. Where re-employment *is* ordered, it is generally because of outrageous conduct by the employer, or sometimes on hardship grounds: *Mullen* v. *Linenhall (1972) Ltd.* (1980). In choosing one or the other form of re-employment, the E.A.T. appears to consider whether the applicant has in some measure been guilty of contributory fault, as for example in *McConnell* v. *John Sisk & Sons* (1981); in such cases re-engagement is the preferred remedy.

If the U.D.A. is to provide any serious degree of job security in the face of arbitrary action by employers, it is undoubtedly essential that greater precedence be given to the re-employment remedies. A combination of a reluctance to award reinstatement or re-engagement and a tendency to award comparatively low compensation casts serious doubts on the effectiveness of the U.D.A.

8 Redundancy

INTRODUCTION

Dismissals are not just sanctions or disciplinary measures used by employers; an employer may for example decide to let go some of his workforce because of economic considerations or because of technological changes. The dismissal of workers in these cases does not relate to any dissatisfaction with their conduct or work performance, but is caused by the fact that the employer no longer requires, or can afford, their service. In such circumstances the concept of redundancy arises, and here the law has provided certain safeguards for the workers concerned. This chapter will deal with redundancy payments and with the obligations to be discharged by employers in the event of multiple redundancies.

THE REDUNDANCY PAYMENTS ACTS

The notion of a redundancy payment was, in these islands, first introduced in the United Kingdom in the Redundancy Payments Act 1965. This Act provided for a lump sum payment, calculated on the basis of length of service, to employees who satisfied certain conditions and who had been dismissed by reason of redundancy. The policy behind this legislation was at the time not particularly clear, a fact which was apparent in the speech by the then Minister of Labour, Mr. Ray Gunter, in the House of Commons during the Second Reading of the Bill (*Hansard* Commons Vol. 711, April 26, 1965). The reasons which he advanced for the legislation included the desire "to make it easier for workers to change their jobs in accordance with the needs of technological progress," or "to encour-

161

age mobility of labour by reducing resistance to change" thus allowing a more efficient use of the national workforce; but he also pointed out that the Bill marked "a very significant step forward in the way we think about the status of the industrial worker," so that it might be seen as some form of recognition of a worker's proprietary interest in his job.

The compatibility of these views of redundancy payments was doubted by K. W. Wedderburn (1966) 29 M.L.R. 55. The purpose of the 1965 Act, he thought, was either "relief of hardship (which might encourage mobility of labour,)" or else "compensation for expropriation (which might not, since the longer the tenure, the higher the payments)." He concluded that "the Act was plainly drafted hurriedly and did not receive extensive parliamentary debate." In fact the same writer has noted elsewhere that "the rationale of the curious Act of 1965 is still shrouded in mystery": *The Worker and the Law* (1971 p. 125).

However, although there may have been doubts about the policy behind the introduction of redundancy payments, it was clear that the British trade unions and employers supported the idea, and this support was evident at the time in Ireland as well. Almost as soon as the 1965 Act had been passed in Britain, the Irish Labour Party introduced in the Dail the Redundant Workers (Severance Pay and Compensation) Bill, but while this failed to secure a Second Reading the Government introduced its own Bill two years later which, based to a large extent on the British 1965 Act, became the Redundancy Payments Act 1967. The then Minister for Labour, Dr. Patrick Hillery, explained in the Dail that the Act's main purpose was "to provide financial help to workers who lose their jobs on account of redundancy and financial help to unemployed workers who have to move from their home areas to secure employment" (*Dail Debates*, Vol. 228, May 30, 1967). The 1967 Act has been amended three times, in 1971, 1973 and 1979.

THE MEANING OF "REDUNDANCY"

Under section 7(2) of the 1967 Act, as amended by the 1971 Act, an employee is dismissed by reason of redundancy if the dismissal is attributable "wholly or mainly" to the following:

"(a) the fact that his employer has ceased, or intends to cease, to carry on the business for the purposes of which the employee was employed by him, or has ceased or intends to cease, to carry on that business in the place where the employee was so employed, or

(b) the fact that the requirements of that business for employees to carry out work of a particular kind in the place where he was so employed have ceased or diminished or are expected to cease or diminish, or

(c) the fact that his employer has decided to carry on the business with fewer or no employees, whether by requiring the work for which the employee had been employed (or had been doing before his dismissal) to be done by other employees or otherwise, or

(d) the fact that his employer had decided that the work for which the employee had been employed (or had been doing before his dismissal) should henceforward be done in a different manner for which the employee is not sufficiently qualified or trained, or

(e) the fact that his employer had decided that the work for which the employee had been employed (or had been doing before his dismissal) should henceforward be done by a person who is also capable of doing other work for which the employee is not sufficiently qualified or trained."

For the purposes of section 7(2)(c) an employer creates a redundancy situation where, under section 7(4A), he replaces an employee by a member of his—*i.e.* the employer's—family. Finally, section 16(3) of the 1967 Act provides that the dismissal of an employee by one company may amount to redundancy where the redundancy exists in respect of the business of associated companies if these are taken together.

(1) Presumption of redundancy

It is not in fact necessary for the employee, in a hearing before the Employment Appeals Tribunal (see Chapter 9), to prove that the above conditions are satisfied in respect of his dismissal. Section 10(*b*) of the 1971 Act provides that

> "an employee who has been dismissed by his employer shall, unless the contrary is proved, be presumed to have been so dismissed by reason of redundancy."

The onus of proving that the employee has been dismissed for reasons other than redundancy therefore rests with the employer, or with the Minister for Labour where the latter disputes the employee's entitlement to a redundancy payment (see below). Since cases are frequently taken to the E.A.T. involving claims both under the Redundancy Payments Acts and the Unfair Dismissals Act 1977 employers may have to rebut two contradictory presumptions in the same case.

How the presumption of redundancy works in practice has been demonstrated in a number of cases. In an early case, *Gaffney* v. *Bohemian F.C.* (1969), the employer claimed that the dismissal was for unsatisfactory work, absenteeism and bad timekeeping. However, the Tribunal found that since the applicant had during his employment never been made aware of any complaints about his work the presumption of redundancy applied. In *Kelly* v. *Dillon* (1979) the employer gave as reasons for the dismissal unpunctuality and laziness, as well as the fact that he "did not have any work"; the E.A.T. again found that, in the absence of specific evidence to the contrary, the employee was dismissed for redundancy.

The English Court of Appeal has further held that even where an employee was employed for a fixed term and knew when he was being taken on that at the end of that term the demand for his work would have ceased, he could still claim a redundancy payment when he was dismissed as expected: *Nottinghamshire County Council* v. *Lee* (1980).

(2) Replacement of employee

It is sometimes said that the best test of whether there has been a redundancy is to ask whether the dismissed employee has been replaced by the employer, but while this is undoubtedly a useful pointer it is by no means conclusive. As the E.A.T. has put it, "non-replacement, although of great importance as a factor to be considered, is not always of overriding importance": *Kenny* v. *Hoctor* (1980). It could for example be that an employer has operated what the English E.A.T. has called a "transferred redundancy," that is to say where one employee takes the job of another, who in turn is dismissed: *Elliot Turbomachinery Ltd.* v. *Bates* (1981); furthermore, as Sachs L.J. put it in *Hindle* v. *Percival Boats Ltd.* (1969), "an employer is entitled to come to a genuine conclusion that despite the requirements of his business he prefers to have a vacancy in his staff rather than to take on an unsuitable replacement."

(3) Mixed motives

In the *Hindle* case the English Court of Appeal further concluded (with Lord Denning MR dissenting) that the employer's reason for dismissing the worker must be considered subjectively, so that the presumption of redundancy is displaced if the employer can show that the reason which motivated him was something other than redundancy, even if that reason was "unwise or based on a mistaken view of facts" (Sachs L.J.). On the other hand the E.A.T. in Ireland has awarded redundancy payments to a number of employees who were nominally—and, for all we know, from the employer's point of view genuinely—dismissed for something else, but since there was a redundancy situation at the place of employment the Tribunal applied the presumption of redundancy: see *e.g. Dowdall* v. *Andrew Dunne & Sons Ltd.* (1977), and *Kelly* v. *W. Tallon Ltd.* (1980). It may therefore be that the onus goes beyond what is implied in the *Hindle* decision.

(4) Changes in work practice

It should also be noted that although, as mentioned above, changes in work practice can be a ground for redundancy, this does not apply where an employer, in the words of Widgery J. in *North Riding Garages Ltd.* v. *Butterwick* (1967), merely "insists on higher standards of efficiency than those previously required." An entitlement to a redundancy payment only arises in these circumstances under section 7(2) of the 1967 Act (as amended) where the work is to be done in a different manner "for which the employee is not sufficiently qualified or trained," as, for example, "if a motor manufacturer decides to use plastics instead of wood in the bodywork of his cars and dismisses his woodworkers" (Widgery J. in the *Butterwick* case).

CONTINUITY OF EMPLOYMENT

It is important for a number of reasons to determine the period of continuous employment of a particular employee with a particular employer (or with particular employers, see below). First, section 7(5) of the 1967 Act, as amended by the 1971 Act, provides that the applicant for a redundancy payment must have been employed by the dismissing employer for "a period of 104 weeks' continuous employment," but excluding any period with that employer before the applicant reached the age of 16. Secondly, it is vital for the purposes of calculating the amount of a redundancy payment to know the exact length of the employee's continuous employment.

(1) Presumption of continuity

What is meant by the term "continuous employment" is explained in Schedule 3 of the Act; furthermore, there is also, under section 10(*a*) of the 1971 Act, a presumption of continuity so that the burden of proof is on the employer if he wants to dispute that the applicant has been continuously employed for a particular period. This was illustrated by the case of *Kelly* v. *Tokus Grass Products* (1981). The employee was absent through illness for a period of three years. During all of this time he sent medical certificates and there was no formal dismissal. Eventually he resumed his work for the employers; another 22 months later he was made redundant. The E.A.T. decided that he was entitled to a redundancy payment, since in the absence of any formal dismissal at the time of his illness the presumption of continuity had not been displaced. A similar decision has been reached by the English Employment Appeal Tribunal: *Southwood Hostel Management Committee* v. *Taylor* (1979). Furthermore, in the case of *Sheehan* v. *Dwane* (1983) the Irish E.A.T. held that the applicant had not, by staying away from work for a week "in protest against an employee of the respondent," interrupted his continuity of employment, since the employer did not take any action at the time which could be construed as dismissal.

(2) Continuity and work interruptions

Paragraph 4A (inserted by the 1979 Act) of the Schedule provides that any period of notice due under the Minimum Notice and Terms of Employment Act 1973, but not given by the employer, must be added to the actual period of continuous employment, and paragraph 5 lists a series of events which, for the purposes of the legislation, do not interrupt continuity of service; these include specified periods of sickness, lay-off, holidays and strikes. Furthermore, where an employee is made redundant but resumes his employment with the same employer within 26 weeks his employment is deemed to be continuous. In all this it must be noted that these provisions apply regardless of the contract of employment, and are in addition to what the contract may itself provide.

An interesting feature of the case of *Kelly* v. *Tokus Grass Products* was that the period of illness of the employee (*i.e.* three years) was much longer than the 78 weeks which, under the 1967 Act, are specified as not breaking continuity; nevertheless Kelly was awarded a redundancy payment. This serves to emphasise again the existence of the presumption of continuity, and therefore the mere fact that the period of sickness, lay-off, and so forth, is longer than that set out in Schedule 3 does not necessarily mean that there is no continuous service. Two decisions of the E.A.T. (both relating to lay-off) underline this: *Creagh* v. *Lee Footwear Ltd.* (1980) and *Coleman* v. *F.K.M. General Engineering* (1981).

(3) Changes of ownership and transfers

The Acts also provide for certain safeguards which apply where there are changes in ownership of the company or business. For example, where a trade or business or an undertaking is partly or wholly transferred "from one person to another" the transfer does not disturb the continuity of employment of the existing workforce (para. 6 of Sched. 3, as amended). It has been held by McWilliam J. in the High Court that in such a case (provided that there is no dismissal under s.20 as explained below) continuity is preserved even if the new owner expressly disclaimed liability for the employee's previous service on the change of ownership: *Minister for Labour* v. *Clarke* (1977). On the other hand the E.A.T. has suggested, in *Murphy* v. *Doyle* (1978), that the old and new owners can decide between themselves as to who is to be liable under the Redundancy Payments Acts, as long as one of them assumes liability; it is a bit difficult to see, however, how the liability of the old employer, should that be the agreed solution, could apply beyond the transfer date so that continuity would be preserved.

Under section 20 of the 1967 Act, where an employee is dismissed in connection with a change of ownership of a business (or part of it) but is re-employed immediately by the new owner the case is treated as if the old employer had continued to employ him, provided the terms of employment stay the same; in such circumstances the *new* employer will, under section 20(5A) (which was inserted by the 1971 Act) be estopped from denying continuity should the issue arise, unless he informs the employee within 26 weeks of the change of ownership of his intention to deny continuity. Apparently the dismissal in connection with the change of ownership can be implied, as in the case of *McSorely* v. *Mogul of Ireland Ltd.* (1983), in which the applicant was merely asked to sign an "employment form" by the new owner. In the *McSorely* case the E.A.T. further explained that the concepts of "business" and "change" of ownership, used in the section, should be interpreted flexibly. An example of such flexibility was the case of *Tease* v. *McMahon Brothers Ltd.* (1982), in which the respondents had merely bought the premises, as distinct from the business, in which the applicant worked. But since they had also kept the workforce, the E.A.T. found that continuity had been preserved by virtue of section 20.

Section 6 of the 1971 Act further applies section 20 to cases where the "control or management" of a business changes, without there being a change of ownership. In addition, under section 16 of the 1967 Act the immediate re-engagement of an employee by an "associated" company will not disturb continuity. Companies are "associated" if one is a subsidiary of the other, or if both are subsidiaries of a third company. However, because of the use of the term "company" the section will not apply where either of the employers concerned is not a body corporate. In the case of *Bailey* v. *John McInerney* (1982), for example, the employee of a company was transferred to the respondents, who operated as a partnership and were directors and shareholders of the company; about 18 months later he was dismissed, but the E.A.T. was not prepared to accept that section 16 could apply, since the respondents were not a "company." The E.A.T. has also held that the section does not apply to a transfer from one company to another where both companies are controlled by the same *persons* as shareholders: *McGuinness* v. *National Film Distributor 1962 Ltd.* (1982).

In a more general way, continuity can be preserved even where there is a straightforward transfer from one employer to another and there is no change of ownership and no association between the employers. However, before this can apply section 9(3) of the 1967 Act requires that the re-employment be immediate, that it take place with the agreement of the employee and the two employers (*i.e.* old and new) concerned and that a written statement be given by the new employer to, and accepted in writing by, the employee, specifying *inter alia* that there is to be continuity: see *Moran* v. *J. O'Gorman & Co. Ltd.* (1975, E.A.T.).

For the purposes of the Acts continuity of employment is however broken where an employee accepts a redundancy payment and then resumes the employment relationship or is transferred to another employer (s.23 of the 1967 Act). However, Costello J. in the High Court has held that continuity is not broken in such circumstances if the employee returns the redundancy payment, always assuming of course that the other requirements of the Act are met: *O'Toole* v. *James O'Keefe & Co. Ltd.* (1981).

(4) The Acquired Rights Directive

The above provisions on change of ownership must be seen alongside the European Communities (Safeguarding of Employees' Rights on Transfer of Undertakings) Regulations 1980, implementing EEC Council Directive 77/187 (see Chapter 4). The Regulations provide that, in the case of a transfer of an undertaking, the "obligations" of the transferor move to the transferee. The British E.A.T. has held, in *Premier Motors (Medway) Ltd.* v. *Total Oil Great Britain Ltd.* (1983), that this includes the obligations under the redundancy payments scheme, so that the Regulations must be taken to preserve continuity in all cases to which they apply. This apparently means, according to *Premier Motors*, that the transferee is liable to pay a full redundancy payment for the period of continuous employment with the transferor even where he refuses to re-employ one of the latter's employees. The Regulations *permit* such a non-re-employment or dismissal under regulation 5(1) if it is "for economic, technical or organisational reasons entailing changes in the workforce," but do not thereby exempt either employer from liability under the 1967 Act.

(5) Casual labour and redundancy

In a recent test case, *Dublin Cargo Handling Ltd.* v. *Minister for Labour* (1983), the E.A.T. held that dockers in the deep sea section of Dublin port could claim continuous employment despite the essentially casual nature of their service, involving intermittent periods without work. In fact, in this context Dublin dock workers are governed by a separate statutory instrument, the Redundancy Payments (Dublin Port Dockers) Regulations 1971, under which the various stevedores are treated as being technically one employer for the purposes of redundancy payments; this was a crucial factor influencing the E.A.T. determination. Nevertheless, it is at any rate arguable that the decision could have implications for other employments of an essentially casual nature, again provided that the other requirements of the Redundancy Payments Acts are met.

ELIGIBILITY FOR REDUNDANCY PAYMENTS

The main burden to be discharged by an employee in dispute with his employer over eligibility for a redundancy payment is to show that he has in fact been dismissed, or in certain circumstances (as we

shall see below) that he has been laid off or put on short-time.
Apart from that, eligibility depends on some other requirements
being satisfied as well. Broadly speaking, the employee must
have been in continuous full-time employment, insurable under
the Social Welfare Acts, for a minimum period of 104 weeks (see
ss.4 and 7 of the 1967 Act as amended). The requirement of
full-time employment means that, under section 4(2) as
amended, the applicant must not be a worker "who is normally
expected to work for the same employer for less than 20 hours in
a week."

Section 3 of the 1971 Act, as amended by the 1979 Act, further
provides that an employee who on the date of the termination of his
employment has reached the current qualifying age under the Social
Welfare Act 1952 for an old-age pension (currently 66 years) is not
eligible for a redundancy payment. However, an employee who is
below that age but has been retained in employment beyond the
normal retirement age of that employment remains eligible: *Byrne* v.
Coates (Ireland) Ltd. (1978).

Furthermore, there are special rules for certain categories of
workers including apprentices and persons normally working outside the State, and the 1967 Act does not apply to close relatives
of the employer, or to employment in a private dwelling house or
on a farm where both the employer and the employee reside. Section 47 of the Act provides that the Minister for Labour can, after
consultations, set up "special redundancy schemes" for employees
not eligible under the Act, and section 15 of the 1971 Act (as
amended in 1979) deals with the administration of such schemes.
Lastly, Schedule 2 of the 1967 Act deals with special rules applying to a redundancy situation arising out of the death of the
employer.

It should be noted that under section 8 of the 1967 Act an
employee dismissed for redundancy, who has in the preceding four
years been laid off for an average annual period of more than 12
weeks, will become eligible for a redundancy payment only after a
similar period has expired from the date of dismissal (or lay-off, if it
is a redundancy by lay-off) without his being re-employed. In such
cases an employee must not unreasonably refuse an offer of re-
employment made during that period.

Finally, under section 51 of the 1967 Act the entitlement to a
redundancy payment cannot be waived, and "any provision in an
agreement" (including a contract of employment) that purports to
do so is void: see *Ward* v. *Talbot (Ireland) Ltd.* (1983).

REDUNDANCY AND MISCONDUCT

Of course, a dismissed worker will only be entitled to claim a redundancy payment if the reason for his dismissal is redundancy. This being so, it might appear odd that the Act specifically provides in section 14 that where an employer, "being entitled to terminate [the] employee's contract of employment without notice by reason of the employee's conduct," actually does dismiss him without notice, or with shorter notice than normally required, or with full notice accompanied by a statement that notice would not have been required, the employee will not be entitled to a redundancy payment. However, if the reason for the dismissal is misconduct then it is not redundancy, so that there would not in any case be an entitlement to a redundancy payment, whether or not the misconduct was sufficiently grave to justify summary dismissal under the contract of employment, and regardless of the amount of notice which was or was not given.

For example, in *O'Reilly* v. *Antigen Ltd.* (1983) the applicant, who was under notice of dismissal for redundancy, blockaded the factory entrance with his car in protest at his treatment, and when suspended, tried to force his way on to the premises. The E.A.T. held that his subsequent dismissal fell under section 14, since "his first dismissal was caused by his conduct." However, that really means no more than that it was *not* caused by the redundancy, so that section 14 cannot have made any difference to the outcome. The only circumstances in which the section might be relevant is where the employer is *entitled* to dismiss summarily for misconduct, but *actually* dismisses for redundancy, as where after a notice of redundancy has been given the employer discovers the existence of serious misconduct.

Subsection (2) then specifies that participation in a strike following on a notice of dismissal for redundancy does not allow the employer to dismiss the employee and at the same time invoke section 14 to justify a refusal to pay a redundancy payment. Section 14 of the Act is taken verbatim from the British legislation, as currently contained in section 82(2) and section 92 of the Employment Protection (Consolidation) Act 1978, and these sections have in turn been analysed by the British Employment Appeal Tribunal in the case of *Simmons* v. *Hoover* (1976), drawing on some previous decisions. The Tribunal pointed out that the sections had been described as "notorious" and that their interpretation had "caused considerable difficulty"; it concluded that the purpose of these provisions was to exclude certain persons from the general entitlement to redundancy payments and to ensure that where this applied "the employee is put on notice that he is being dismissed otherwise than in the ordinary course of the contract." Section 14(2) (in Ireland) is then merely an exclusion from an exclusion, and it does not confer any original rights; the British Tribunal further held that it only applies where a strike begins *after* the redundancy notice has been served, not to one which had already started and which then continued. Despite all this it must be said that section 14 of the Act is unclear both in its purpose and in its interpretation; it is not easy to see why such an unsatisfactory provision was copied *verbatim* from the English Act, and it is a clear candidate for amendment.

FACT OF DISMISSAL

In many respects the most difficult hurdle an employee claiming a redundancy payment from an unwilling employer is likely to have to cross is the need to prove that there was in fact a dismissal. "Dismissal" for the purposes of the redundancy payments scheme is defined in section 9(1) of the 1967 Act (as amended) as (a) termination by the employer of the contract of employment; (b) non-renewal on its expiry of a fixed-term contract; and (c) termination of the contract by the *employee* in circumstances which are "such that he is entitled so to terminate it by reason of the employer's conduct." The last of these is known as "constructive" dismissal (see below) and is approached in a similar way to constructive dismissal under the Unfair Dismissals Act 1977.

It must also be noted that an employer may argue that there was no dismissal in circumstances in which various contractual doctrines such as frustration or repudiation might be thought to apply. There is less evidence of such arguments being raised in redundancy cases than in unfair dismissal cases, but there have been a small number of examples. In the case of *Lynch* v. *J. Geraghty & Sons* (1981) the applicant was replaced when, after an accident, he told the employer that he would be absent "for a long time." The E.A.T. found that the contract of employment had been frustrated and that there was no dismissal. In fact, even if there had been no dispute about the fact of dismissal it would be difficult to see how the applicant could have succeeded in his claim for a redundancy payment, since the employer would presumably have had little difficulty in showing that the reason for dismissal was something other than redundancy.

Apart from constructive dismissal, an employee may resign and still get a redundancy payment in one other set of circumstances. Under section 10 of the 1967 Act (as amended in 1979), an employee who has been given notice of dismissal may, within the minimum period required (*e.g.* by the contract or by statute) for the employer's notice, give a shorter counter-notice. For the purposes of the redundancy payments scheme he will be taken to have been dismissed by the employer, unless the latter has required him to withdraw the counter-notice and he has "unreasonably" refused to do so. The date of dismissal will be the date on which the employee's notice expires.

Finally, it should be noted that where an employee is laid off for a period prior to the termination of his employment, he will not be deemed to have resigned by taking up temporary alternative employment elsewhere, provided that he is prepared and able to return to his original job as soon as the lay-off had ended; this was decided by the E.A.T. in the case of *Moran* v. *West of Ireland Security Ltd.* (1983).

CONSTRUCTIVE DISMISSAL

The case law, such as there is, on constructive dismissal suggests that it is not easy for an employee who has himself terminated his contract to succeed in a claim for a redundancy payment. It is possible that the circumstances which make up a constructive dismissal are less likely to occur in a redundancy situation than in unfair dismissal cases, except perhaps where an employer unilaterally redefines the terms and conditions of employment as a response to economic difficulties, or where he is prepared to use devious methods to avoid paying his share of the lump sum. In fact the cases are not very instructive, for while they show a reluctance on the part of the E.A.T. to construe section 9(1)(c) widely, there have been no general statements of the legal principles involved, in contrast to some of the cases under section 1 of the Unfair Dismissals Act 1977. Since the definitions used by the two Acts are not identical it must be considered doubtful whether decisions on one can be used in interpreting the other.

An example of where a redundancy was held to have arisen despite the employee's resignation was the case of *Matthew* v. *Donnellys Ltd.* (1977), in which an already given notice of redundancy had been "suspended," prompting the resignation. Similarly in *Margay* v. *Fingal Manufacturing Co. Ltd.* (1981), when the employers unilaterally introduced a three-day working week, the applicant

announced that she was "withdrawing from her contract of employment"; the E.A.T. held that this amounted to constructive dismissal
for redundancy. In *Meneely* v. *S. J. Bigger Ltd.* (1978) the E.A.T.
found that the employer's non-payment of agreed wage rates constituted a constructive dismissal.

However, a different conclusion was reached in the case of *Russell*
v. *Demag Industrial Equipment Ltd.* (1980). There were apparently
strong signs (not elaborated on in the report) that the respondent
company was facing closure, and in these circumstances the applicant terminated his contract, claiming a redundancy payment. The
E.A.T. found that this was a resignation, not a dismissal. A similar
decision was reached in the case of *Earls* v. *Edward Lee & Co. Ltd.*
(1980), in which the applicant resigned since he feared that his job
was going to be down-graded; the E.A.T. felt that his resignation
was, at least, premature, and no entitlement to a redundancy payment arose.

If one can draw any conclusion from this, it is that signs or warnings of a future or even imminent redundancy situation do not enti-
tle the employee to resign and then claim a redundancy payment, so
long as there is merely a climate of uncertainty and insecurity, as
distinct from a clear indication of the employer's intention to dismiss
the employee. This is particularly significant in recessionary times
when employees might be tempted prematurely to cut their losses
and look for work elsewhere. This point was also made in the British
case of *Morton Sundour Fabrics Ltd.* v. *Shaw* (1967); it was illustrated in
the Irish case of *Deegan* v. *Irish Biscuits Ltd.* (1980), in which the
respondent company had in fact declared its intention of cutting
back the category of staff to which the applicant belonged and had
commenced negotiations with the relevant trade union; not only
that, but the applicant was, when he resigned, given ambiguous
information concerning his entitlement to a redundancy payment.
Nevertheless his claim before the E.A.T. failed, and he was held not
to have been dismissed.

CHANGES IN THE PLACE OR NATURE OF THE WORK

Another difficult question is whether transferring an employee to
another place of work amounts to constructive dismissal for the purposes of the Redundancy Payments Acts. There are two dimensions
to this problem, one being the location of the place of employment
and the other the nature of the work to be carried out at the new
place by the employee. If an employee is merely being asked to carry

out substantially the same work, for the same pay, at a place very close to where he worked previously (*e.g.* another part of the same building or plant) there is clearly no ground for resigning and claiming a redundancy payment.

(1) Transfers

However, there are some English cases which suggest that transfers of a more serious nature may amount to constructive dismissal. In *O'Brien* v. *Associated Fire Alarms* (1968) the Court of Appeal held that the dismissal of employees who refused to move from Liverpool to Scotland was a dismissal for redundancy, and it would therefore seem possible to argue that a resignation because of such a transfer would be a constructive dismissal; but this would clearly depend on other factors, and in particular on the terms of the contract and whether these envisaged some degree of mobility.

(2) Changes in work practice

In another recent case the English E.A.T. held that moving a skilled worker to another department involving unskilled work only was a constructive dismissal: *Millbrook Furnishing Industries Ltd.* v. *McIntosh* (1981). But Browne Wilkinson J. also pointed out that there was no constructive dismissal "if an employer, under the stresses of the requirements of his business, directs an employee to transfer to other suitable work on a purely temporary basis and at no diminution in wages" (p. 311). It should of course be stressed that in all cases of constructive dismissal an employee will only be awarded a redundancy payment if all the other requirements of the Acts relating to redundancy are met.

SUITABLE ALTERNATIVE EMPLOYMENT

Section 15 of the 1967 Act, as amended by the 1971 and 1979 Acts, excludes from the entitlement to a redundancy payment all those employees who have been offered a renewal of their contracts or new contracts of employment, either with the same terms, or with different terms which constitute an "offer of suitable employment," where they "unreasonably refuse" the employer's offer. In other words, where an employee who is being made redundant receives an offer of suitable alternative employment which is to take effect (in the case of the same contractual terms) at or before the date of dismissal or (in the case of different terms) not later than four weeks after the date of dismissal, he will lose his entitlement to a redundancy payment if he unreasonably refuses that offer.

Where an employer offers alternative employment in terms which differ from those of the previous job, the offer must under section 15(2)(a) be made in writing. If the employer neglects to do this, he will not be able to claim that the employee is excluded from the entitlement to a redundancy payment, even if the latter has quite unreasonably refused a perfectly suitable alternative job; this has been held by the E.A.T. in a number of cases, including *Burke* v. *Irish Sisters of Charity* (1980); *Brennan* v. *Cross Channel Carriers Ltd.* (1979); and *Stockil* v. *Ranks (Ireland) Ltd.* (1980).

(1) Suitability of employment

Overall, the crucial point under section 15 is what constitutes an "unreasonable" refusal of alternative employment or, seen from another angle, what is a "suitable" alternative job. As is the experience in so many other contexts, the case law of the E.A.T. discloses very few statements of legal principle, and all one can do is to present the Tribunal's reaction to one or two sets of facts. In *Farren* v. *Edward Lee & Co. Ltd.* (1980) the respondent company was taken over by a chainstore group and the applicant, who was trained as a shop assistant, was offered a new job which largely involved operating a cash register (but little else). She refused, and the E.A.T. held that her refusal was not unreasonable and that she was entitled to a redundancy payment.

A similar decision was reached in the case of *Gallagher and Colleran* v. *O'Mahony* (1980), in which the applicants had been employed as garage mechanics. They were offered new jobs involving fuel sales only, and their refusal was held not to have been unreasonable. Furthermore in *Fitzgerald* v. *Hally & Sons Ltd.* (1982) it was held that a new job which, unlike the former position, did not involve free transport to work could be refused without prejudicing the right to a redundancy payment. Work in a different place some distance from the original place of work, and thus involving a lot of extra travelling and expense, can also be reasonably refused: *McLaughlin* v. *Alliance and Dublin Consumers' Gas Co. Ltd.* (1979).

Apart from the above cases involving less advantageous terms of employment, an employee can also reasonably refuse alternative jobs for which he is not adequately qualified or trained. For example, in *Stafford* v. *Stafford* (1983) the applicant's employment as a farm worker came to an end and he was offered the job of lorry driver; he was held to be entitled to refuse this since he did not have the necessary driving licence. On the other hand, the E.A.T. has held that a change in the terms of employment which was permitted under an express or implied term of the contract cannot be reasonably refused: *Lynch* v. *Donnelly's (Dublin) Ltd.* (1978).

If one were to attempt tentatively to abstract some general conclusion from the above, it might be that an alternative job which involves any significant reduction of responsibility or worsening of terms and conditions of employment (including pay and benefits in kind) is not suitable alternative employment for the purposes of the Acts and can be refused quite reasonably. Furthermore, the British E.A.T. had held that the employee's decision in such cases should be judged objectively—*i.e.* from the employee's own point of view at the time when the decision was made: *Executors of J. F. Everest* v. *Cox* (1980). The question therefore is whether the employee acted reasonably in the light of the facts known to him and his perception of those facts at the time when the offer of alternative employment was made. A refusal can therefore be reasonable even if it was based on an incorrect assessment of the circumstances, provided that it was an honest assessment.

(2) Trial periods

The Redundancy Payments Acts also allow employees to "try out" alternative jobs to test their suitability. Section 15(2A) of the 1967 Act (inserted by the 1971 Act) provides as follows:

> "Where an employee who has been offered suitable employment and has carried out, for a period of not more than four weeks, the duties of that employment, refuses the offer, the temporary acceptance of that employment shall not solely constitute an unreasonable refusal for the purposes of this section."

What this means is that if an employee temporarily accepts an offer of alternative employment and works in the new job for not longer than four weeks, but then refuses the offer, his temporary acceptance does not make the ultimate refusal unreasonable. However, this is a negative provision, in that it does not make the refusal reasonable: it merely means that the employee does not burn his bridges by trying out the new job for a while.

It appears in fact that it is not necessarily fatal if the employee waits beyond the end of the four week period before signalling his refusal. In *Crawley* v. *Trophies (Ireland) Ltd.* (1981) the applicant worked in the new job for two months before finally rejecting it, but the E.A.T. found that his refusal was still not unreasonable. The decision is somewhat unsatisfactory, since the E.A.T. did not state what exactly it was basing its decision on. However there were special circumstances involved in the case, including a move to England; in the ordinary course of events one would not expect the E.A.T. to allow trying-out periods going beyond the statutory four weeks, since this would generate great uncertainty in the employer-employee relationship.

Section 15(2B), inserted by the 1979 Act, also provides that an alternative job involving a "substantial" reduction in pay or working hours of up to 50 per cent. can be accepted temporarily by an employee for a period not exceeding 52 weeks; during that time it will not be taken as an acceptance of an offer of alternative employment.

LAY-OFF AND SHORT-TIME

In most cases an employee who intends to claim a redundancy payment will have to show that he has been dismissed. However, in certain circumstances employees who have been laid off or put on short-time are eligible as well. In such situations common law questions relating to the contract of employment can arise (see Chapter 3); it should be noted, for example, that the imposition of short-time by an employer may amount to a repudiation of the contract, thus entitling the employee to claim *dismissal* for redundancy: see *Treanor* v. *Stedfast Ltd.* (1980)

"Lay-off" is defined in section 11(1) of the 1967 Act as a cessation of employment caused by the employer's inability to provide work, but where the employer believes that this is temporary and he gives the employee notice to that effect *before* the cessation. "Short-time" is defined in section 11(2) (as amended by the 1979 Act) as a reduction in remuneration or hours of work by 50 per cent. in any week caused by diminished requirements for the work the employee performs under his contract of employment, provided that this is temporary and the employer gives notice to that effect prior to the reduction. The Act does not however apply to any lay-off or short-time which is "wholly or mainly attributable to a strike or lock-out," regardless of where the strike or lock-out has occurred: section 13(4)(b).

In all cases the employer must give the notice required *before* the beginning of the lay-off or short-time. He cannot for example dismiss an employee and then claim afterwards that it was a lay-off: *Kavanagh* v. *Johnston and McInerney Ltd.* (1977, E.A.T.). Furthermore, his belief that the fall-off in demand for the employee's work is temporary must be "reasonable in the circumstances"; so for example, if a cessation of work clearly looks like being permanent, a lay-off notice will be taken to be a dismissal: *Magee* v. *Solarship (Ireland) Ltd.* (1981, E.A.T.). Similarly, where the employer initiates a "lay-off" clearly knowing that the cessation of employment is permanent, his action will amount to a repudiation of the contract which, as a constructive dismissal, gives an entitlement to a redundancy payment: see Costello J. in *Industrial Yarns Ltd.* v. *Greene* (1983).

Where the above conditions are met the employee may be entitled to a redundancy payment under section 12 of the 1967 Act (as substituted by the 1971 Act), but only if the lay-off or short-time has continued for a period of four or more consecutive weeks, or at least six non-consecutive weeks within a period of 13 weeks. The employee must then give to the employer something called a "notice of intention to claim" within four weeks of the lay-off or short-time having ceased. If he terminates his contract of employment by giving the correct notice within that same period he will also be deemed to have given "a notice of intention to claim." If these procedural requirements are not complied with there is, in the absence of dismissal, no entitlement to a redundancy payment: see *e.g. Perry* v. *George Little & Sons Ltd.* (1982).

Where an employee gives a notice of intention to claim, the employer can under section 13 give within seven days a counter-notice refusing a redundancy payment. However, under section 13(1) this has effect only if on the date of the employee's notice it was "reasonably to be expected" that he would within four weeks "enter upon a period of employment of not less than thirteen weeks" without lay-off or short-time; only then will the employer's counter-notice allow him to escape the obligation to pay a redundancy payment. However, if at the end of the four-week period the employee is still on lay-off or short-time, the employer's counter-notice is inoperative since the essential condition of section 13(1) has as a matter of fact not been met: see *Keddy* v. *James A. Gibb Ltd.* (1982).

REDUNDANCY PROCEDURES

In a case where there is no dispute between the employer and the employee about the fact of or the reason for dismissal or the entitlement to a payment, the procedure to be followed is relatively straight-forward. Under section 17 of the 1967 Act (as amended) the employer must give notice in writing to the employee of the proposed dismissal at least two weeks beforehand and must send a copy to the Minister for Labour; it is a criminal offence not to comply with this provision, and it will also lower the amount of the rebate given to the employer out of the Redundancy Fund (see below).

The employer must in addition, on or before the date of dismissal, furnish the employee with a certificate known as the "redundancy certificate" (on a special form available from the Department of Labour). It is vital for an employer to issue this; Kenny J. held in the case of *Minister for Labour* v. *O'Connor and Irish Dunlop Ltd.* (1972) that payment of a lump sum without the certificate did not necessarily discharge the employer's statutory obligation. As soon as the dismissal takes effect the employer must finally pay the lump sum.

If the employer has furnished a redundancy certificate but paid no money, then under section 32 of the 1967 Act (as amended in 1971) the employee can, if he has "taken all reasonable steps (other than legal proceedings) to obtain the payment of the lump sum from the employer" and has failed or the employer is insolvent or has died, get his payment directly from the central Redundancy Fund (see below). In such cases, section 32(3), as amended, provides that the Minister for Labour becomes the legal bearer of all the employee's rights and remedies in relation to the redundancy lump sum, or whatever part of it has been paid out of the central fund, so that he can seek to recover the sum (minus the appropriate rebate) from the employer, or from the employer's estate where he is deceased. The Minister is also entitled to claim, under section 32(5), "in the bankruptcy, arrangement, administration of the insolvent estate or winding up (as the case may be)" where the employer is insolvent.

However, when there is a dispute between the parties this is taken to the Employment Appeals Tribunal. The procedures of the Tribunal are outlined in Chapter 9, below, but it should be noted here that, under section 24 of the 1967 Act (as amended), an employee will lose his entitlement to a payment unless he brings a claim in writing within 52 weeks of the date of dismissal. This period can be extended by the E.A.T. to 104 weeks if the failure to bring a claim in time was "due to a reasonable cause," and can be extended further if the reason for the delay was connected with the employer's failure to comply with his statutory obligations relating to the giving of notice or the redundancy certificate where there was a change of ownership or transfer of the employee. In other cases the E.A.T. has held that the employee's ignorance of his statutory rights is a "reasonable cause" justifying an extension of the time limit to 104 weeks: *Kelly* v. *Brian Kenna* (1982).

CALCULATION OF THE LUMP SUM

The amount of the lump sum is determined by a calculation set out in Schedule 3 of the 1967 Act, as amended. It consists of:

(a) a sum equivalent to the employee's "normal weekly remuneration"; plus

(b) half of his normal weekly remuneration for each year of continuous employment between the date on which the employee turned sixteen years old and the date on which he turned forty-one (or up to the termination of the contract of employment); plus

(c) his full weekly remuneration for each year of continuous employment from the date of his forty-first birthday until the dismissal, *i.e.* up to the termination of the contract.

However, a number of things need to be taken into account in this calculation. First, it must be noted again that it is based on the employee's "continuous employment," so that breaks in continuity of the kind discussed earlier will lower the sum. Service for the purposes of the calculation will then run from the date of commencement of employment after the break in continuity. It should also be noted that there is a distinction between "reckonable" and "continuous" employment, in that paragraphs 8 and 10 of the Schedule exclude certain absences from work from "reckonable service": they are not counted for the purposes of calculating the amount of the lump sum, even though they do not necessarily disturb continuity.

Secondly, the basic unit is the employee's "normal weekly remuneration," which is determined in accordance with paragraphs 13 to 24 of the Schedule (as amended). Broadly, it consists of his fixed gross earnings plus his average weekly overtime earnings (if any). If the employee's pay has been reduced without his consent, then the former earnings must be used for calculating the payment: *Valentine* v. *Castle Hosiery Ltd.* (1971). On the other hand, the British E.A.T. has held that back-dated pay increases agreed after the date of dismissal cannot increase the lump sum: *Leyland Vehicles Ltd.* v. *Reston* (1981). There are also special rules for determining the normal weekly remuneration of workers whose pay is not fixed, who are paid by piece rates or who are entitled to payments such as bonuses or commissions; the provisions on these should be consulted in the Act.

Finally, there is an upper limit to the amount of earnings on which the calculation can be based. Under the Redundancy Payments (Lump Sum) Regulations 1983 (amending para. 2 of the Schedule) "any part of an employee's earnings per annum in excess of £11,000 shall be disregarded" for the purposes of the calculation. In other words, if an employee earns, say, £15,000 per annum, his redundancy lump sum will be calculated as if he were on a salary of £11,000. For persons earning less than £11,000 the actual salary is taken. This upper limit is varied from time to time, so that it is always advisable to check it with the Department of Labour.

It must also be noted that the lump sum is calculated in accordance with the law *at the date of dismissal*. If an employee brings a case to the E.A.T. he cannot benefit (or suffer) from legal changes made by the Oireachtas or the Minister between the date of dismissal and the date of the hearing: *Cowpar* v. *Clover Meats Limited* (1979).

It might be asked whether the amount of the statutory redundancy payment is really adequate; in Britain, for example, the statutory rates are significantly higher. It must further be noted that many lump sum payments negotiated voluntarily between employers and trade unions in collective agreements are significantly above the statutory minimum level, and indeed there is a general expectation among unionised workers that it should be so. Recently the Irish Transport and General Workers' Union claimed that four to six weeks' pay per year of service was the general trend in negotiated redundancy settlements. The Federated Union of Employers disputed the figure but did acknowledge that in the majority of agreements two weeks' pay per year of service was paid (*Irish Times*, October 8, 1983). As the system operates, therefore, it might be said to discriminate against those relatively few employees who only secure the statutory minimum, frequently because they are not union members.

THE REDUNDANCY FUND

The employer does not actually have to pay all of the redundancy payment himself but will, if all the required procedures are properly carried out, get a rebate from a central fund known as the Redundancy Fund. This was set up under Part III of the 1967 Act. The fund is administered by the Minister for Labour and is financed through weekly contributions by employers for each employee currently in employment and advances made by the Minister for Finance from time to time as the need arises. Under the Protection of Employees (Employers' Insolvency) Bill 1984 the Fund is to be renamed the Redundancy and Employers' Insolvency Fund. In addition to the rebates discussed below, this Bill (necessitated by EEC Council Directive 80/987) when enacted will provide for certain payments out of the fund to employees whose employers have become insolvent. The payments (relating to debts under employment contracts, statutory debts under protective legislation, and so forth), their calculation and mode of payment are specified under section 5 of the Bill.

However, the main function of the Redundancy Fund will continue to be to provide rebates in redundancy cases. Under section 29 of the 1967 Act (as amended in 1979) an employer making a redundancy payment is normally entitled to a rebate out of the Fund of 60 per cent. of the statutory payment, but this can be reduced down to a lower limit of 40 per cent. if the employer has not given the proper notice to the employee and the Minister. However, an employer will get no rebate if he has paid a lump sum to an employee who was not entitled to it under the Acts, even if the E.A.T. on the basis of incorrect information awarded a payment; nor will he get a rebate for any amount paid above the statutory sum calculated in the manner described above: see *Scotts Food Ltd.* v. *Deciding Officer* (1980, E.A.T.), and *Cormac Murray Ltd.* v. *Minister for Labour* (1977, E.A.T.).

If the Minister for Labour feels that the redundancy payment was in any way improperly or inappropriately paid, he will refuse to pay any rebate out of the Fund. The Minister, it might be noted here, is also entitled to be represented in E.A.T. proceedings, since he has a vested interest in the outcome of these cases. In some of these matters the functions of the Minister may be carried out by officials in his Department known as "Deciding Officers." An employer dissatisfied with a decision taken on behalf of the Minister may bring an appeal to the E.A.T.

VARIOUS PROVISIONS OF THE ACT

A small number of final points need to be made about the redundancy payments scheme.

(1) Winding up or insolvency

Redundancies may frequently take place in circumstances where there appear to be few chances of actually securing a payment. In such cases the employee may, as already noted, be able to secure his payment directly from the Redundancy Fund, but there are additional safeguards as well. Under section 42 of the 1967 Act (as amended in 1979) the employer's debts under the Act in respect of redundancy payments are counted as debts which have priority in the distribution in the assets of a company (under the Companies Act 1963) or in the distribution of the property of a bankrupt.

(2) Time off while under notice

Under section 7 of the 1979 Act an employee who has been given notice of dismissal for redundancy (and who has been employed for two years) may, during the two weeks before the notice expires, take "reasonable time off" during working hours to seek or be trained for future employment, on full pay. The employer may in such circumstances seek evidence that the employee is actually using the time off in the intended manner. Where an employer refuses unreasonably to allow time off, the matter can be taken to the E.A.T., which may award compensation recoverable as a contract debt.

COLLECTIVE REDUNDANCIES

It is necessary finally to comment briefly on the employer's procedural obligations in the case of collective redundancies, as provided for in the Protection of Employment Act 1977. This legislation was necessitated by Ireland's membership of the European Economic Community and more particularly by the EEC Council Directive 75/129 on Collective Redundancies. The purpose of the Directive, as outlined in Article 2, is to ensure that where an employer dismisses a certain number of workers within a specified period "for one or more reasons not related to the individual workers concerned," he must observe certain procedures. These are consultation with the workers' representatives, and the notification of the impending redundancies to the public authorities of the State. The 1977 Act is intended to implement this Directive, and it applies to dismissals for redundancy as defined in section 7 of the Redundancy Payments Act 1967 (as amended).

(1) Application of the Act

Under section 6 the Act applies to a situation where in a period of 30 days a number of employees are dismissed for redundancy in the same "establishment." The minimum number of dismissals needed to bring about the Act's application varies depending on the size of the total workforce. In an establishment normally employing 21 to 49 employees (inclusive) the Act applies if at least five are dismissed within 30 days; at least 10 in an establishment employing 50 to 99; at least 10 per cent. in an establishment employing 100 to 299; and at least 30 persons in an establishment employing 300 employees or more. This means that the Act does not apply at all to establishments employing 20 persons or less, nor does it apply to, say, redundancies within 30 days of less than 30 employees in a large establishment of 300 or more employees.

An "establishment" for the purposes of the Act is defined in section 6(3) as a "location" where an employer carries on business; each location is taken separately where an employer operates at more than one. Section 6(3)(b) defines "location" by giving a number of examples, including "workplace, factory, mine, quarry, dockyard, . . . office, shop" and so forth. The section also specifies that the total number of employees counted should include those "who are based at the establishment but who also perform some of their duties elsewhere." Under section 8 the total number is calculated by taking the average number of those employed within the last 12 months.

As already noted, the Act applies to dismissals for redundancies. It does not apply however to certain categories of persons, such as persons employed under fixed-term contracts where these expire, State employees, local government officers or employees of bankrupt persons or companies being wound up under a court order.

(2) The employer's obligations

The main obligations under the Act are summarised as "consultation and notification." Taking the latter obligation first, under section 12 the employer must, if he "proposes to create collective redundancies" as explained above, notify in writing the Minister for Labour at least 30 days before the first dismissal takes effect of his proposal, and a copy must be sent to the "employees' representatives" (*i.e.* usually their trade union). If he fails to do this, or if he effects the redundancies before the 30 days have expired, he is guilty of an offence. It must be noted that the Act does not adopt the Directive's approach of allowing a reduction of the period of notice in certain special circumstances.

Under section 9 of the Act the employer must, also at least 30 days before the first dismissal, enter into consultations with the employees' representatives "with a view to reaching an agreement." "Consultations" must include a discussion on the way in which the redundancies are to be implemented and, significantly, on whether they can be avoided, reduced or the consequences mitigated.

For the purposes of these consultations the employer must provide certain written information, including the reasons for the redundancies, the number of employees affected and the period during which the dismissals are to take effect. Again, non-compliance with any of these obligations is, under section 11, a criminal offence.

Furthermore, the employer must keep adequate records and show these on request to an "authorised officer" appointed by the Minister for Labour. The latter officers may inspect the premises where persons are employed to check that the Act's provisions are being implemented. It should also be noted that the Act cannot be derogated from or waived in a contract of employment or a collective agreement.

(3) Comments

The Act is to some extent an unsatisfactory piece of legislation. It follows the rather curious tradition of some Irish protective statutes of enforcement via Department of Labour prosecutions. Indeed, short of that it provides no remedies, in contrast with the scheme of "protective awards" available under Part IV of the British Employment Protection Act 1975, which also deals with collective redundancies; it may to that extent be an inadequate implementation of the EEC Directive.

It is also to some extent not clear exactly what the substantive requirements of the Act are. Section 9 requires consultation "with a view to reaching an agreement." This follows the wording of Article 2 of the EEC Directive, and it may perhaps be equated with the American statutory concept (under the National Labor Relations Act 1935) of "bargaining in good faith." However, the Act gives no guidance on how this should be approached in individual cases. How, for example, should one assess a situation in which an employer bases his decision to make workers redundant on an economic assessment of his enterprise from which he is unwilling to depart but which the union rejects? When in addition to this the onus of acting against a recalcitrant employer is on the Department of Labour and its officials, who do not have the same vested interest as an affected trade union in contesting the employer's position, it is possible to envisage a less than satisfactory outcome in a number of cases.

Furthermore, it appears that the Department of Labour will not prosecute an employer who, while giving the correct notice and appearing to be ready to "consult," has already taken irrevocable decisions which pre-determine the date, extent and precise nature of the proposed redundancies. At least one such case occurred in 1982, and if the Department's policy is to be continued the substantive obligation to consult is rendered quite meaningless. In another case the Department refused to prosecute an insolvent company which closed down with just one day's notice; the refusal was justified because, as was explained in a letter, "it does not appear to the Minister that any useful purpose would be served by initiating a prosecution." Clearly that is not a satisfactory approach.

Another difficulty arises in the context of the duty to consult. The Act provides that consultations should take place with "employees' representatives." These in turn are defined in section 2 as "officials (including shop stewards) of a trade union or of a staff association with which it has been the practice of the employer to conduct collective bargaining negotiations." In section 9 it is further stated that the representatives should be persons "representing the employees affected by the proposed redundancies."

None of this presents any difficulties if one union represents all workers in the establishment. But it is much more difficult if there are several unions and/or associations and if there are some non-unionists. For example, if an employer proposes to make redundant a number of non-unionists in a plant where he negotiates with several trade unions, whom exactly must he consult, if anyone? One must presume that the intention of the Act is to make *some* consultation obligatory in all collective redundancies, so that it should be wise for an employer to consult *all* unions which have negotiation rights, regardless of which one, if any, has the affected workers in its membership. After all, even the remaining workers (those not to be dismissed) could be said to be "affected by the proposed redundancies." However, the Act does not spell this out. In any case it is doubtful, as the Federated Union of Employers has pointed out, whether there is in the Act adequate protection for non-unionists (*FUE Opinion on Protection of Employment Bill 1976*, February 4, 1977).

Finally, it must be asked whether the combination (prompted by the EEC Directive) of requiring a minimum number of dismissals before the Act applies, with the number varying depending on the size of the workforce, and the use of the "establishment" as the basic unit, is either wise or desirable. It could allow some employers to manipulate the number and location of dismissed employees so as to avoid any obligations. It would have been much better to require the employer to notify and consult in all cases of dismissal for redundancy. On the other hand, the Federated Union of Employers has taken the view that the 1977 Act is already too onerous and, in that it applies to as few as five dismissals in firms employing 20 to 50 persons, that it amounts to "a direct form of discrimination against smaller firms whose resources are inadequate to meet the [Act's] requirements" (*FUE Opinion*, see above).

9 Tribunals

INTRODUCTION

One of the features of the new generation of protective statutes
which began with the Redundancy Payments Act 1967 and are concerned largely with dismissal and employment equality is the new
system through which these Acts are enforced. Previously protective
legislation was enforced by way of criminal prosecutions brought by
an inspectorate based, for the most part, in the Department of
Labour; in fact, in those areas where protective legislation had
already developed before 1967 (*i.e.* health and safety, conditions of
work, and so forth) the same enforcement procedures continue to be
used even in more recent statutes.

The old system, relying largely on Department of Labour prosecutions, has arguably not proved to be a success. The imposition of
criminal liability, with fairly minor fines as penalties, does not
encourage a positive frame of mind in those whom the legislation
seeks to control. Furthermore, when the initiative for enforcement
rests with a government department it may, for a variety of reasons,
take a different attitude to a breach of statutory obligations than
those directly affected by the breach, and indeed may lack the
resources and manpower to ensure compliance in every workplace
and in all circumstances. In this context the emergence of a system
in which the legislation is enforced through claims taken by
aggrieved persons to tripartite tribunals was to be welcomed.
Although we are here concerned only with labour tribunals, it may
be noted that they are part of a development which has been in evidence throughout the administrative process, in particular since the
report in Britain of the Committee on Administrative Tribunals and
Inquiries (the Franks Committee, 1957, Cmnd. 218). Tribunals are
thought to provide speedy, inexpensive and informal justice in specialised areas in which the tribunal members have expert knowledge, and the field of employment is an obvious example of where
such attributes are of benefit. In Britain the system of industrial

tribunals was set up under the Industrial Training Act 1964, and following the recommendations of the Donovan Commission (*Report of the Royal Commission on Trade Unions and Employers' Associations,* 1968, Cmnd. 3623, Chapter X) it was extended rapidly into a number of areas of employment law.

In Ireland the operation of quasi-judicial tribunals is affected by the provisions of the 1937 Constitution, under which justice must be administered by the courts of law. However, under Article 37 "limited functions and powers of a judicial nature" can be exercised by non-judicial bodies. This permits the operation as such of tribunals, but it has some consequences in relation to their functions and for the enforcement of their determinations (for a review of the constitutional questions involved, see J.M. Kelly, *The Irish Constitution,* 1984, pp. 363–8).

There are two tribunals operating in employment matters in Ireland, these being the Employment Appeals Tribunal and the Labour Court. It is difficult to see why there should be two tribunals involved and, as we shall see in a moment, the Labour Court was in any case an odd choice for such a role. For some time now it has been argued by interested persons and bodies that the function of adjudicating under protective employment statutes should be exercised in all cases by the same tribunal, and that this should be the Employment Appeals Tribunal (E.A.T.). However, in view of the growing criticism of the way in which the E.A.T. performs its role these arguments have lost their urgency, and a more fundamental review now seems necessary.

THE EMPLOYMENT APPEALS TRIBUNAL

Section 39 of the Redundancy Payments Act 1967 set up the Redundancy Appeals Tribunal to hear applications brought under the Act. It was re-named the Employment Appeals Tribunal under section 18 of the Unfair Dismissals Act 1977. Its procedures are governed by the various Acts under which it has jurisdiction (see below), as well as by the Redundancy (Redundancy Appeals Tribunal) Regs. 1968 (which we shall hereafter refer to as the Redundancy Regs.) and the Unfair Dismissals (Claims and Appeals) Regs. 1977 (the U.D. Regs.).

(a) Composition

The E.A.T. has a chairman, who must be a practising barrister or solicitor of at least seven years' standing, and seven vice-chairmen, who in practice satisfy the same requirement of legal qualification although there is no statutory provision to that effect. There is also an equal number of members nominated by various employers' organisations (including the Irish Employers' Confederation, the Construction Industry Federation, the Federation of Trade Associations and the farming organisations) and by the Irish Congress of Trade Unions. The Tribunal sits in divisions, in accordance with section 39(11) of the 1967 Act. Each division consists of a chairman (or vice-chairman), and one member each from the nominees of each side of industry. Originally there were four divisions, but this has been increased to eight. Two of the vice-chairmen are based in Cork, and the rest in Dublin; the Tribunal does however sit regularly in other towns throughout the State. At each hearing there is also present a clerk, who records the proceedings and assists in other ways but who is not a member of the tribunal.

(b) Jurisdiction

The original jurisdiction of the E.A.T. was under the Redundancy Payments Acts, but it has been extended to cover disputes under the Minimum Notice and Terms of Employment Act 1973, the Unfair Dismissals Act 1977 (the U.D.A.), and the Maternity Protection of Employees Act 1981. An employee bringing an application to the E.A.T. can claim under all of these Acts at the same time, although complications may set in if the applicant is claiming under the U.D.A. or the Maternity Act and, at the same time, under the Redundancy or the Minimum Notice Acts, since the procedures are different under the two former statutes (see below).

The terminology used by the Acts for applications brought under them varies. Under the Redundancy Payments Acts the E.A.T. hears "appeals"; under the Minimum Notice and Terms of Employment Act 1973 disputes about minimum notice are referred to the E.A.T. "for arbitration"; under the U.D.A. and the 1981 Act the E.A.T. hears "claims"; and under the two latter Acts the E.A.T. can also hear "appeals" from decisions of Rights Commissioners (see below). All this leads to the confusing practice whereby the Tribunal varies the description of the party bringing the case depending on the Act under which it is brought—*i.e.* "appellant," "claimant," and so forth. In this book we have used the term "applicant" throughout, since it can cover all of these categories and is a term which has in fact been used by some High Court judges in cases under these Acts.

(c) Bringing an application

Applications to the E.A.T. are made on special forms (RP51A) available from the Tribunal or the Department of Labour; the same form is used for all the relevant Acts. The kind of details which the employee must give include name and address, the name and address of the employer, pay, and so forth. He must also name the Act or Acts under which he is claiming, the grounds of the application, and the redress sought. Finally, the employee must give the name and address of his representative, if any (see below).

In bringing an application, the employee must observe the time limits specified under each Act (except the 1973 Act). It must in particular be noted that section 8(2) of the U.D.A. requires that a notice in writing be given to the Rights Commissioner (see below) or the E.A.T. within six months and that "a copy of the notice shall be given to the employer concerned within the same period." From an early stage the practice developed whereby the applicant gave the notice required to the E.A.T. and the Tribunal passed a copy on to the respondent employer. In the case of *Hayes* v. *B and I Line* (1979) the E.A.T. held that while the onus of giving the copy to the employer was on the applicant, this onus was discharged if the Tribunal in fact sent the copy; it further held that if the copy was not given to the employer within the six months period the E.A.T. was still "at liberty (if it thinks it proper in the exercise of its discretion) to hear and determine a claim."

In *I.B.M. Ireland Ltd.* v. *Feeney* (1982) Judge Ryan in the Circuit Court reached a different conclusion on the latter point. He held that the requirement of section 8(2) of the U.D.A. "is mandatory and requires that the employee shall furnish a copy of the notice in question to the employer within six months of the date of the relevant dismissal" (p. 51). Subsequently, in the case of *State* (*I.B.M. Ireland Ltd.*) v. *Employment Appeals Tribunal* (1983) counsel for the employers argued that the principle should be extended so that a copy of the notice would not have been "given" unless it was given directly by the employee to the employer; it would not be sufficient for the E.A.T. to send on a copy. This was, rightly in our view, rejected by Hamilton J. in the High Court; he held that the onus of giving the copy is indeed on the applicant, but that if it is given to the respondent it does not in fact matter who actually gave it.

Regulation 9(1) of the Redundancy Regulations and regulation 5(1) of the U.D. Regulations provide that the employer must, within 14 days of receiving a copy of the appropriate notice, "enter an appearance"; this means that he must, on a form obtainable from the Department of Labour, give certain details and indicate whether and on what grounds he intends to contest the application. Under regulation 9(2) and regulation 5(2), respectively, the employer is not entitled to take any part in or be represented at the proceedings unless he has thus submitted a notice of appearance; this has been applied in some cases, as *e.g. Wilmot* v. *O'Connor* (1983). In some recent cases, for example in *Connolly* v. *Malone* (1983), the E.A.T. has invited the applicant to "waive" this requirement, but when the applicant in each case refused the Tribunal excluded the employer and found the dismissal unfair; in fact there is nothing in the regulations which suggests that an applicant *can* "waive" this legal requirement, and we would submit that this approach of the E.A.T. is wrong. Furthermore, in *McConnell* v. *McKenna Properties* (1982) the E.A.T., having excluded the employer in relation to the substantive question of unfair dismissal, then did hear him on the question of costs; this again is inconsistent with the very clear wording of the regulations, under which the employer should remain excluded for all of the proceedings.

In relation to all of the notices required of the parties, they are "given" only when received, not when posted. This was held in a number of British cases, *e.g. House* v. *Emerson Electric Industrial Controls* (1980), and also by the Irish E.A.T.: *Cunningham* v. *Crosspan Developments Ltd.* (1980). However, the British E.A.T. has held that a notice is "received" on the day it arrives on the addressee's premises, even if this is after office hours: *Post Office* v. *Moore* (1981).

It has also been held that the failure of the applicant to name the respondent correctly will not invalidate the application if the real respondent received the necessary notice and knew, or should reasonably have known, that it referred to him. In *Gillen* v. *J.V. Hennessy (Ireland) Ltd.* (1982) the notice was sent to a director of the respondents, who indeed replied to it without raising the question of identity; the respondents' subsequent contention that no valid application had been made was rejected by the E.A.T. However, in some cases where the application clearly referred to the wrong person or company as respondent it was held to be invalid: see *e.g. Connolly* v. *Irish Commercial Society Ltd.* (1983).

Finally, it should be noted that where the employer dies after the dismissal, an application may still be brought under the U.D.A. against his personal representative. This was decided by the E.A.T. in *Hutton* v. *Philippi* (1980).

(d) The Rights Commissioners

If there is an application under the U.D.A. or the 1981 Act, it will in the first instance be referred to a Rights Commissioner unless either of the parties objects; issues under these Acts will here be separated from issues under the Redundancy Payments Acts or the Minimum Notice Act, if such are included in the same application. Rights Commissioners are appointed by the Minister for Labour under section 13 of the Industrial Relations Act 1969, and their main task under that Act is to investigate, and issue recommendations to resolve, certain types of trade dispute (usually relating to individual grievances). Their function under the 1977 and 1981 Acts is that of adjudicating in disputes under these statutes and of issuing recommendations.

Very little is published about the procedures and practices adopted by the Rights Commissioners, and indeed there are virtually no statutory guidelines for them to follow. Section 8(1) of the U.D.A. merely provides that a Rights Commissioner must, like the E.A.T., "hear the parties and any evidence relevant to the claim," and must then "make a recommendation." However, how the commissioner conducts the hearing is largely up to him, subject to the general principles of law, such as the requirements of natural justice. Under section 8(6) of the U.D.A. the hearings are held *in camera*, and no written decisions, or reasons for them, are published. If either party objects in writing (in advance of the hearing) to the case being heard by a Rights Commissioner, it is heard directly by the E.A.T. In fact, this now happens in most cases, and in 1982 a total of 916 applications went directly to the E.A.T. (Employment Appeals Tribunal, *Fifteenth Annual Report*, 1982, p. 2).

An application which has been heard by a Rights Commissioner may, and frequently will, still go to the E.A.T. Under section 9 of the U.D.A. either party can, within six weeks of the recommendation being issued, appeal to the E.A.T.; a copy of the notice of appeal must be given to the other party within the same period. In such cases the Tribunal hears the case *de novo*, frequently without reference to the proceedings before the Rights Commissioner.

Under section 8(4) of the U.D.A. an employee may further apply to the E.A.T. where the employer has not carried out a recommendation of a Rights Commissioner. The E.A.T. has held in *Sheehan* v. *Racket Hall Ltd.* (1982) that such an application for implementation can only be initiated after the period for bringing an appeal has elapsed, and that the proceedings may not involve any questions or arguments of substance; for example, the employee may not argue for a different remedy from that recommended by the Rights Commissioner, and the employer may not introduce new evidence. Where, as occasionally happens, the Rights Commissioner oversteps his role under the legislation, for example by recommending *ex gratia* compensation, the E.A.T. cannot and will not order the implementation of such a recommendation: *Loftus* v. *Irish Glass Bottle Co. Ltd.* (1980).

(e) E.A.T. hearings

The procedures adopted at E.A.T. hearings to some extent follow the traditional pattern of court cases, but with a greater degree of informality and some other modifications. Under regulation 11 of the Redundancy Regulations hearings of the E.A.T. are in public, but at the request of either party the Tribunal may order a case to be heard *in camera*; for an example, see *Gillespie* v. *Adtec Teo.* (1979).

Regulation 13 of the Redundancy Regulations provides that:

"A party to an appeal heard by the Tribunal may—
  (i) make an opening statement,
 (ii) call witnesses,
(iii) cross-examine any witnesses called by any other party,
(iv) give evidence on his own behalf, and
 (v) address the Tribunal at the close of the evidence."

Where a party is represented, it is the representative who will carry out most of these activities. Regulation 12 of the Redundancy Regulations provides that a party "may be represented by counsel or solicitor or by a representative of a trade union or of an employers' association or, with the leave of the Tribunal, by any other person." Since the E.A.T. was set up an increasing number of applicants and respondents, but in particular of respondents, have chosen to be represented by legal practitioners. In 1978 32 per cent. of employees and 63 per cent. of employers who were represented at all had legal representation (E.A.T., *Eleventh Annual Report*, 1978, p. 11); in 1982 these figures had become 44 per cent. and 68 per cent. respectively (*Fifteenth Annual Report*, 1982, Annexe 5). This development appears to have contributed significantly to the legalism which is now often experienced at E.A.T. hearings. Where a party wishes to be represented by a person who is not a legal practitioner or an official of a trade union or employers' association, this is, to our knowledge, invariably permitted by the E.A.T., and an advance request before the date of the hearing is not as a rule necessary.

If there is a dispute as to the fact of dismissal the employee or his representative will start the submissions and call his witnesses, if any; in other cases it is the employer. Either party may summarise the case to be presented in his opening statement, but if a burden of proof is to be discharged it cannot be done merely by outlining the case in this statement; additional evidence must be submitted, usually through witnesses. In the case of *Garrett* v. *Coras Iompair Eireann* (1980) the E.A.T. held as follows:

> "The purpose of an opening statement is to give to the Tribunal an outline of the evidence which will be given on behalf of the party whose representative makes the statement. However, an opening statement is not a substitute for such evidence. Purported statements of fact unsupported by evidence, firstly, should not be made and secondly will not be taken into account by the Tribunal in so far as they are so unsupported."

In relation to the evidence which may be used, there are a number of English decisions in which it has been held that the rules applicable in courts of law do not necessarily apply in industrial tribunals. In the case of *Lawrence* v. *Newham London Borough Council* (1977) the British E.A.T. held that a written statement, the author of which was not available for cross-examination, was admissible at the discretion of the tribunal; in *Coral Squash Clubs Ltd.* v. *Matthews* (1979) it held that hearsay evidence was admissible. In the latter case Slynn J. declared that a tribunal "is not bound by the strict rules of evidence but should exercise its good sense in weighing the matters which come before it" (p. 611). In the same way it would be true to say that, in Ireland, these questions are determined at the discretion of the E.A.T.; this is confirmed in part by regulation 15 of the Redundancy Regulations.

Witnesses who are called are examined and cross-examined, and the members of the tribunal may further ask questions of them. Their evidence is, under section 39(17) of the Redundancy Payments Act 1967, normally given under oath. Under section 39(17)(c) the E.A.T. may further order persons to attend a hearing and give evidence, and may also order the discovery of relevant documents.

During the course of a hearing the tribunal will sometimes adjourn the case for a short period to allow the parties to reach a friendly settlement. This happens where the tribunal members feel that the case would be better resolved by such a settlement than by an E.A.T. determination and where the parties appear to be ready to compromise. If a compromise agreement is then reached which disposes of the application, such an agreement is valid and is not rendered void by section 13 of the U.D.A.: *Moran* v. *Microtherm Ltd.* (1982, E.A.T.). This practice of the E.A.T. is undoubtedly useful, but it also shows up the lack of individual conciliation, as carried out by ACAS officers in Britain, before the actual hearing. The introduction of such conciliation in Ireland would be most useful, and the present authors feel that it might be carried out by the Rights Commissioners, instead of their current role.

The decision (or "determination") of the E.A.T. can be given at the close of the hearing, but more usually it is issued some time later in written form. The delays in issuing determinations have grown in recent years, and an interval of about two months between the hearing and the determination is now common. The decision of the E.A.T. must, in line with regulation 17(2) of the Redundancy Regulations, be "recorded"; the British E.A.T. has held, in relation to the identically worded British provision, that this means that the tribunal must give reasons for its decision: *Guest* v. *Alpine Soft Drinks Ltd.* (1981).

The E.A.T. maintains a register of its decisions, which may be inspected free of charge. However, there is no subject index, or even an alphabetical index; as a result it is almost impossible to find relevant cases and the Tribunal itself seems to find it easier to rely on the well reported and indexed decisions of the British courts and tribunals.

(f) Costs

The attractiveness of the E.A.T., such as it is, depends to a major extent on the proceedings being inexpensive for the parties. For this reason regulation 19 of the Redundancy Regulations provides that "the Tribunal shall not award costs against any party." However, under regulation 19(2) costs *may* be awarded against a party who has "acted frivolously or vexatiously." We are aware of only one case in which this has been applied: in *Conway* v. *Westair Aviation Ltd.* (1983) costs were awarded against the employer for his failure to enter a notice of appearance. In Britain the equivalent provision was analysed by the National Industrial Relations Court in the case of *E.T. Marler Ltd.* v. *Robertson* (1973); in relation to applicants, the court found, "frivolous" applies "if the employee knows there is no substance in his claim and that it is bound to fail, or if the claim is on the face of it so manifestly misconceived that it can have no prospect of success"; "vexatious" applies "if an employee brings a hopeless claim not with any expectation of recovering compensation but out of spite to harass his employers or for some other improper motive" (*per* Sir Hugh Griffiths, p. 76). Since it is very important not to deter genuine applicants it is obvious that costs should rarely if ever be awarded, and it is to be welcomed that this appears to be the policy of the E.A.T.

It should be noted that in no case can the costs arising out of legal representation be awarded against either side. Finally, under regulations 20 and 20A (as inserted in 1979) of the Redundancy Regulations certain costs of persons appearing before the E.A.T., including loss of earnings, can be awarded out of the Redundancy Fund (under the Redundancy Payments Acts), or out of funds provided by the Minister for Finance.

(g) Adjournments

Regulation 14 of the Redundancy Regulations provides that the E.A.T. "may postpone or adjourn the hearing of an appeal." The policy of the Tribunal in relation to adjournments sought by the parties was set out in the 1982 *Annual Report* (p. 4): if both parties seek an adjournment immediately after they have been notified of the date of the hearing it is usually granted, otherwise it is usually refused. Because of an increase in applications for adjournments in recent years and the resulting disruption to the E.A.T. schedules, the attitude of the Tribunal has become increasingly tough. Furthermore, the E.A.T. makes no special allowances for the needs of legal representatives. In most cases the parties or parties seeking an adjournment must appear in person at a regular hearing and make the application before the start of the day's proceedings.

(h) Appeals

All the relevant Acts under which the E.A.T. operates permit appeals. Under section 40(*a*) of the Redundancy Payments Act 1967 the Minister may, where a question under the Act is brought before the E.A.T., refer it to the High Court on the request of the Tribunal. Furthermore, a determination of the E.A.T. may, under section 39(14) and section 40(*b*), be appealed to the High Court, but only on a point of law. The same applies to decisions of the E.A.T. under the Minimum Notice and Terms of Employment Act 1973 (see section 11). Relatively little use has been made of these appeal procedures.

Under the U.D.A. appeals may be taken by either party to the Circuit Court within six weeks of the E.A.T.'s determination being issued. If no such appeal is brought, and if the employer in the case has not implemented the determination, then the Minister for Labour may, under section 10(1) of the U.D.A., institute proceedings in the Circuit Court "in his name on behalf of the employee," and the Circuit Court may award "the appropriate redress"; in these latter proceedings costs may be awarded against the employer or the Minister, but never against the employee on whose behalf they are brought. Seven such cases were initiated by the Minister in 1982 (*Fifteenth Annual Report*, p. 3). Finally, following the decision of Ellis J. in *McCabe* v. *Lisney & Son* (1981), it is also possible to appeal from the Circuit Court to the High Court. In such cases, of which there have now been a few, the High Court conducts a full re-hearing.

In unfair dismissal cases an increasing number of cases have been taken to the Circuit Court, generally by employers. In 1982 at least 61 determinations were appealed (E.A.T. *Fifteenth Annual Report*, 1982, p. 2). The procedures for such appeals are governed by a number of statutory instruments, in particular the Circuit Court Rules (No. 1) 1979 and the Circuit Court Rules (No. 2) 1981. The information which filters back from the Circuit Court about the cases is totally and alarmingly inadequate; in three counties no information about Circuit Court appeals is made available at all. In other counties we are told the total number of appeals (in aggregate only), but there are no reports and there is no information about the reasons for these decisions; indeed, for persons wishing to do research on them it is not as a rule even possible to know exactly which cases (as distinct from how many) were appealed. In this book, where we have referred to Circuit Court decisions, we have had to rely on a number of informal sources and on some media reports. Assuming that these are accurate, the standard of the proceedings and the quality of the decisions do not impress. It is clear that all aspects of the Circuit Court role are highly unsatisfactory, and we would support the call, which has come from trade unions in particular, to remove the Circuit Court from unfair dismissal cases. Furthermore, appeals from the E.A.T. to the courts in general should be permitted only on points of law.

THE LABOUR COURT AND SEX DISCRIMINATION

The Labour Court was set up under section 10 of the Industrial Relations Act 1946, and it holds all its main functions under that Act (as amended). Broadly, its role is to promote collective bargaining and resolve industrial conflict. When the Anti-Discrimination (Pay) Act was passed in 1974 it gave to the Labour Court the role of adjudicating in disputes under its provisions, and a similar role was subsequently provided for under the Employment Equality Act 1977. In the first years of this new jurisdiction the Labour Court was mainfestly uneasy in its role, and in its 1978 *Annual Report* (p. 10) it noted that in sex discrimination cases "the Court finds itself involved with legal aspects of its actions and its decisions thus depriving it of the flexibility which it enjoys when dealing with cases referred to it under the Industrial Relations Acts."

In fact, it would not be unfair to say that the quality of the Labour Court's early decisions was less than what might have been desired. The decisions were often hard to understand and were frequently not backed up by the giving of reasons, a practice which makes sense when mediating in industrial disputes but not when adjudicating on statutory entitlements. There was also some evidence of the Court seeking to encourage compromises rather than declaring the parties' rights. However, the passage of time has changed the picture somewhat, and it is now accepted by most commentators that the Labour Court is performing its role well. The present authors have not been able to welcome all of the Court's decisions in the area of sex discrimination (see Chapter 6), but we feel that in general its procedures are good and, of late, its decisions well argued. It is to be noted that the Employment Equality Agency, which had in 1978 advocated that this jurisdiction be transferred to the E.A.T., has recently declared a change of mind: subject to some changes being introduced, the Agency now favours the retention of this role by the Labour Court (*The Role of the Labour Court in Enforcement Procedures under Equality Legislation—Recommendations for Change*, 1984).

(a) Composition and workload

The composition of the Labour Court is in many ways similar to that of the E.A.T. It is a tripartite tribunal, consisting of a chairman and three deputy chairmen, as well as four members nominated by trade unions and four nominated by employers' organisations. However, the chairman and the deputy chairmen do not need to have, and in fact do not have, any formal legal qualifications; this is because when the Court was given its original functions in 1946 it was thought advisable to keep lawyers away from its proceedings. However, it might now be asked whether this lack of legal expertise prejudices the Labour Court's ability to handle the interpretation of statutory rights and obligations. Like the E.A.T., the Labour Court sits in divisions, with three members in each division.

The Court, as already noted, spends most of its time dealing with industrial disputes under the Industrial Relations Acts. The scale of this will be understood if we consider that, in 1982, the Court issued 975 recommendations in trade disputes, and only 21 determinations under the 1974 and 1977 Acts. It is clear from this where the weight of the Court's business lies.

(b) Bringing an application

The procedures for bringing applications are, in theory at any rate, different under each of the two Acts. Under the 1974 Act, where there is a dispute about an equal pay entitlement it may be referred to an Equality Officer under section 7 of the Act, who investigates a dispute and issues a recommendation. Disputes under the 1977 Act are, under section 19, referred to the Labour Court itself, which can refer the application *either* to an Industrial Relations Officer *or* to an Equality Officer; the latter may issue a recommendation. Under both Acts, a recommendation of an Equality Officer can be appealed by either party to the Labour Court.

The 1974 Act does not provide for time limits for bringing an application, but under section 19(5) of the 1977 Act an application must be brought "not later than six months from the date of the first occurrence of the act alleged to constitute the discrimination"; the Labour Court can extend this "where reasonable cause can be shown." In *Slievadara National School* v. *O'Connor* (1980) the Court found that the employer's reluctance to communicate with the applicant in relation to the form under section 28 (see below) was a "reasonable cause" for the delay. In this case it was also pointed out, without any conclusion being reached on the matter, that it is not always easy to determine the date of an act of discrimination. This does not in practice appear to have presented any problems to date, but it is not hard to envisage a case in which a dispute about this could arise. For example, in the case of an allegedly discriminatory refusal to select for employment, it could be argued that the first act of discrimination was the decision to select someone else, or that it was the previous discriminatory interview, or that it was a company policy decided some months before, and so forth. The Act does not provide a solution to this problem. It is our view that the relevant date should be when the employer takes the final decision to implement the act said to constitute the discrimination—in the above example, the date of the selection for employment of the other person.

Under section 28 of the 1977 Act the applicant may, prior to lodging her application, seek from the respondent a written statement setting out "the reason for the act believed by the employee to have constituted discrimination"; special forms are available for this from the Labour Court. The respondent must, under the section, provide the statement as sought, but rather curiously the Act imposes no penalty for non-compliance. If the respondent's reply does not satisfy the applicant, she may then lodge her application, enclosing the forms. This procedure does not apply where the application concerns an allegedly discriminatory dismissal.

Both Acts also provide for the possibility of the Employment Equality Agency (E.E.A.) bringing applications. Under section 7(2) of the 1974 Act the E.E.A. can refer a dispute to an Equality Officer where it feels "that an employer had failed to comply with an equal pay clause" (see Chapter 6) and where no application has been, or is likely to be, brought by an employee. Similarly, under section 20 of the 1977 Act proceedings under the Act can be initiated by the Agency. These functions were originally vested in the Minister for Labour but were transferred to the E.E.A. under section 36 of the 1977 Act. Furthermore, under section 48 of the Act the Agency "may at its discretion provide assistance" to an applicant under the 1974 or the 1977 Act where "an important matter of principle" is involved or where the applicant cannot be expected adequately to present the case without assistance; an applicant who desires assistance may contact the Agency. However, the E.E.A. may only assist in applications brought before an Equality Officer or the Labour Court; appeals to the High Court (see below) are not covered.

Finally, as a matter of practice parties may be represented by legal practitioners or an official of a trade union or an employers' association. No statistics have been made available, but the trend towards legal representation which we noted in our discussion of the E.A.T. has not been in evidence in the case of the Labour Court, although in some cases solicitors or barristers have appeared. The representation of applicants by trade unions is very common.

(c) Group applications

Where there is discrimination the discriminatory practices are frequently applied by employers against all female (or male) employees, rather than just against specific individuals. It follows from this that if a woman (or a man) has a grievance under either the 1974 Act or the 1977 Act, it is likely that other women (or men) in the same employment have similar grievances. Individual claims, leading merely to individual redress, may not be sufficient to deal with an employer who is discriminating on a major scale.

The power of the Employment Equality Agency, noted above, to initiate proceedings, and indeed its power to conduct investigations under section 39 of the 1977 Act, helps to deal with this problem. For example, under section 20 of the 1977 Act the E.E.A. can refer to the Labour Court discrimination which "is being generally practised against persons," discriminatory advertisements, and attempts to procure discrimination. In using this power the Agency is in a position to tackle discrimination at the root, rather than just incidents of it. Where discrimination appears to be widespread, an E.E.A. investigation, which is carried out by a specially nominated investigation team, can examine all the employer's policies and practices; a recent example of such an investigation was that into allegations concerning Arthur Guinness Son & Co. (Dublin) Ltd. initiated in 1981. All these powers of the Agency have been used somewhat sparingly, but this is due in part to constraints upon its resources (see E.E.A., *Annual Report*, 1982, pp. 28–9).

However, in general it is of crucial importance to consider the approach of the Equality Officers and the Labour Court to applications involving a collective aspect. The greatest problems have arisen under the Anti-Discrimination (Pay) Act 1974, mainly as a result of the case of *Medeering Ltd.* v. *ITGWU* (1978). In the course of hearing the appeal the Court sought legal advice which concluded that "each individual woman's claim for equal pay with a man" must be judged "as a separate issue thus ruling out an approach which would judge the generality of the work done by a group of women with the generality of the work done by a man or a group of men in the same employment" (Labour Court, *Thirty-Second Annual Report*, 1978, p. 11). What this means is that while a number of applicants may jointly bring applications, these must be handled in such a way as to preserve the principle of individual, rather than collective or group, rights under the Act.

Procedures for bringing group applications under the 1974 Act are outlined in a Labour Court memorandum, most recently published in the 1982 *Annual Report* (Appendix XI). Where the work carried out by all the applicants is identical only one job description will need to be provided or considered, but the name and address of each applicant will have to be given and, technically, separate decisions will be issued in respect of each. Where the work is different as between the applicants, a separate investigation is carried out into the work of each applicant and that of the chosen comparable person of the opposite sex. As a result of these developments the ability of the legislation to counter structural discrimination has been further prejudiced.

(d) Equality Officers and Industrial Relations Officers

Applications under both Acts—other than applications concerning allegedly discriminatory dismissals, which under section 26 of the 1977 Act go straight to the Labour Court—are processed at first instance by officers of the Labour Court known as Equality Officers. The office was created initially under the 1974 Act under the title of Equal Pay Officer, and this was changed to Equality Officer under section 18 of the 1977 Act. Hearings before Equality Officers are held *in camera*, and the officers may inspect the premises at which applicants work and may observe the work in progress. Section 6(4) of the 1974 Act empowers an Equality Officer to require the production of certain documents and to make copies of them; obstruction or non-compliance is a criminal offence. At the end of his investigation an Equality Officer issues a recommendation under section 7(3) of the 1974 Act and section 19(3) of the 1977 Act.

Section 19(2) of the 1977 Act allows the Labour Court, in cases under that Act, to "settle the dispute through an industrial relations officer" before, or instead of, referring it to an Equality Officer. Industrial Relations Officers are officers of the Labour Court whose main function, under the Industrial Relations Act 1969, is to conciliate in trade disputes. It is quite unclear why they were introduced into the scheme of the Employment Equality Act; disputes here, as we have noted before, are about statutory entitlements, and conciliation—that is, encouraging the conclusion of compromise settlements—is manifestly out of place. In fact, the Labour Court has not recently made use of Industrial Relations Officers in employment equality cases (see Labour Court, *Thirty-sixth Annual Report*, 1982, p. 10); only 13 cases have ever been referred to IROs, and almost no disputes were resolved through this method.

(e) Labour Court hearings

Where an Equality Officer has issued a recommendation, any party may, under section 8(1)(*e*) of the 1974 Act or section 21(2)(*d*)

of the 1977 Act, appeal within 42 days of the date of the recommendation to the Labour Court. The Labour Court will then investigate
the dispute, and the procedures used in such investigations are more
or less the same as those used by the Court for the investigations of
trade disputes under the Industrial Relations Acts. The parties are
required in advance of the hearing to make written submissions setting out their arguments and to send these to the Court. These submissions are then read out at the hearing. The Labour Court has
further held that the party bringing the appeal against an Equality
Officer's recommendation has the onus of "convincing the Court
that it should be upset": *Pretty Polly (Killarney) Ltd.* v. *I.T.G.W.U.*
(1979).

In most respects Labour Court hearings are very informal, and
the Court is bound by almost no procedural rules other than by the
general principles of law; it is required to observe the principles of
natural justice and may not use expert evidence, such as that of the
Irish Productivity Centre, without disclosing the substance of such
evidence to the parties and allowing them to make submissions on it:
State (Cole) v. *Labour Court* (1983, High Court). On the other hand
the Court has the power, under section 20(4) of the Industrial Relations Act 1946, to summon witnesses, examine them under oath and
require them to produce relevant documents; these powers are
rarely used. Hearings of the Court are as a rule held *in camera*, but
can at the request of a party be held in public: see section 8(1)(c) of
the 1974 Act and section 21(3) of the 1977 Act.

The Labour Court can also hear applications for the implementation of Rights Commissioner recommendations. Section 8(1)(a) of
the 1974 Act and section 21(1) of the 1977 Act allow a party to an
application, where an Equality Officer has issued a recommendation, to "appeal to the Court for a determination that the recommendation has not been implemented": for an example of such a
case, see *Central Bank of Ireland* v. *A.S.T.M.S.* (1980). The hearing
proceeds in the same way as an appeal. Finally, under section 8(4) of
the 1974 Act and section 24 of the 1977 Act a party can complain to
the Labour Court that a determination of the Court itself has not
been implemented. If the Court considers the complaint to be well
founded, it may order the implementation of the determination, and
after two months from the date of the order (or, where applicable,
the date of an order of the High Court on appeal, see below) non-
compliance becomes a criminal offence. To date only one prosecution has been brought in such a case (see E.E.A., *The Role of the
Labour Court, op.cit.,* p. 17).

(f) The courts of law

Section 8(3) of the 1974 Act and section 21(4) of the 1977 Act permit a party to a sex discrimination case to appeal from a determination of the Labour Court to the High Court on a point of law; the Acts do not specify any time limits for bringing such appeals. Furthermore, where a person is prosecuted for the commission of any of the offences provided for under the Acts (including those relating to dismissals), the proceedings will of course be conducted in a court of law.

Apart from the appeals provided for in the Acts, it is also possible to seek a State-side order from the High Court in relation to Labour Court proceedings under the 1974 and 1977 Acts. For such cases the decision in *State (Stephen's Green Club)* v. *Labour Court* (1960) is not a precedent, since the Court's function under the 1974 and 1977 Acts is fundamentally different from its function under the Industrial Relations Acts, in that it gives legally binding determinations under the former Acts. In the case of *State (Cole)* v. *Labour Court* (1983) Barron J. granted an order of *certiorari* quashing a determination of the Labour Court, and in *State (Employment Equality Agency)* v. *Labour Court* (1983) the E.E.A. was granted a conditional order of *mandamus*. However, in *State (Casey)* v. *Labour Court* (1984) O'Hanlon J. held that, in the ordinary course of events, sex discrimination cases should come before the High Court only by way of appeals on points of law under the Acts. *Certiorari* (in this case) should be granted only, he held, where certain issues arise, *i.e.* "the issue as to whether the Labour Court in making its determination acted without jurisdiction, or in excess of jurisdiction, or without regard to the principles of natural and constitutional justice, or was induced to make its determination by fraud or perjured evidence, or has made a determination which contains an error of law apparent on the face of the record." This decision, though unfortunate in view of the rather questionable determination of the Labour Court which O'Hanlon J. was being asked to quash (the *Ballindine School* case, see Chapter 6), was in our view correct; it is in every way desirable to minimise the contact between sex discrimination cases and the courts.

Index